X 5219

Library Service

ENFIELD WORKING FOR PEOPLE
LEISURE SERVICES

Please remember that this item will attract overdue charges if not
returned by the latest date stamped above. You may renew it by
personal call, telephone or by post quoting the bar code number and
your personal number. I hope you enjoy all of your library services.

Peter Herring, Head of Arts and Libraries

O/P 01/00

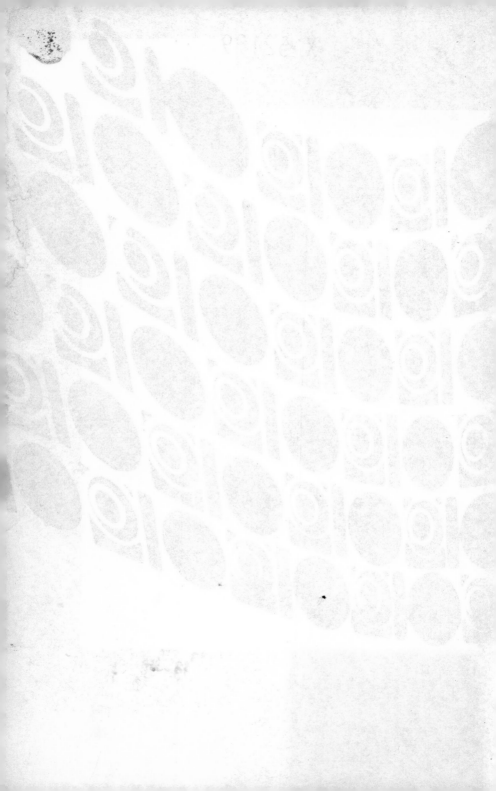

Hypnosis

H. B. GIBSON

Hypnosis

ITS NATURE AND THERAPEUTIC USES

PETER OWEN · LONDON

ISBN 0 7206 0334 x

The passage from Sigmund Freud's 'Hypnosis',
in *The Complete Psychological Works of
Sigmund Freud*, Vol. 1, is reproduced by
permission of The Hogarth Press.

PETER OWEN LIMITED
73 Kenway Road London SW5 0RE

First British Commonwealth Edition 1977
© H. B. Gibson 1977

Printed in Great Britain by
Bristol Typesetting Co. Ltd
Barton Manor St Philips Bristol

To Gosaku Naruse

who has illuminated many issues

CONTENTS

ILLUSTRATIONS

Illustrations are reproduced by courtesy of the following: The Wellcome Institute (1); Associated Newspapers Group Ltd (3); Hatfield Polytechnic (4, 6); Messrs Baillière Tindall Ltd (5, 7).

I *What Is Hypnosis?*

What do we mean by hypnosis or hypnotism? When people use the words they are not very clear about their real meaning and often use them in a figurative sense. They may say for example, 'I was so hypnotized by the music, that I forgot how late it was getting;' or, 'I was hypnotized by his manner of giving the speech, and so at the time I didn't realize what nonsense he was talking.'

The *Oxford Dictionary* gives the definition, 'Hypnosis . . . 1. The inducement or the gradual approach of sleep. 2. Artificially produced sleep; esp. the hypnotic state 1882.' But most people are not concerned with dictionary definitions; they use words to mean what they have grown up to understand by them. If asked what they mean by the word 'hypnotized', most people will give such meanings as 'put in a trance', 'fascinated' and 'under someone's influence'.

Usually, the concept of hypnosis is first encountered in childhood. The first relevant experience recalled by this author was being shown that one can hypnotize a chicken by catching it, putting its beak to the ground and then drawing a chalk line away from it. The chicken goes remarkably quiet and behaves for a few minutes as though it believes that the point of its beak is tied by a thread – the chalk line – so that it cannot escape. It does not struggle. After a while the chicken moves its head and, apparently discovering that it is free after all, runs away.

This childhood demonstration of hypnosis was fascinating, and led to repeated experiments in the chicken run. It seldom failed and seemed to work just as well when a piece of stick was substituted for the chalk line. Later on it became apparent that the line or stick was quite unnecessary; all that was needed was to immobilize the bird. Much later, reading revealed that these demonstrations used to be a popular amusement in the seventeenth century, and possibly determined some part of the public's attitude to hypnosis. These childhood experiments led the author to think of hypnosis as involving a victim, a creature like a chicken that is apparently so stupid that you could hoodwink it into thinking that it could not escape when it could. Hypnosis therefore appeared to be a matter of dominance over a gullible victim.

This belief was reinforced by my reading that snakes hypnotize their victims so that they become immobile and an easy prey, or even approach with terrified fascination the death that awaits them. In one of Kipling's books he has the snake hypnotize monkeys who are thus drawn to the jaws of the predator.

There are many accounts of the alleged ability of snakes to hypnotize, and country people imagine that they catch their prey by first fascinating them with their glittering eyes. What truth there is in this old idea will be discussed in a later chapter on animal hypnosis. Men are also credited with the power of subduing wild animals by hypnotizing them with a brave, unblinking gaze, and the author was most impressed by Ballantyne's *The Gorilla Hunters* where the hero, temporarily disarmed, intimidated a lion in the jungle by staring fixedly into its eyes, and compelled it to slink away. It seemed evident that the eyes could be the agent of hypnosis, although the local dogs did not seem to respond when stared at.

A number of Victorian novelists such at Hawthorne, Dickens, du Maurier, Melville and Poe wrote of hypnosis as though it were a mysterious and occult force and encouraged the belief that it was somehow connected with the alleged phenomenon of telepathy. Probably these authors were as ignorant of the true facts about hypnosis as were the bulk of their readers, but because of the enormous popularity of their novels, they have helped to form the public image of hypnosis. This highly fictional background to hypnosis has led some people to believe that in reality it is all a myth, to be discounted as being on a par with fortune telling, astrology and spiritualism. This over-sceptical view is probably less common today because most people are better educated, and more able to distinguish between scientific fact and pre-scientific myth.

The ancient idea that hypnosis and the alleged phenomenon of telepathy are in some way connected, deserves some scrutiny. It arises from the belief that hypnosis consists of one mind dominating another, the hypnotist's 'will' replacing that of his subject. This is untrue, as we shall see later, but on the face of it it appears plausible that if hypnosis is a matter of one mind controlling another, the way it takes place is not important, and so why not by telepathy? Many important figures in the history of European medicine and psychology have believed in the possibility of telepathic hypnosis. Pierre Janet, an eminent French psychiatrist who died early in this century, at one time convinced himself that he was able to put one of his patients into a hypnotic state at unexpected times when she was not present, merely by concentrating his thoughts upon her. His contemporary, Professor Bernheim, considered and did not reject the idea of hypnosis by telepathy, but honestly admitted that it had never worked for him!

Otto Wetterstrand[1] wrote, regarding Bernheim: 'Some of his French colleagues and others, however, have proved this possibility, but its apparently exceptional occurrence has deprived it at present, perhaps, of practical usefulness for therapeutical purposes.'

Many readers may be surprised to learn that the evidence for the very existence of telepathy is by no means good. From time immemorial men have believed in the reality of telepathy, but this in itself is not a very convincing argument. They have also believed in the existence of hobgoblins and werewolves, but we tend to be sceptical about these creatures today. The current reasons for believing in the reality of telepathy are twofold. First, what may be called domestic and personal evidence, and second, the efforts of a band of persistent ESP researchers, sometimes associated with university departments.

For a start, let us admit that we would like to believe in the reality of telepathy. It would get us away from the drab realities of everyday life and open up exciting possibilities. Most of us have a favourite telepathy story, how we, or our Welsh aunt, were able to achieve knowledge of some momentous happening without any natural means of communication. People who are closely tied emotionally like twins, devoted mothers and lovers are often supposed to be able to transcend the ordinary channels of communication. Because many people are so wedded to their personal telepathy story it is difficult for them to be open-minded about the subject, to admit to themselves that perhaps chance and coincidence played a role in what they remember as happening, and to ask (a sensitive question), has the story perhaps grown a little in the repeated telling of it?

The other sort of evidence, that from the centres of ESP research, has been very influential in convincing the man in the street that at least telepathy is recognized as a respectable 'thing' that can be investigated. He cares little about the apparently boring experiments in card-guessing that go on in such places, but he reasons that if serious professors are devoting their time to such activities and grant-giving bodies are putting up substantial sums of money to finance them, then surely the existence of telepathy is a proven fact. It should be noted that other serious professors do not think that it is a proven fact. In the opinion of Professor C. E. M. Hansel[2] there is not a shred of scientifically acceptable evidence to support belief in telepathy. Considering all the research effort that has been given to the question in laboratories at least since the beginning of the century, the layman is entitled to be highly sceptical about the laboratory-based evidence. If he does 'feel' that telepathy probably exists, his feeling is more likely to be based on personal and domestic incidents. Apart from the occasional bare-faced frauds which are unmasked in the groves of academe, ESP research is the dullest and most sterile of academic exercises.

Hypnosis has no logical connection with allegedly telepathic phenomena. The presumed connection dates from the very early ideas about mesmerism, when the mind of the mesmerized person was supposed to be able to become free of the constraints of space and time, and to be able to peek into other people's minds, just as it could read from closed books, according to some. The fact that there is no logical connection between hypnosis and telepathy does not deter modern researchers in ESP from trying hypnosis with their subjects, in the belief that it is some sort of magic and will enable them to get results better than chance.

The role of popular fiction in promoting sensational and inaccurate ideas about hypnosis in the public mind is not so much in evidence today. Nowadays people may acquire a somewhat more realistic knowledge of the nature of hypnosis from television programmes which give them better factual information. It should be noted that British television does not permit the actual induction of hypnosis to be shown. It was tried experimentally on closed-circuit TV in the 1950s and found to be so effective that some of the limited circle of viewers went into a trance. One can imagine the effect if it were broadcast to millions.

Another important source of misinformation about hypnosis is stage performances where a version of hypnosis is exploited for public entertainment. This has been illegal in Britain for nearly twenty years now. Stage hypnotism, as practised by a variety of performers, is never quite genuine, for the genuine state is often less interesting than what can be produced with a bit of showmanship. A common procedure is to get a large audience to clasp their hands above their heads, with the fingers interlocked, and then to give strong suggestions that it will be impossible to unclasp the hands when a challenge is made. Among an audience of some hundreds there will always be a few who do not unclasp their hands, and these people will be invited on to the stage, where the hypnotist begins to try other tricks with them.

Such tricks usually involve the stage hypnotist making his victims behave in an undignified manner, thereby raising easy laughs from the audience. This is by no means typical of hypnosis. In reality, when people are in a hypnotic state they are no more prone to act as buffoons than when they are in their normal state of waking consciousness. However, the sort of person who goes to a variety performance and offers himself as a stooge to a stage hypnotist is generally a rather unusual individual to begin with. The gesture of acting as though he cannot unclasp his hands, or really being unable to unclasp them, is a sort of signal that he actively wants to make a public exhibition of himself.

Where stage hypnotism differs from the real thing is largely in the slickness and the showmanship. The stage hypnotist has not got the time to produce many real effects, nor does this greatly matter to him. He is a showman and it is his job to crowd as much entertainment and raise as many laughs as he can in the limited time allotted to him. To some degree he relies on the tricks of the conjurer rather than the skills of a hypnotist to produce many of the effects. They could perhaps be produced by genuine hypnosis, but it might take a very much longer time and require a genuinely susceptible subject rather than the sort of exhibitionist who is more often his subject. The showman knows very well that part of the audience realizes that a lot of the performance is mere bluff, but they are there to be entertained and not out of a serious interest in hypnosis. Many tricks, such as demonstrating 'hypnotic anaesthesia' by passing the flame of a cigarette-lighter under an allegedly hypnotized man's hand, rely entirely on showmanship, for the way the trick is performed ensures that it would not hurt *anyone's* hand.

Although stage hypnotists deliberately rely on conjuring and showmanship to give their audiences what they want, many are also skilled and self-taught hypnotists who use genuine hypnosis in practising hypnotherapy with patients who come to them for treatment. The efficacy of such treatment may be no less than that achieved by some professional people with medical and other degrees after their names.

An amusing account of stage hypnosis is given by Mark Twain.[3] He recounts how in 1850, when he was fourteen years of age, a travelling mesmerist put on a show at his village. He sat among the stooges who were being tested for susceptibility but failed to show any signs of it, much to his disappointment, for he was eager to show off in public. To his annoyance, another village lad, Hicks, was remarkably susceptible and went through a spectacular performance, night after night on the stage. This made Hicks very renowned and popular in the village, much to our young hero's envy.

He relates : 'On the fourth night temptation came and I was not strong enough to resist. When I had gazed at the disk for a while I pretended to be sleepy and began to nod. Straightway came the professor and made passes over my head and down my body and legs and arms, finishing each pass with a snap of his fingers in the air to discharge the surplus electricity; then he began to "draw" me with the disk, holding it in his fingers and telling me I could not take my eyes off it, try as I might; so I rose slowly, bent and gazing, and followed the disk all over the place, just as I had seen the others do. Then I was put through the other paces. Upon suggestion I fled from snakes, passed buckets at a fire, became excited over hot steam-boat races, made love to imaginary girls and kissed them, fished from the platform and landed mud cats that outweighed me – and so on, all the customary marvels. But not in the customary way.'

He found that because he was not really hypnotized but shamming, he was a much more effective performer on the stage than Hicks, whose limelight he had stolen. Hicks was apparently a genuine hypnotic subject, and genuinely hypnotized people do not always make as entertaining and marvellous a show as the hypnotist and audience might wish. Apparently this travelling mesmerist was rather ignorant of many of the true facts of hypnosis and tried to do tricks with telepathy, staring at the back of Hicks' head and attempting to convey commands by telepathy, of course without success. When he came to do this with the young Mark Twain, the latter saw from the expectant faces of the audience that he was expected to do something, and so, rather than sit there in mute torpor as Hicks had done, he jumped up and did the first thing that came into his head. This was to seize a stage prop, an old rusty revolver, and with well-simulated frenzy, chase another boy, who was an enemy of his, right out of the theatre.

The audience was, of course, greatly impressed by this exhibition of the hypnotist apparently controlling his subject by telepathy, and there was a storm of applause. The hypnotist, who was as surprised by this antic as anyone else, was nevertheless quick to take advantage of the incident, and addressed the audience thus : 'That you may know how really remarkable this is and how wonderfully developed a subject we have in this boy, I assure you that without a single spoken word to guide him he has carried out what I mentally commanded him to do, to the minutest detail. I could have stopped him at any moment in his vengeful career by the mere exertion of my will, therefore the poor fellow who has escaped was at no time in danger.'

Mark Twain also relates how he endured agonies without even wincing while people stuck pins in his arm, because the hypnotist wanted to show off induced analgesia. Hicks, the real hypnotic subject, winced considerably when they stuck the pins in his arm, for the hypnotist had apparently neglected to induce analgesia properly.

Twain tells how, thirty years later, he told his old mother of the imposture he had perpetrated as a boy, but the old lady, who had witnessed his antics on the stage, simply refused to believe that he had been shamming! Now as Mark Twain was a great humorist and teller of tall stories, it is doubtful how much credit we should give to the authenticity of his account, particularly as he follows it by an even more improbable tale of a mesmerist in London who stripped an unwilling victim of his clothes by means of mesmerism. However, the tale is instructive in that it shows that a century ago or longer, the various antics of stage hypnotism were being employed by travelling entertainers who, partially ignorant of the real facts of hypnosis, tried to perform impossible feats such as telepathic influence which are supposed to occur in hypnosis, and were sometimes apparently successful by trickery.

According to various people who have investigated the matter, like Marcuse,[4] stage hypnotists sometimes employ the same susceptible, or at least compliant, subjects again and again at successive performances, without necessarily informing the audience that it is simply a well-rehearsed act.

What people think about hypnosis, and how their attitudes and expectancies about it have been formed, have been discussed at some length, but now readers will want to know what the phenomenon really is, and how it is understood and employed by medical doctors and behavioural scientists in modern times. Strangely enough, there is no one accepted definition of hypnosis among scientists, nor is there complete agreement about what the phenomenon consists of. Instead, there are different approaches to its study, and different theoreticians would explain it in rather dissimilar ways. It will therefore be helpful to describe a number of different approaches to the topic, which vary according to the sort of scientists concerned, and their somewhat different areas of research.

The early experiments in the hypnotizing of animals naturally led people to think of hypnosis as a form of sleep. The hypnotized chicken might be thought of as in a sort of sleep, and various small mammals that can similarly be hypnotized by immobilization also appear to be suddenly plunged into sleep. The great Russian physiologist Pavlov certainly accepted that hypnosis was a form of sleep.[5]

Pavlov, whose work in the conditioning of dogs is well known, was mainly interested in how the stimuli received by the brain cause 'excitation' (and hence mental activity, learning and alertness) or 'inhibition' (hence passivity, forgetting and sleep). He noted that sometimes when teaching a dog to acquire a conditioned response – that is, a particular activity resulting from a previously unconnected stimulus – the animal would suddenly go to sleep at a somewhat unexpected time. He studied this matter further and worked out the special conditions that would send an animal to sleep or, in other words, hypnotize it.

For Pavlov and his followers, hypnosis in animals and in humans is the same thing. It depends on the spreading of 'inhibition' over the thinking part of the brain, the cortex. Viewing hypnosis as a form of sleep dependent on spreading inhibition raises the puzzle of how a deeply hypnotized person can be active both physically and mentally. How is such activity compatible with the supposed inhibition of the brain? Pavlov explained this in terms of what may seem a rather naïve picture of the brain's cortical surface being under partial or patchy inhibition. There were 'sentinel points' which remained in a state of excitation, and thus the hypnotist could still maintain contact with the subject and communicate any idea to him that he wished. Although the anatomical and physiological reality of such a condition would hardly be accepted today, it does convey the idea of what appears to be happening in the hypnotized person. The hypnotized subject may be almost totally unaware of most of what is going on around him, yet he is intensely aware of a narrow range of stimuli that are called to his attention by the hypnotist, and of the ideas that are suggested to him.

The same picture of patchy excitation also fits in with the behaviour of the natural sleepwalker. He is out of bed and moving around with his eyes open, yet it is not difficult to see that he is not fully conscious of where he is or what he is doing. He may have an odd, blank look on his face and does not appear to react properly to his surroundings. He may be possessed of one dominant and incongruous idea – say of finding the ticket office as he leaves his bedroom and wanders around the landing, under the impression that he is lost on a railway station.

Pavlov's idea of 'sentinel points' remaining alert in an otherwise somnolent brain of the sleeping or hypnotized person, is borne out by another sort of event which must be familiar to us all in some form, according to our interests and way of life. Consider the doctor and his wife who have a young baby. Because of their respective habits and duties, their 'sentinel points' will be different and react to different stimuli. The husband will awake immediately at the sound of the telephone, for it means a night call which it is his job to attend to, while his wife may sleep on, hardly disturbed. But if the baby cries it is more likely that the wife will be instantly alert, while her husband goes on sleeping.

Pavlov's view of the basic identity of sleep and hypnosis, and of hypnosis in animals and man being much the same phenomenon, has been strongly criticized. Early on it was found that the pattern of electrical brain waves, which can be recorded with the EEG (electroencephalograph) machine, showed that the physiological state of the hypnotized person was not quite the same as that of a sleeping person.[6] However, some of the very latest work with more sophisticated techniques of recording the EEG pattern, which will be mentioned in a later chapter, makes us less sure about rejecting the sleep model of hypnosis. In fact, research has now made us question whether we really know very precisely what we mean by 'sleep'.

The general consensus of opinion, which serves us very well, is that the sleeping person shows the general characteristics of being relaxed, with closed eyes, and is largely unresponsive to stimuli coming from his environment. On awakening, he knows that he has been unconscious of his surroundings for a while, and he may possibly report on the subjective experience of dreaming. No one objects to our regarding sleep as an 'altered state of awareness', nor did they before the EEG machine was invented and it became possible to show that the pattern of brainwaves in sleep is rather different from that obtained in waking consciousness.

However, since we have begun to take such refined physiological measures as EEG, we have learned that sleep is by no means a unitary state. There are at least four stages of sleep, each discernible by the characteristic EEG pattern, and a fifth stage, generally known as REM (rapid eye movement) sleep. In this latter condition, the muscles of the eyes are flickering to the extent that an observer can see the eye movements taking place beneath the closed eyelids. If a sleeper is awakened when the REM condition is observed, there is an increased probability that he will report that he has been dreaming.

In spite of the activity of the eye muscles in REM sleep, the rest of the body is extraordinarily limp and relaxed, except the hands and feet, which may show occasional twitching.

REM sleep has also been called 'paradoxical sleep'. In general, the ease with which one wakes from sleep depends upon the stage one is in, stage one being the lightest and stage four the deepest stage of sleep. REM sleep is very similar to stage one sleep as far as the EEG pattern goes, but it is relatively difficult to arouse a person from it. In spite of the body being so relaxed in this paradoxical sleep, the brain is very active, as shown by circulatory changes, and with male subjects it is reported that the penis is erect in 80 per cent of observed cases. Perhaps Freud's theories about the sexual nature of dreams get some support from this latter finding!

Interestingly enough, the same differences between the two main types of sleep may be observed in other animals. If the domestic cat is observed as she sinks into sleep on the hearthrug, it may be seen that she generally falls asleep with her chin on or between her front paws, and her head more or less horizontal. Later, when she goes into the REM stage, she falls into a very different posture, lolling on her side and going extraordinarily limp. Occasional twitches of the paws may be observed. EEG studies of cats have shown that they are very similar to humans in the stages of their sleep.[7] This evidence concerning the similarity of man to other animals in the physiological mechanisms of sleep lends some support to the idea that human hypnosis and animal hypnosis may not be so very different in some basic respects.

The critics of the idea that hypnosis may be considered as a sort of sleep state now have to contend with the awkward finding that whereas we used to consider that a person was either awake or asleep, we must now acknowledge that there are several sorts of states he may be in when we refer to him as 'asleep'. Even such a well-recognized state as sleepwalking, which occurs in about 6 per cent of us at some stage in our lives, and which much resembles hypnosis, is now admitted to be of such an ambiguous nature that experts are not certain how to classify it. At a conference on sleep and altered states of awareness,[8] Professor Jacobsen referred to sleepwalking thus : '. . . we don't like to call this period when the sleepwalker is walking, "awake". We don't like to call it "sleep". We just don't know; we're not that certain about definitions.'

We do not need to complicate the picture further by considering here the various other sorts of altered states of awareness that can be induced by drugs, fever or mental illness. Let it suffice that we enter different states of consciousness at different times, and some of them are generally regarded as sleep states. The language which has grown up around hypnosis, and which the layman partly understands, treats hypnosis as though it were a sleep state, and the critics of this view now have to define exactly what they mean by 'sleep'. When a hypnotist tries to induce hypnosis, he generally talks about drowsiness and sleep to his subject, and later on when he wants to restore the subject to a normal state of consciousness he tells him to wake up – and he does.

Professor Ernest Hilgard at Stanford University, who is one of the greatest living authorities on hypnosis, considers that hypnosis can usefully be regarded as an altered state of awareness, but he does not agree with Pavlov's rather literal concept of the identity of sleep and hypnosis, or with the partial identity between human and animal hypnosis. Hilgard's work[9] and that of his wife Josephine Hilgard,[10] has centred around the interesting fact that there is a great difference between people in their capacity to experience hypnosis. Contrary to popular opinion, there is no great difference between hypnotists in their power to induce hypnosis, since it depends on technique rather than on any personal talent, but hypnotic susceptibility is a very stable personality characteristic. What underlies the ability to experience hypnosis is little known, however, and has been the subject of much research.

Ernest Hilgard's theory of hypnosis is relatively straightforward. He regards hypnosis as an altered state of consciousness in which physiological mechanisms may well be implicated. It is not, in his opinion, merely a state of high suggestibility, as some other psychologists would maintain. What is meant by 'suggestibility' is a technical matter, and is rather different from the loose meanings given to it in everyday speech. The matter will be discussed in detail in Chapter 9, but for the present it will be sufficient to stress that in the technical sense the word is not to be equated with 'gullibility' when used in connection with hypnosis. It is more a matter of a person's capacity for receiving ideas. The older word 'acceptivity' is now rarely used, which is a pity; in Baudouin's[11] somewhat picturesque description : 'In a word, *it is not the conscious but the subconscious which accepts.* The idea, instead of being confronted with others and judged from an intellectual and volitional viewpoint, is granted hospitality like a welcome stranger.'

Ernest Hilgard's view is that in the altered state of awareness which we call hypnosis, people have a much enhanced capacity for 'suggestibility' or 'acceptivity', and it is this innate capacity which makes possible the transition to the altered state. His work has been so extensive that it is difficult to define just what has been his major contribution, but his name is prominently associated with the important field of the measurement of hypnotic susceptibility.

There is a maxim in psychology that if something exists, it exists in some quantity, and if we are to study it properly we must try to measure it. Measurement of hypnotic susceptibility dates from the late nineteenth century when it became evident that there is a good deal of variability between people in the degree to which they can respond to hypnosis. Various research workers have tried to find out, by testing large numbers of people, just what variations in response there are to various tests of hypnotizability. It has been necessary to publish normative data, specifying very exactly what the precise methods of giving the tests have been, and the exact criteria for scoring the subjects' responses. Much that psychologists have learned in the matter of the accurate testing of intelligence has been put to good use in devising reliable tests of hypnotizability.

Much of this effort may seem rather dull work, depending as it does on the patient hours, days and weeks of trying to hypnotize hundreds of people in exactly the same way and recording and analysing elaborate statistics about their responses. Such work has been entirely necessary in making progress from the days when all that was known about hypnosis depended upon the unreliable memories of doctors and others who were doing their best to cure or alleviate patients' troubles, or having fun in drawing-room exhibitions of hypnosis.

It is to the credit of research workers like Ernest Hilgard that over years of patient work they have amassed a great deal of information about hypnotic susceptibility that is reliable and is now put to good use in research laboratories all over the world. Ever since the time of Bernheim,[12] who in 1884 devised a nine-point scale of hypnotizability, research workers have been borrowing from and improving on the work of others. It should be noted that such scales of hypnotizability imply that people are hypnotized to different 'depths' of hypnosis, just as we talk about different depths of sleep. This is rather a crude way of looking at either sleep or hypnosis, for is stage four sleep deeper or less deep than REM sleep? In reality hypnosis is not a single phenomenon, and people are affected by it in different ways, but at the risk of being a little superficial we can talk meaningfully about different degrees of hypnosis. After all, we accept that people are more and less intelligent, although psychologists will explain that there are meaningful differences between different *sorts* of intelligence.

Perhaps the most useful and widely used of modern scales measuring hypnotizability are the Stanford Scales.[13] These measure different forms of behaviour before, during and after hypnosis, such forms of behaviour being traditionally associated with what is meant by hypnosis. Some examples of items on a scale may usefully be given by way of illustration.

Eye closure : the administrator asks the subject, who is comfortably seated in a chair, to gaze at a spot on the ceiling and attend carefully to what is being said to him. He suggests that he is becoming more and more relaxed, sleepy and heavy and that his eyelids are becoming heavier and heavier, so heavy that he will be unable to keep his eyes open and they will close of their own accord. These suggestions, which go on for some time, follow an absolutely standard form of words and are actually read from a booklet (although the administrator tries to make them sound as natural as possible !). If at the end of a certain paragraph, the subject still has his eyes open, he has 'failed' the item. If his eyes have closed before the end of that paragraph, he has 'passed'. It should be noted that failure to close the eyes spontaneously does not mean that the subject will not be hypnotized later – he may achieve quite a deep trance although he was slow to begin it.

Arm immobilization : later, after more suggestions of relaxation and drowsiness, the administrator suggests that one of his subject's arms is becoming so heavy, so impossible to lift that he will find that he simply cannot lift it up from where it rests on the arm of the chair. The subject is then challenged to try to lift up his arm and if he manages to get it up an inch or more he has 'failed' the item. About 85 per cent of experimental subjects fail this item, but the other 15 per cent really do not seem to be able to raise their arms.

Hallucination : the administrator suggests that there is a mosquito flying around and that one can hear its high-pitched noise. He suggests that it lands on the subject's hand and is tickling and is going to bite. If the subject make no overt response such as flinching or trying to brush away the imaginary mosquito, he 'fails' the item. Surprisingly, about 35 per cent of experimental subjects actually pass this item, though many of them say afterwards that even though they did not think it was a real mosquito, they could not resist brushing it away.

Post-hypnotic amnesia : before the administrator comes to the end of his tests, he tells the subject very definitely that he will be unable to remember *anything* of what has been going on, after he 'wakes up'. Later on, he questions the subject very closely about what he can remember, and if he succeeds in remembering more than three out of ten items he 'fails' the amnesia item. This is a difficult item to score, for the criteria for pass or fail depend on how hard the administrator presses for the subject to remember, and instructions for this are not easy to standardize. Some subjects are totally without memory of what has been going on, and such subjects are generally very much affected by other hypnotic tests. Right at the end the administrator says, 'Listen carefully to what I say. Now you can remember *everything*.' This post-hypnotic communication generally wipes away the last trace of the amnesia, but not always. Sometimes full memory can only be restored by re-hypnotizing the subject so that, back in the hypnotic state, memory returns and can be retained on awakening.

These four items, out of a scale of twelve, have been described in some detail to illustrate the fact that hypnosis does not consist of just one sort of thing. Different feelings and behaviours are illustrated, like feeling unable to keep one's eyes open, an enormous heaviness of the arm, experience of a hallucinated mosquito tickling one's hand and losing one's memory of what one has just been doing. All these different, dream-like experiences are connected, for if one scores positively on one of them it is more probable that one will score positively on others.

Considering the test as a whole, a few people who are highly susceptible pass all twelve items, and an equally small number pass none at all. Most people score somewhere in the middle – just as in intelligence tests.

It must not be thought that research psychologists such as Ernest Hilgard are merely interested in the techniques of measuring hypnotic susceptibility. Such tests are merely tools, although very necessary tools making possible a general exploration of the whole field. Hilgard discusses hypnosis in three aspects : in terms of the kind of development of the individual which leads him to be relatively susceptible or insusceptible to hypnosis; the kind of interaction between two people that occurs in hypnosis; the kind of state it is compared with other states of awareness.

In discussing the developmental aspects of hypnosis, Ernest Hilgard puts forward the view that all of us begin life with a strong capacity for hypnosis and that events in our own developmental history determine the degree to which we retain that capacity. The evidence that his wife, Josephine Hilgard, has gathered supports this view, and an evaluation of the evidence will be made later in this book.

Concerning the interactive aspects of hypnosis, Hilgard notes that, providing the hypnotist is perceived as a reasonably responsible person whom the subject is prepared to trust, it is the situation and not the hypnotist that matters. His personal characteristics are of very little importance. With repeated inductions of hypnosis, the subject learns to enter a hypnotic state much more quickly, but the degree to which he is affected does not alter much. Hilgard stresses that hypnosis is not the same for everyone, and that different people may enter a hypnotic state through rather different paths. For some, it may be through their well-developed capacity for becoming deeply involved in active adventure; for others, it may be through their capacity for fantasy, developed early on by becoming absorbed in reading and vicariously enjoying the lives, adventures and emotions of others.

In discussing what sort of state of awareness hypnosis is, Hilgard is less definite in his views. He makes the point that the hypnotic trance is normally achieved through the suggestions of the hypnotist, and so the degree of 'suggestibility' (or 'acceptivity' as Baudouin proposed) is an important factor in hypnotic induction. But the hypnotic trance is more than just a state of heightened suggestibility. As mentioned earlier, Hilgard does not concur with Pavlov that the hypnotic trance is a sleep-state, but he admits that it is rather too early to say much about its physiological correlates. Instead, he holds on to the old idea of Janet[14] and Morton Prince[15] that the hypnotic state is characterized by various partial dissociations of awareness. Dissociation implies that a person's consciousness can operate, as it were, in various unconnected compartments. At the descriptive level this is fine, and portrays the situation in which the hypnotized person can be seemingly unaware of features of his environment which have been screened out by the suggestions of the hypnotist. Also, post-hypnotically he may have memories of what has been going on under hypnosis which are simply not available to his waking consciousness. But although we may reject the naïve physiological model of patchy cortical excitation and inhibition which derives from Pavlov, no better one has been put forward as an explanation of dissociation.

Hilgard's theory of hypnosis has been discussed at some length because it is probably the simplest way a non-specialist can understand how most psychologists view the phenomenon, but it is not the only theory. Some other psychologists take a different view, a view which may strike the reader as very strange. At first sight it may seem that they are denying the existence of hypnosis altogether. Take the viewpoint of two psychologists, Theodore Sarbin and William Coe.[16] They approach the study of hypnosis from the point of view of social psychologists, reasoning that hypnosis is just another sort of social interaction taking place typically between two people. Our lives consist of many different sorts of social interactions in which we play all sorts of different roles. We do not, of course, consciously think, 'Now I am going to play the role of a boss (or a husband, a friend, a chairman, a hospital patient etc.) so I must put on an appropriate act.' Yet we do indeed act, and feel, very differently according to the role we are playing at different times. These social psychologists suggest, therefore, that in hypnosis the subject is just playing a new role, the role of a 'hypnotized subject' in the way that the hypnotist defines it. They do not suggest that hypnosis is mere pretence or 'play-acting', for the hypnotized subject enacts his role quite as genuinely as he enacts any other of the many roles he plays in life.

This view of hypnosis is part of a way of regarding all human behaviour as a sort of dramatic performance, even to the extent that all the emotions we experience are merely those which we think we ought to feel in the part. Therefore, when the hypnotized person flinches and tries to brush away the pretend mosquito that the hypnotist has told him is tickling his hand, even though he afterwards reports that he felt it tickling him, heard it humming and felt apprehensive about the possibility of being bitten – all this is merely the result of his vividly acting a part.

Can we reasonably accept such a view as plausible? Well, let us consider an experience which is common to many of us. We are watching a film or a play in which something very moving is taking place. Little Nell is nobly sacrificing herself for the sake of her old parents, while Sir Jasper gloats – we feel anger and pity; the tears come pricking to our eyes and our hearts beat faster. It is all very well to remind ourselves that Little Nell is really a paid actress who will probably have a drink with Sir Jasper when they have washed the greasepaint off; we know this perfectly well, but these are real, salty tears in our eyes and the pulse really is beating faster. So with half our mind we believe in the tear-jerking scene before us, and respond with appropriate emotions. Is this not comparable to the real tickle and slight fear which the hypnotized person feels when he is told that a mosquito is on his hand? Perhaps he believes in the reality of the mosquito with only half his mind, but the peculiarity of hypnosis is that the sceptical half of the mind is not in evidence – it appears to have gone to sleep.

Those who regard hypnosis in terms of playing a dramatic role so vividly that we believe in it, have to answer the question why some people, even when they try very hard to be hypnotized, are able to experience only very little. Their answer is that people vary in the degree to which they are capable of losing themselves in enacting a new role. This does not get us very far in understanding the mechanisms of hypnosis.

Apropos of the connection between acting ability and hypnotic susceptibility, many people will understand the difference between so-called 'technical' acting and 'method' acting. The technical actor is trained to remain outside his part, to study very carefully what he must do to produce the required effect on the audience. He does not really get emotional in an emotional part, he only seems to and his simulated emotions are very carefully contrived. The method actor, by contrast, is trained to throw himself wholly into his part and to feel with some degree of passionate conviction the emotions the character he is playing would feel. Josephine Hilgard's researches with students of drama showed, as one might expect, that those who were method actors were more susceptible to hypnosis than those whose acting was technical.

One of the most sceptical, as well as the most prolific of writers and researchers on hypnosis is Professor Xenophon Barber. His book *Hypnosis: A Scientific Approach*,[17] published in 1969, lists seventy publications (mainly journal articles) of which he is the sole or joint author. Barber's scepticism is such that he frequently puts words like 'hypnosis' in quotation marks to signify that his concept of the term is entirely different from that of other people.

Barber is a stern critic of all who make advanced claims for the power of hypnosis. Many of his experiments have been designed to show that many of the effects which are claimed to be due to hypnosis can be produced by other means. His favourite device is what he calls 'task motivational instructions', which he claims can often be as effective as hypnosis. The instructions are like a pep-talk which he gives to his subjects before an experiment. In this talk he makes it plain that unless they feel and act as he will suggest that they feel and act, they are failing to come up to expectations, wasting time and making him look silly! This strong moral pressure directed towards his subjects (who are often his own students) tends to produce a high degree of conformity to what he suggests, and many of the effects which other researchers produce with hypnosis, Barber gets with his task motivational instructions.

One may detect a flaw in Barber's general method and in the deductions he makes. Suppose subjects *report* some such phenomenon as an absence of pain to a rather slight noxious stimulus, either with hypnotic suggestions of numbness or following Barber's task motivational instructions – are the two conditions comparable? In the former case one may believe that hypnotic suggestion really did remove the experience of pain in those susceptible enough to be influenced by it, but in the latter case common sense suggests that the subjects really did experience the pain but dared not admit it. The negative report of the latter might well be due to Barber's telling them that they would not feel pain if they really tried, and that if they did they were making his experiment a failure, wasting time and making their professor look silly! Most of us will tell a convenient lie if we are under sufficient moral pressure.

It is on the issue of the experience of pain that Sarbin and Coe's role enactment theory of hypnosis also falls down. If a surgical operation is performed under hypnosis with absence of pain being induced solely by suggestion, then in their theory such absence of the usual signs of pain can only be due to the patient's superb acting. He hates being cut as much as the next man, but he *acts the role* of someone who is not in any pain. This stretches our belief in the powers of acting rather far. At one time or another most of us have tried desperately to act 'bravely' and not to show pain when hurt, and know very well how difficult this is. The records of the last century, which will be discussed in the next chapter, show cases of amputations being performed painlessly under hypnosis before the days of anaesthetics, and it is difficult to believe that this was due merely to role enactment on the part of the amputees to spare the feelings of the poor surgeons!

Further light on the question of how much hypnosis depends

upon the hypnotized subject acting a role that is expected of him comes from the ingenious experiments of Professor Martin Orne.[18] Many of his experiments have taken the form of comparing the performance of two groups of subjects, those who are really hypnotized and those who simulate hypnosis. The latter are told by experimenter A that experimenter B will not know in advance who are the real subjects and who are subjects instructed to try to deceive him by deliberately acting the part of hypnotized subjects, although retaining their full waking consciousness.

The results of these experiments with real subjects and simulators are controversial, as are many scientific experiments, but there is fairly good evidence that the 'reals' and the simulators act differently in various subtle ways. The performance of the simulators is often too good to be true and they betray themselves by acting logically where real hypnotic subjects would act with the superb illogicality of a dreamer. For instance, a person who is really deeply hypnotized can be made to see an imaginary person sitting in a chair in front of him, with such clarity that he believes the figure to be real, and can describe him in detail. If the subject is then asked to describe the back of the chair in which his hallucination is sitting, he will also do this, without showing any surprise that Mr X., while still sitting there, has gone quite transparent. This simple acceptance of the impossible is known as 'trance logic', and is reminiscent of what we experience in dreams. Simulating subjects, by contrast, tend to betray themselves by clinging to consistency and logicality in their responses, and asked to describe the chair-back in such a situation are likely to say something like, 'I can't see the back of the chair because Mr X. is sitting in it.' The evidence from such experiments tends to make us doubt whether hypnosis is really an extension of vivid acting and trying to play a prescribed role. It seems more likely that the mind of the hypnotized subject is functioning in a very special manner analogous to, although not identical with, dreaming.

The fact that these various researchers into hypnosis are sceptical and critical of one another's theories is all to the good as it allows one to form a balanced view of hypnosis. Many people still regard hypnosis as a mysterious and uncanny thing, and connect it with the occult and supernatural, for many of the phenomena associated with it – induced insensitivity to pain, apparent regression to child-hood personality, hallucination of objects which are not there, selective blindness to objects which are there, the wiping out of recent events from the memory – make them feel that something preposterous is going on. In actual fact, what is slightly preposterous is the ordinary set of assumptions about human behaviour and experience which most people hold. When we witness or experience hypnosis, we are getting a broader perspective of the reality of the human mind, and even of bodily function, and its possibility for a greatly enlarged range of experience.

People who have been hypnotized, and think about the experience afterwards, generally connect it with all sorts of half-forgotten events in their lives, and with experiences which are by no means novel to them. In reality, we are not quite the rational beings we think we are, alternating daily between sleep and waking consciousness. Some of the basic mechanisms of hypnosis are, to a greater or lesser extent, part of our daily lives which we do not recognize. Hypnosis opens the doors on a better understanding of ourselves, and indicates how we can achieve more fulfilment of our individual potentialities.

We have discussed hypnosis in terms of an analogy with sleep, but all hypnotic states are not identical. It should be noted that there is a form of hypnosis known as an 'alert trance' in which the hypnotist stresses an active and exclusive concentration on a single idea as a means of evoking the trance, rather than making the subject relaxed and drowsy.[19] An alert trance has something in common with the open-eyed reverie that some people fall into spontaneously, a condition in which they are dominated by a single mental preoccupation, and they are utterly lost to the world while it lasts.

Allied to spontaneous self-induced states of reverie is the technique of self-hypnosis which can be learnt with practice. It is not always necessary for a hypnotist to be present for a state of hypnosis to be achieved. The hypnotist can teach a subject to put himself into a trance, by training him to react to some special signal or circumstances which become powerfully associated with the hypnotic induction. This is very useful for some therapeutic purposes, such as training an expectant mother to put herself in hypnosis as an aid to an eventual comfortable delivery.

Oriental peoples often have a greater understanding of and acceptance of hypnosis, due to its traditional associations with religious practices in the East. Naruse[20] points out that: '. . . the name of hypnosis had not been so much spoiled by the so-called stage hypnotists or amateur hypnotists, as in Great Britain or the USA. The hypnotic phenomena, therefore, were readily accepted by Japanese psychologists and physicians as an object of scientific study.' Apart from Zen meditation, which is closely allied to the hypnotic trance, the mechanisms of hypnosis have been traditionally used in Japan and China as part of the training leading to greater mental and physical efficiency.

Although no completely integrated theory of hypnosis is yet possible, and the controversies between different psychologists will still flourish, it is possible now to make a fairly coherent statement about what is going on in hypnosis within the general framework of modern psychology.

What we ordinarily experience, and hence how we behave, is determined by the interaction between what stimulates us both from without and from within the store-house of our own minds. From without we have the stimulation of what we see, hear, and so on, in our immediate surroundings at the moment. From within we have the stimulation from all our past experiences stored in memory. When we are 'asleep' (if one may still use so ambiguous a term!) we are little affected by stimulation from without, although we may grunt and turn over if prodded in the ribs and told to stop snoring, and even weave the prod into our dreams. But dreams consist almost wholly of a jumbled pastiche of that inner stimulation. When 'awake' we are busy sorting out the huge volume of that outer stimulation, using our inner stimulation (which represents past experience) to make some sort of sense of it. The waking mind, then, is constantly employed in reality-testing, filtering out from the blooming, buzzing confusion around us coherent impressions which are meaningful to us personally. What we actually perceive is not entirely that which is there before our eyes and in our hearing, but is partly our own version of it, modified according to what we expect to see and hear. It is this necessary distortion of reality which leads to our experience of such things as visual illusions and conjuring tricks.

Some people are reluctant to admit to themselves that they do not experience reality at first hand, as it were, but only their own privately edited version of it. In the opinion of some philosophers, which need not concern us here, our own privately edited version of the universe *is* the only reality. However, these basic facts of perception have been explored and illustrated by psychologists pretty thoroughly. 'Going to sleep', then, involves giving up this constant process of sorting and editing. Instead, we shut out some of the outer stimulation by closing our eyes and relaxing our bodies. In sleep perhaps some editing of the inner stimulation goes on (Freud made much of this) but not much, and it does not worry us if we sit down to tea with a talking sheep who is wearing our uncle's wrist-watch. We are resting from reality testing.

When a person is hypnotized, the ordinary prerequisite is that he should agree to put himself in the hands of the hypnotist to the extent that he just lounges and listens and accepts whatever experiences occur. The hypnotist suggests that he relaxes, gets drowsy and goes to sleep, and this is precisely what he begins to do, giving up his waking activity of reality testing, filtering and editing all the stimuli he receives, and letting the hypnotist's voice become the substitute for his own thoughts. The hypnotist may tell him that his left arm is beginning to stiffen, to get light and to float up in the air, and since the hypnotist's words have replaced his own inner channels of communication, that is precisely what he does experience, and the arm floats up, perhaps to his own slight amazement.

Many subjects who have been hypnotized report afterwards that they vaguely remember feeling a slight surprise at what was happening to their own bodies, but this surprise is typical only of the *early* stages of hypnotic induction when the hypnotist's voice has already begun to determine the nature of reality, but the subject's critical faculty has not entirely subsided.

In this common form of hypnotic induction the subject starts to fall asleep, but the process is not complete, for the hypnotist keeps talking to him, continuously talking, keeping up a steady flow of communication and screening out the subject's own sources of inner stimulation. The subject's universe of experience becomes almost entirely limited to what the hypnotist is saying to him, and if when the hypnotic trance is well developed, this stream of words tells him that a duck is sitting in his lap, he experiences the duck with all the clarity of a vivid dream. And also, as in a dream, he does not find it in the least surprising that a duck should be sitting in his lap.

If the hypnotist tells the subject that he will now have a dream, dream he does, drawing on his own flow of inner stimulation in place of the hypnotist's flow of words which is now suspended. If the hypnotist simply stops talking and leaves the hypnotized subject alone, it is likely that he will fall into a true sleep and eventually awake in his own good time.

Although the hypnotist continuously defines and thus controls reality, the subject is still *himself*. He does not experience any changes in his standards or moral judgements whatever the hypnotist says, even though he may have been regressed to childhood and is experiencing a return of his childhood personality. The hypnotized subject is not an automaton; he still retains his unique personal identity, and may refuse to accept suggestions which are out of keeping with his particular and habitual preferences.

All the above information should help to clarify the relations between the hypnotic state and the various states of altered consciousness, including those we group together as 'sleep' and have as their common factor a lowered responsiveness to outer stimulation in the way of information processing and reality testing. Whether we choose to refer to hypnosis as a *form* of sleep is quite immaterial and it merely a matter of verbal usage.

Have, then, the chickens which the author hypnotized as a child come home, so to speak, to roost? Have they anything at all in common with the people hypnotized in later years for one purpose or another? Obviously the differences are more in evidence than the similarities. The chickens had no choice in the matter : they were seized and immobilized and experienced some minutes of strange passivity in contrast to their normal activity. The humans experienced the state of hypnosis by their own volition, and indeed they could not have experienced it if they had not been actively co-operative.

The childhood assumption that there is something of dominance-submissiveness in human hypnosis, as many fictional stories lead one to believe, has to be revised. Hypnotic subjects use the hypnotist for their own purposes, and one can consider the relationship in the same terms as any other mutual social relationship.

Having noted all these obvious points of difference between animal and human hypnosis, there remains, however, the interesting fact that in most of our important human activities – eating, loving, striving, relaxing and varying our states of consciousness – we are making use of the primitive mechanisms of our animal ancestry, and hypnosis may be no exception to this generality. The topic of animal hypnosis is sufficiently important to be the subject of a later chapter.

He who would study hypnosis today may at first be struck with the apparent scarcity of readily available books and journals concerned with the subject. But if he follows up his interest he will find that there has been no lack of writing on this topic; there is literally too much, and the problem is to get at it and to separate the wheat from the chaff. Ellenberger[21] reports that in 1888, '. . . publications became so numerous that it was impossible to keep up with them. Max Dessoir added a supplement with 382 new titles to the 801 titles of his bibliography of modern hypnotism of 1888.' Today one gets the impression that much of real worth has been forgotten, and modern writers sometimes seem unaware of the great heritage of knowledge that is available. The present book is offered as a simple answer to the question of what hypnosis is, a question to which there is no short reply.

REFERENCES

1 O. G. Wetterstrand, *Hypnotism and its Application to Practical Medicine*, trans. H. G. Petersen, London: Knickerbocker, 1902.

2 C. E. M. Hansel, *ESP: A Scientific Evaluation*, London: MacGibbon & Kee, 1966.

3 Mark Twain, 'The Mesmerist', in B. DeVoto (ed.), *Mark Twain in Eruption*, New York: Grosset & Dunlap, 1922.

4 F. L. Marcuse, *Hypnosis: Fact and Fiction*, Harmondsworth: Penguin Books, 1959.

5 I. Pavlov, 'The identity of inhibition with sleep and hypnosis', *Scientific Monthly*, 17, 1923, pp. 603–608.

6 F. J. Evans, 'Hypnosis and sleep: techniques for exploring cognitive activity during sleep', in E. Fromm and R. E. Shor (eds.), *Hypnosis: Research Developments and Perspectives*, New York: Aldine Atherton, 1972.

7 M. Jouvet, 'The states of sleep', *Scientific American*, February, 1967.

8 S. S. Kety, E. V. Evarts, and H. L. Williams (eds.), *Sleep and Altered States of Consciousness*, New York: Williams & Watkins, 1967.

9 E. R. Hilgard, *Hypnotic Susceptibility*, New York: Harcourt, Brace & World, 1965.

10 J. R. Hilgard, *Personality and Hypnosis*, Chicago: University of Chicago Press, 1970.

11 C. Baudouin, *Suggestion and Autosuggestion*, London: George Allen & Unwin, 1920.

12 H. M. Bernheim, *Hypnosis and Suggestion in Psychotherapy*, trans. C. A. Herter, 1888, New Hyde Park, N.Y.: University Books, 1963.

13 A. M. Weitzenhoffer and E. R. Hilgard, *The Stanford Hypnotic Susceptibility Scale. Forms A and B*, Palo Alto, Calif.: Consulting Psychologists Press, 1959.

14 P. Janet, *The Major Symptoms of Hysteria*, New York: Macmillan & Co., 1907.

15 M. Prince, *The Unconscious*, New York: Macmillan & Co., 1916.

16 T. Sarbin and W. Coe, *Hypnosis: a Social and Psychological Analysis of Influence Communication*, New York: Holt, Rinehart & Winston, 1972.

17 T. X. Barber, *Hypnosis: A Scientific Approach*, New York: Van Nostrand Reinhold Co., 1969.

18 M. T. Orne, 'On the simulating subject as a quasi-control group in hypnosis research: what, how and why', in E. Fromm and R. E. Shor (eds.), *Hypnosis: Research Developments and Perspectives*, op. cit.

19 F. J. Vingoe, 'The development of a group alert-trance scale', *International Journal of Clinical and Experimental Hypnosis*, 16, 1968, pp. 120–132.

B

20 G. Naruse, 'Recent developments of experimental hypnosis in Japan', *Psychologia*, 2, 1959, pp. 20–26.

21 H. F. Ellenberger, *The Discovery of the Unconscious*, London: Allen Lane, 1970.

Such, in brief, is the history of hypnotism. All sciences alike have descended from magic and superstition, but none has been so slow as hypnosis in shaking off the evil associations of its origin.

c. l. HULL, *Hypnosis and Suggestibility*, 1933.

One of the most common misconceptions about hypnotists is that they stare into the eyes of their subjects and make 'passes' with their hands, as though they were stroking the air. George du Maurier's famous novel *Trilby*[1] has an illustration of the evil Svengali putting the girl into a trance by waving his long fingers at her as he intones, '*Et maintenant dors, ma mignonne.*' The popular belief in the 'passes' of the hypnotist arose through the early practices of the mesmerists, who thought they could convey a supposed fluid of 'animal magnetism' to their subjects through the movement of their hands.

The words 'hypnosis' and 'hypnotism' were first coined by the Scottish doctor James Braid, who worked in Manchester. He referred to the phenomenon first as 'neurypnology', seeking a Greek equivalent of the earlier term 'nervous sleep'. This was in 1842.[2] What Braid was doing was to make scientifically respectable a much older body of knowledge, speculation and myth, which had come to be known by the name of mesmerism.

Many people suppose that Mesmer, from whom the word mesmerism derives, was the originator of hypnotism in Europe. Mesmer, however, did not use hypnosis, or only unintentionally as a result of his other practices. Nevertheless an historical account of the development of hypnosis in Europe must consider the work of Mesmer and his followers, for out of their fumbling efforts, mistaken and inappropriate though they often were, the scientific study of hypnosis and its application was eventually to develop.

Franz Anton Mesmer studied medicine in Vienna, and in 1766 wrote a dissertation on *The Influence of the Planets on the Human Body*. He was to write a number of other dissertations on the same theme. His ideas were not original, for he was greatly influenced by the work of Father Hehl, a Jesuit professor of astronomy at Vienna who experimented with the supposed effects of magnets on the human body in a effort to cure sickness. Mesmer also plagiarized

35

the work of an English doctor, Richard Mead,[3] who had published similar speculations much earlier. Most of these eighteenth-century magnetizers were drawing on the ancient superstitions and folk-lore surrounding the wondrous properties of the lode-stone and the magnet, and connecting them with the ideas of astrology. In an age when mysticism and science were still closely linked, it was not difficult to concoct a lot of impressive-sounding theory with which to impress the gullible.

The orthodox medical world of Vienna rejected Mesmer's theories with ridicule, and he moved to Paris in 1777. There he had considerable success treating the diseases of the rich and imparting his method to students who, it is said, paid him a fee of one hundred louis d'or each.

Mesmer's method was not hypnosis. Instead he used a system of elaborate hocus-pocus designed to impress his patients that they were receiving the curative magnetic fluid, and that they would react in the way that Mesmer assured them that they would. An element of hypnosis was no doubt present in the treatment of some suggestible patients, but no understanding of it or deliberate attempt to foster it was part of Mesmer's method.

In group sessions the patients stood around a large tub or *baquet* which contained water, magnets and iron filings. Iron rods protruded from the tub and each patient held such a rod. Sometimes the circle of patients would be connected one to the other by a rope which was supposed to unite them in a magnetic circle. Soft and soothing music was played to them, and at some stage in the proceedings Mesmer would enter the room dramatically, impressively attired. He would approach one patient, make 'passes' in the air with his hands and eventually touch her. This produced a 'crisis' – the patient would go into a convulsion, and emerge from it feeling much better in health. It has already been mentioned that these 'passes' were supposed to direct a stream of the 'magnetic fluid' on to the patient. Belief in the reality of this fluid was so great that one patient reported to Dr Ricard, her mesmerist : 'At each pass you direct towards me I see a little column of fiery dust which comes from the end of your fingers and seems to incorporate itself in me. Then when you isolate me I seem surrounded by an atmosphere of this fiery dust . . .'[4] Other mesmerized subjects reported seeing similar marvels, including visible flames coming from the ends of magnets.

Mesmer undoubtedly had considerable success in his treatment of some patients, but records do not exist showing just what types of maladies were cured or improved by the treatment. All that we know about medicine today indicates that the disorders with which he was probably most successful were those which are now known as hysterical. These disorders can take almost any form but they are entirely functional, that is, there is no underlying physical basis for them. They come and go very much as a result of the patient's emotional well-being. Hysterical disorders are often dramatically cured by the impressive drama of a faith healer, and this was the sort of thing that Mesmer was doing. That the patients regularly went into a curious convulsive 'crisis' when Mesmer touched them was no doubt due largely to group suggestibility. They saw what happened to other patients and knew what was expected at the critical moment, so convulse they did.

Mesmer's work received no more friendly reception from the orthodox medical world of Paris than it had in Vienna. As one who treated the diseases of the rich, Mesmer came to the attention of the influential people at the court, and King Louis XVI ordered that a Commission of Inquiry should be appointed from the Faculté de Medicine and the Acadamie Royale des Sciences to investigate mesmerism. This commission had Benjamin Franklin, then representative of the United States at the court of King Louis as its president, and included such well-known scientists as Lavoisier the chemist and the famous Dr Guillotin. It was not Mesmer himself but his pupil and colleague D'Eslon who demonstrated and explained the practices of mesmerism and the theory of animal magnetism to the commission. Mesmer wisely departed to Switzerland before the findings of the commission were made known.

The commission was very businesslike in its investigation, and devised objective scientific tests of all the phenomena which were claimed by the mesmerists. Their conclusions were quite definite : 'Therefore, having demonstrated by decisive experiments that the imagination without magnetism produces convulsions, and that the magnetism without the imagination produces nothing, they have concluded with a unanimous voice, on the question of the existence and the utility of the magnetism, that the existence of the fluid is absolutely destitute of proof, and that the fluid, having no existence, can consequently have no use.'[5]

In short, the commissioners saw through the hocus-pocus of Mesmer's elaborate methods. They found no evidence which suggested that there might be a magnetic fluid, and their view of the situation seems to have been very shrewd. What effects there were, and there were certainly many strange behaviours to be observed, resulted, in their belief, from the patients' imagination. It was no new thing to observe that the power of the human imagination could produce very marked physical changes without any conscious fraud or pretence on the part of the imaginer. Had Mesmer understood what he was doing he could probably have produced even greater effects by using some of the simpler methods of hypnosis. Unfortunately the suspicion remains that Mesmer was more interested in the louis d'or than in his patients' health, a tendency which is still manifest in some corners of medicine today. Many of Mesmer's writings give the impression that he was both a liar and a charlatan who had realized that with sufficient cool effrontery one can trade on the gullibility of a large section of mankind.

Opinion today is by no means unanimous about Mesmer. He has his defenders and Altschule[6] claims that a small group of psychoanalysts regard him as one of the founders of their craft. The late Wilhelm Reich, an unorthodox psychoanalyst whose works are enjoying a new vogue of republication,[7] took over many of Mesmer's ideas in the 1940s. He refurbished them, calling animal magnetism 'orgone energy', and even resuscitated Mesmer's idea of the *baquet* as an 'orgone accumulator'. He died insane in an American prison, a martyr in the eyes of some of his followers.

The followers of Mesmer tended gradually to drop the more flamboyant trappings of the treatment, but they continued to believe that the changes they produced were due to the supposed magnetic fluid rather than the psychological mechanism following on expectancy, imagination and hypnotic susceptibility. The first clear account of hypnosis induced by a mesmerist is that of the Comte de Puységur's treatment of a shepherd boy.[8] He used the usual rituals of 'passes' to magnetize the young man, who was confined to his bed with a bad chest, and found that he passed into a state then known as 'magnetic somnambulism'. The fact that the man became deeply hypnotized and exhibited all the classic signs of an altered state of consciousness in which he was perfectly lucid and completely suggestible, and had no memory at all of the event after he was awoken, is clearly recorded.

That the phenomenon of hypnosis was by no means unknown in the eighteenth century (as indeed it had been known in various forms from time immemorial) is attested by a very intelligent pamphlet published under the anonymous initials of M.F. in 1785.[9] The author refers to magnetic somnambulism as '. . . an intermediate state between sleep and wakefulness, which has the characteristics of both, and produces also a great number of phenomena which belong to neither.' This is not a bad description of the hypnotic state, the only error being that the author attributed it to magnetism. As well as observing correctly many of the classic phenomena of hypnosis, he also attributed to the hypnotist a totally unreal capacity of being able to control the subject by thought alone. This supposed connection between hypnosis and such unproved mystical phenomena as clairvoyance and telepathy was prominent in the days of the magnetizers, and has not died out even today.

This eighteenth-century pamphlet, besides taking it for granted that hypnosis resulted from the power of magnetization, makes an interesting reference to Franz Mesmer. 'Even at the present, there are several Magnetizers who are very talented, who do not regard Somnambulism as being an essential part of Animal Magnetism, or separated from it, indifferently. M. Mesmer himself has always seemed to me of this last opinion.'

Thus Mesmer was unaware of, and uninterested in, what must have been the major effective component of his treatment in a great number of cases.

Mesmerism, shorn of many of the trappings of the *baquet*, the soft music and the showmanship, came to be used by a few British doctors not only as a general therapy, but for the very practical purpose of removing pain in surgical operations. In the days before the discovery of chemical anaesthesia, surgery was always a grisly business, patients sometimes dying of the shock of pain in major operations like amputations. The magnetizers discovered that if they could produce a sufficiently deep hypnotic trance by means of their procedures, then not only could surgical operations be performed painlessly but a good deal of the trauma of surgical shock could be eliminated.

It is extremely difficult to get at the true facts, but it appears that the British doctor John Elliotson was performing painless surgical operations at University College Hospital, London, up until 1838 when it was resolved 'That the Hospital Committee be instructed to take such steps as they shall deem most advisable, to prevent the practice of Mesmerism or Animal Magnetism in the future within the Hospital.' (Resolution of the Council of University College, 27 December, 1838.)

Dr James Esdaile, working in India, published in 1852 an astonishing record of the surgical operations he had performed painlessly with 'mesmeric anaesthesia'.[10] Hypnosis was also used in dentistry. In 1837 Jean Etienne Oudet presented to the French Academy of Medicine details of the painless extraction of teeth in 'magnetic sleep'. Dr William Curtis wrote to *The Critic* as follows : 'On Tuesday, Feb. 4th, before a numerous company assembled to witness the operation, I extracted a large molar tooth without the knowledge of the patient whilst in a magnetic sleep. The patient is a girl . . . only mesmerized a few times . . .'

It may be difficult for us to comprehend why, in the era before the introduction of chemical anaesthesia, such practices were not welcomed by the medical profession in general, but the fact is that they were treated with ridicule and bitter hostility by the medical establishment. We may understand the position better if we consider that orthodox medical men were concerned to free themselves from past connections with astrology and magic and to establish an image of themselves as being strictly scientific.

If we read the writings of Elliotson, we begin to comprehend why his practices were outlawed at University College Hospital. His writings are vague and rambling, and full of anecdotes which simply do not ring true in the ears of any reasonable man. If we grant that he did indeed practise painless surgery by 'magnetizing' his patients, we wonder why he had to claim so much more. He appears to have regarded mesmerism as a cure-all, and naïvely ends his long account of eight cures as follows : 'These are all the Cases of insanity and St Vitus dance that have been treated with mesmerism by myself or, to my knowledge, by my friends. I have therefore no failures to relate or I would relate them.'[11] We would find his and his friends' curing by mesmerism a little more credible if they admitted the occasional failure, but it should be recorded that Elliotson was no money-seeking charlatan. He never received a fee for practising mesmerism and he appears to have been moved by the highest of motives, but like many enthusiasts he was unscientific in his approach and was probably self-deceiving.

Among the mesmerists of the early nineteenth century there were many absurd and eccentric characters. There was the Baron du Potet de Sennevoy who invented a magic mirror which, he claimed, threw people into convulsions, and who mixed his mesmerism with medieval magic. There was Baron Charles von Reichenbach who claimed that he could magnetize people so that they could see magnetic emanations coming from the hands of the mesmerist and from magnetic apparatus. Indeed, such curious crankiness still exists in a lunatic fringe today, who claim that hypnosis is just another manifestation of the occult.

It is no wonder that sensible people have always been rather wary of the whole topic of hypnosis, considering its antecedents, and that in the days of the mesmerists medical men reacted so strongly that many refused to believe in the reality of the quite genuine phenomena which could have contributed usefully to their craft. The fact that chemical anaesthetics such as ether and chloroform came into use in the middle of the century, meant that medical men could comfortably forget the disturbing facts of hypnotic analgesia that Elliotson, Esdaile, Curtis and company were trying to force upon their attention.

The story of how hypnosis became respectable in the later years of the nineteenth century is typical of the scientific climate of the time. James Braid, the Scottish physician working in Manchester, was well aware of the work of the mesmerists, and indeed had written a criticism of Baron Reichenbach's theories.[12] Although Braid probably guessed quite shrewdly that suggestibility, the vivid acceptance of an idea by one person from another, was at the root of most of the phenomena to be observed, he first chose to represent publicly that it was all a purely *neurological* matter. To attribute everything to the properties of the nervous system was to be scientifically respectable. He wrote :

'The various theories at present entertained regarding the phenomena of mesmerism may be arranged thus : – First, those who believe them to be owing entirely to a system of collusion and delusion; and a great majority of society may be ranked under this head. Second, those who believe them to be real phenomena, but produced solely by imagination, sympathy and imitation. Third, the animal magnetists, or those who believe in some magnetic medium set in motion as the exciting cause of the mesmeric phenomena. Fourth, those who have adopted my views, that the phenomena are solely attributable to a peculiar physiological state of the brain and the spinal cord. . . .

'I shall merely add that my experiments go to prove that it is a law of the animal economy that, by the continued fixation of the mental and visual eye on any object in itself not of an exciting nature, with absolute repose of body and general quietude, they become wearied; and, provided the patients rather favour than resist the feeling of stupor which they feel creeping over them during such experiment, a state of somnolency is induced, and that peculiar state of brain, and mobility of the nervous system, which render the patient liable to be directed so as to manifest the mesmeric phenomena. I consider it not so much the optic, as the motor and sympathetic nerves, and the mind, through which the impression is made. Such is the position I assume; and I feel so thoroughly convinced that it is a law of the animal economy, that such effects should follow such condition of mind and body, that I fear not to state, as my deliberate opinion, that this is a fact which cannot be controverted.'[13]

Braid related how he had induced the hypnotic state (and he firmly replaced the word *mesmerism* by *hypnotism*) in various people, including his own wife, simply by getting them to stare at a fixed point for a few minutes and thus '. . . paralysing nervous centres in the eyes and their appendages and destroying the equilibrium of the nervous system, thus producing the phenomenon referred to.'

Braid's original theory of hypnosis was thus entirely mechanical.

He held that it was an interesting property of the nervous system that if exhausted in the way he described, an hypnotic state would ensue. His account of his experiments is almost certainly erroneous. All that we know about hypnosis today makes it extremely unlikely that things happened quite the way he said. However, Braid did not make the absurd and monstrous claims that the mesmerists did – that a mesmerized person could read the time from a watch held behind his head, read from closed letters or a shut book, perceive what was happening miles away, and accurately diagnose the diseases of others although ignorant of medical knowledge. Reading Braid we are aware of having come into modern times, even if we cannot completely believe his reports. His errors of reporting were probably due to faulty scientific method and an enthusiastic bias.

Braid conceded that '. . . there exists great difference in the susceptibility of different individuals, some becoming rapidly and intensely affected, others slowly and feebly so.' This is an important acknowledgement about hypnotic susceptibility upon which much later research was to focus. However, he made everything seem much more simple than it is, declaring that anyone who adhered closely to all the rules of his method was bound to have almost total success in inducing a hypnotic state. It is a real possibility that over a century ago people in general were more hypnotizable than they are today. The researches of Josephine Hilgard[14] and others have shown how different degrees of hypnotic susceptibility may be partly dependent on the whole process of the child's growing up in a complex environment, and his interaction with his parents and others. In the modern world, the various pressures that are put on us as we grow up tend to make us less susceptible to hypnosis. In the simpler life of the nineteenth century, with their very different attitude to many things, including the upbringing of children, it is likely that people were psychologically different from today. Such facts as the much greater prevalence of hysterical disorders attest to this subtle difference.

The remarkable cures by the use of hypnosis alone, cures of partial blindness and deafness for instance, which Braid describes, may very well be due to the fact that the patients' disorders did not depend on a purely physical pathology but were of an hysterical nature. Yet Braid did not make the sweeping claims that the mesmerists did. He merely stated that 'we have acquired an important curative agency for a *certain class* of diseases, I desire it to be distinctly understood, as already stated, that I by no means wish to hold it up as a universal remedy.'[15] This rationality left room for further advance.

The fact that Braid's neurological theory of hypnosis was almost wholly erroneous is of little importance. What counted was that it was based on the facts of anatomy and physiology known at the time. It enabled the scientists who had derided the extravagances of the mesmerists to the extent that they would not even attend demonstrations of painless surgery, to think again. It is questionable whether Braid really believed for very long in the neurological theory which he originally propounded. By the time he came to publish *The Power of the Mind over the Body* in 1846, he had done enough experimental work to demonstrate clearly that a hypnotic state, with all the attendant phenomena, could be achieved by the technique of verbal suggestion alone. He made acute criticisms of the mesmerists on these grounds, demonstrating that if a hypnotized subject were to overhear the hypnotist predict that he would make a certain movement when touched appropriately – the prediction being quite arbitrary – the prediction would generally be fulfilled as the hypnotized subject does what is expected of him.

Braid was not the first eminent writer to contest the claims of the mesmerists that the reactions they produced in people depended on a supposed 'magnetic fluid'. Twenty years before Braid started writing, Alexandre Bertrand, who had practised mesmerism, asserted that the magnetic fluid did not exist, and that all the subject's reactions depended on his imagination. In 1826 Bertrand's book *Du Magnetisme Animale en France* explained that magnetism was '*une pure chimère*'. However, this purely psychological theory of hypnosis, which Bertrand referred to as '*l'extase*', was not enough to convince sceptics that the phenomenon itself was real. It required Braid's neurological theory, expressed with all the jargon of the science of the time, to make the medical world take hypnosis seriously.

Braid's over-simple theory of hypnosis came to the attention of the great French neurologist Professor Jean Martin Charcot, at the Salpêtrière Hospital in Paris. Charcot was a man of great eminence, and had collaborators who were to become equally well known : Pierre Janet, Sigmund Freud and Alfred Binet, later famous for his IQ test. Practised against such a distinguished and academically respectable background, no one would dare to allege that hypnosis was merely the plaything of cranks. Charcot did not make the mistake that Elliotson (originally a reputable and eminent doctor) had done in associating personally and in print with every sort of contemporary occultist and weirdie.

A good number of patients at the Salpêtrière Hospital suffered from hysterical disorders, and Charcot was engaged in formulating a theory of hysteria. It appeared to him that hypnosis was very similar to hysteria, for many of the hypnotic phenomena that can be elicited by suggestion – paralyses, insensitivity to pain, amnesia, loss of vision and so on – are like the symptoms occurring in hysterical disorders.

Braid's early theories appealed to Charcot, for here was a possibility of weaving all these phenomena into a grand and all-explanatory theory depending on the properties of the nervous system. This same task was later tackled with rather more success by the Russian physiologist Pavlov. The result of Charcot's theorizing was to teach a number of half-truths and downright errors. Firstly, Charcot accepted Braid's early contention that hypnosis could be produced by sheerly mechanical means, and neglected Braid's later findings that the role of expectancy and suggestibility was critical. Secondly, he taught that hypnosis was a pathological condition which could be induced only in those who were hysterically disturbed. This elementary error arose from the fact that he experimented with the disturbed patients of the Salpêtrière and had no experience of hypnosis in normal people. Thirdly, he maintained that hypnosis was more easily produced in women than in men, an error which derived from Charcot's preoccupation with hysteria, a type of disorder that has been traditionally supposed to characterize the female sex, the name 'hysteria' coming from the Greek word for the womb. Finally, and most surprisingly, he taught that hypnotic and hysteric phenomena could be influenced by magnets and metals, a crude error that linked him with the early work of the magnetizers. He had no first-hand knowledge at all of 'metalloscopy', as it was called, and relied entirely on the reports of incompetent collaborators.

How such an eminent professor came to mix such nonsense with his otherwise impressive teaching deserves some consideration. It followed partly from his exalted status within the hospital. He was too important to do the actual hypnotizing himself, or to be conversant with what actually went on behind the scenes. He left all the preparatory work to his assistants, and he would appear in the lecture theatre to demonstrate with patients in a hypnotic state which he himself had not induced. This lecture theatre appears to have been open to the public and all sorts of lay people, including actors, journalists, writers and dilettanti who had the time to spend at an interesting performance. It is possible that in some cases the patients were putting on a show for the entertainment of the audience.

Here we come to a problem which is of perennial significance in research. Famous professors, bowed down by the huge weight of their responsibilities, tend to leave much of the donkey-work of their investigations to research assistants, and are not always quite aware of how these assistants conduct themselves. They have to take the results which their assistants offer on trust. If it is well known that a certain professor holds some particular theoretical views, rather than incur his possible displeasure by offering him findings which flatly contradict him, there is a very human tendency to offer him results which fit in with those views. All this can take place without there being any real conspiracy to deceive or any conscious dishonesty among the research assistants. Thus, famous professors with an axe to grind tend to be supplied with the facts which confirm their expectations, unless they are shrewd enough to do much of the donkey-work themselves. Charcot did not do any of the mundane tasks of research. It is reported that he never actually hypnotized a single patient himself, but merely took control when hypnotized patients were ushered into his presence. Perhaps this is an exaggerated report.

His theory was that hypnosis consisted of three stages which took place in a fixed order; the phases of catalepsy, of lethargy and of induced somnambulism. In the phase of catalepsy the subject was supposed to exhibit an extreme plasticity of his muscles, so that he would retain whatever position one chose to put his limbs in, like a puppet. In lethargy he was in a profound stupor and did not react even to sudden loud noises or shocks. In the final somnambulistic state he could behave actively and reasonably, but was entirely under the command of the hypnotist. Later research has shown that Charcot was not correct in what he taught, for people do not really go through these invariant stages when being hypnotized. However, Charcot's belief were not wholly illusory. Many techniques designed to produce somnambulism, or the 'deepest' state of hypnosis, depend on first producing muscular catalepsies and then getting the subject into a deeply lethargic, sleepy state. The final condition of somnambulism may or may not follow in the subject who appears superficially to be deeply asleep.

Charcot's teaching, influential throughout Europe though it was, was not the only major development in hypnosis at that time. Two professors at the University of Nancy, Liébault and Bernheim, were pursuing a very different path. Liébault's experience had been acquired as a country doctor working often with peasants and labouring people. He found that the power of verbal suggestion was very great indeed, and could be used therapeutically in a wide variety of cases.

Liébault and Bernheim saw no reason to postulate any particular neurological mechanisms to account for hypnosis. The subject 'went to sleep' simply because the hypnotist implanted the idea of sleep in his mind. Although they found that suggestions given in hypnosis were particularly powerful, they claimed that with or without

hypnosis they succeeded in conveying effective therapeutic suggestions in at least 90 per cent of their patients. Interestingly enough,
although they carried out extensive research with both patients and
with normal people, they were not much concerned with a phenomenon which now seems of absorbing interest, the inhibition of pain
by hypnosis. Bernheim reported that 'hypnotism only rarely succeeded as an anaesthetic',[16] a finding in strong contrast to the
impression that had been created by the mesmerists.

The doctors of the Nancy school, whose approach to hypnosis was
entirely psychological in contrast to the neurological approach of
the Paris school, had considerable influence on the future of
psychiatry rather than that of general medicine. The medical profession, which was making great strides in the control and treatment
of disease by means of drugs, vaccines and surgery, had little use for
the psychological aspects of medicine. Psychology as a science was
little developed at that time, and the study of hypnosis was largely
in the hands of those doctors who had a special interest in the so-
called nervous diseases which presented in their practices. Previously
psychiatry had been concerned almost wholly with patients who
were so seriously insane that they had to be cared for in lunatic
asylums or by private nurses. Now more attention was beginning to
be paid to sufferers who, although perfectly sane, had their lives
made miserable by neurotic afflictions and psychosomatic disorders.
The word 'neurasthenia' was coined by George Beard in 1868.

Research carried out by men whose training was clinical rather
than scientific was bound to lead to many interesting and ambitious
speculations which were nevertheless erroneous with regard to the
facts they were supposed to be based on. Pierre Janet, a pupil of
Charcot's, did not accept his master's neurological theories entirely,
and made much more intelligent use of hypnosis as a technique of
investigation. Janet's theory was that neurosis resulted from a lack
of the mental energy which should hold the mind together in a state
of wholeness and integration. He regarded the artificially produced
state of hypnosis as a condition of 'dissociation' – one part of the
mind functioning independently from other parts. For instance, the
patient under hypnosis may be brought to remember things of which
he is normally unaware when in his normal waking state. Con-
versely, he can be made to forget things of which he is normally
well aware (for instance his own name). Janet found that patients
suffering from neurotic disorders often had surprising gaps in their
memories about themselves. They appeared to have forgotten a
great number of things – mainly incidents of a particularly painful
and unpleasant nature. Under hypnosis these memories could be
regained and, by suggestion, communicated to the waking con-

sciousness, thus leading the patient to a greater understanding of himself and his troubles.

With our present-day sophistication we may suggest that there is a world of difference between a person really forgetting an incident, or a whole related series of incidents, and a reluctance to discuss these incidents with a psychiatrist, or to outwardly acknowledge their existence. In the repressive times of the nineteenth century so many topics were simply not discussed, out of shame, that one wonders how much Janet's patients had truly 'forgotten' and how much they simply preferred not to acknowledge to him. That these incidents could be brought out into the open by hypnosis was all to the good, but here a danger arises. For the probing hypnotist may unwittingly create memories for events which never took place. For instance, a highly suggestible patient might 'remember' an incestuous affair with her uncle at the age of ten, which never took place and owed more to the fantasies of the psychiatrist than to her childhood history.

Allied to the dissociation of consciousness which, in Janet's theory, could be produced by hypnosis, or occurred naturally in the pathology of hysteria, is the phenomenon of multiple and alternating personalities with 'fugue states'. In these latter cases the person takes flight from his problems by apparently forgetting huge areas of his past, and even forgetting his own identity. William James describes the case of a clergyman who disappeared from his home and set up as a shopkeeper in a strange town, running a successful business and apparently forgetting his own identity as a clergyman and all that went with it. Eventually the clergyman personality reasserted itself and he suffered amnesia for his shopkeeping activities.[17] He seemed to be unable to integrate the two aspects of his personality and could only alternate, as it were, between being two different people.

In the nineteenth century multiple personalities appear to have been more common than they are today, as indeed were all forms of hysterical disorder, and they caught the public's fancy. R. L. Stevenson's book *Dr Jekyll and Mr Hyde* was a popular imaginative novel based on this theme. Morton Prince devoted a whole book to the subject.[18] In more recent years multiple personalities have been out of fashion, and when people show the classic symptoms psychiatrists are more prone to treat them as dishonest humbugs rather than as interesting cases to be investigated by means of hypnosis.

That the public interest in the Jekyll and Hyde syndrome has not waned is shown by the great success of the book, and subsequently the film, *The Three Faces of Eve*, which was published in the 1950s.[19] This is the true story, related by two American psychiatrists, of a young married woman who was leading a double life, alternat-

ing between being a dull, mousy housewife ('Eve White') and a lively
spendthrift who lived for superficial kicks ('Eve Black'). When she
suffered a neurotic breakdown, her doctors used hypnosis to investigate the case and revealed all the classic features of a dissociated
personality which would have gladdened the hearts of Pierre Janet
and Morton Prince.

It is interesting that research in hypnosis in the later nineteenth
century opened up considerable interest in the psychopathology of
neurotic disorders, and indeed, in the fundamental nature of
consciousness itself, but went no further. Hypnotherapy was not to
become an important technique in either physical or psychological
medicine. As time went on, interest waned rather than increased,
and doctors thought that they had discovered all there was to know
about hypnosis – a judgement that now strikes us as naïvely pre-
mature. Hypnosis attained respectability but hardly favour in the
medical world.

In 1892 that pillar of respectability, the British Medical Association, received the Report from the committee it had appointed 'to
investigate the nature of the phenomena of hypnotism; its value as
a therapeutic agent; and the propriety of using it'.[20] The committee
reported favourably on hypnosis as a therapeutic agent in the relieving of pain, procuring sleep and relieving many functional ailments. They advised, as might have been expected, that when used
for therapeutic purposes hypnosis should be employed only by
qualified medical men, but even so, they added a prohibition
characteristic of the time, '. . . that under no circumstances should
female patients be hypnotized except in the presence of a relative or
a person of their own sex'.

That the use of hypnosis as a therapeutic agent declined rather
than increased towards the end of the century indicates an important
aspect of the relations between doctor and patient upon which the
medical profession depend for their status in the eyes of the public.
When a good deal was known about hypnosis it became apparent
that there are wide individual variations between people in their
hypnotic susceptibility. There are no very obvious advance indicators
as to whether a person will be susceptible to hypnosis, and so if a
doctor tries to hypnotize a patient and fails completely, he suffers
a loss of prestige in the patient's eyes. Whatever other treatments he
then tries with the patient, including prescribing bottles of coloured
water, his efforts are likely to be met with some scepticism. Doctors
who used hypnosis began to devise techniques whereby their failures
would not be so obvious, but it was nevertheless a problem threatening to their prestige.

The problem of the insusceptible patient was one of the reasons why Sigmund Freud gave up hypnosis and elaborated the alternative technique of psychoanalysis, a technique that became so popular with psychiatrists that it effectively ousted hypnotherapy from favour.

Freud, like Mesmer before him, came from Vienna to Paris in search of wider horizons, but unlike Mesmer, he had the wit not only to re-hash the theories of his forerunners but to study and make use of the work of his contemporaries. Eventually, he outstripped them all in theory-building.

Freud studied under Charcot at the Salpêtrière and worked with Janet. He also studied hypnosis at Nancy under Bernheim, and translated the latter's book on hypnosis and psychotherapy into German. He was thus well aware of the contemporary theories of hypnosis and able to adapt current practices to his own work. His own methods of hypnosis are conveyed in an article he wrote in 1891 for a medical dictionary, before he had become quite disenchanted with hypnotherapy,[21] but even here he indicates the nature of his frustrations in the therapeutic use of hypnosis :

'We can never tell in advance whether it will be possible to hypnotize a patient or not, and the only way we have of discovering is by the attempt itself. There has been no success hitherto in bringing accessibility to hypnosis into relation with any other of an individual's attributes. All that is true is that sufferers from mental disease and degenerates are for the most part not hypnotizable and neurasthenics only with great difficulty. . . . The second alternative, however, is that no influence, or only a slight degree of it, has been established, while the physician has behaved as though he had a successful hypnosis before him. Let us picture the patient's mental state at this point. He has promised at the start of the preparations to stay quiet, not to speak any more and to give no indication of confirmation or denial; he now notices that, on the basis of his consent to this, he is being told that he is hypnotized; he is irritated at this, feels uncomfortable at not being allowed to express his irritation; no doubt, too, he is afraid that the physician will begin suggesting to him too soon, in the belief that he is hypnotized before he is. And now experience shows that, if he is not really hypnotized, he does not keep the compact we have made with him. He opens his eyes and says (resentfully as a rule) "I am not in the least asleep!" A beginner would now regard the hypnosis as a failure, but someone with experience will not lose his composure. He will reply, not in the least angrily, as he once more closes the patient's eyes : "Keep still. You have promised not to talk. Of course I know that you are not 'asleep' nor is that in the least necessary. What would have been the sense of my simply making you fall asleep? You would not understand when I speak to you. You are not asleep, but you are hypnotized, you are under my influence; what I say to you now will make a special impression on you and will be of use to you." After this explanation, the patient usually [*sic* !] becomes quiet and we make the suggestions to him; for the moment we abstain from looking for physical signs of hypnosis, but after this so-called hypnosis has been repeated a number of times, we shall find that some of the somatic phenomena which characterize hypnosis will emerge. In many cases of this kind it remains to the end doubtful whether the state we have provoked deserves the name of "hypnosis".'

To a man of Freud's dominating personality such failures to hypnotize must have been very galling. He did not apparently appreciate that, through no fault of his own, some attempts to hypnotize were inevitably bound to fail, since the capacity to achieve hypnosis depends on the subject more than on the hypnotist. The technique of psychoanalysis which he went on to substitute for hypnotherapy contained no such hazards for the physician, and it is small wonder that it came to be accepted by so many psychiatrists as a preferable alternative. In psychoanalysis there is no attempt on the part of the therapist to do more than be a patient listener, commentator and interpreter of whatever the patient chooses to say or not to say while lying on the couch, and no guarantee is given as to how the treatment will progress. It may take years; the patient cannot definitely expect a progressive improvement as he would in hypnotherapy or any other form of therapy. Freud showed his genius in such an invention.

This is hardly the place to discuss the advantages and disadvantages of psychoanalysis as compared with hypnotherapy, from the point of view of either the physician or the patient. It merely suffices to point out that the huge amount of clinical effort which went into the study and practice of hypnosis in what has been called the 'golden age' of hypnosis in the last quarter of the nineteenth century came to be largely replaced by psychoanalysis and various other forms of psychotherapy. Our forebears approached the study of hypnosis with enthusiasm, some dedication and a great deal of miscellaneously divided effort. Their work advanced psychological medicine considerably but it raised more questions in psychology than it answered. It remained for a later age, using the humdrum methods of modern scientific investigation, to tackle more effectively the fascinating questions which the nineteenth-century masters had left unanswered.

REFERENCES

1 G. du Maurier, *Trilby*, London: Unicorn Press, 1894.

2 J. Braid, *Satanic Agency and Mesmerism Reviewed*, Manchester: 1842.

3 F. A. Pattie, 'Mesmer's medical dissertation and its debt to Mead's "de Imperia Solis ac Lunae" ', *Journal of the History of Medicine*, 2, 1956, p. 275.

4 A. P. Sinnet, *The Rationale of Mesmerism*, Boston: Houghton, 1897.

5 B. Franklin *et al.*, *Report of Dr Benjamin Franklin and Other Commissioners Charged by the King of France with the Examination of the Animal Magnetism, as now Practiced at Paris*, trans. from the French with an historical introduction by William Godwin, London: 1885.

6 M. D. Altschule, *The Roots of Modern Psychiatry*, New York: Grune & Stratton, 1965.

7 C. Ryecroft, *Wilhelm Reich*, London: Fontana, 1971.

8 A. M. J. Chastenet de Puységur, *Récherches, Expériences et Observations Physiologiques sur l'Homme dans l'Etat de Somnambulisme Naturel*, Paris: 1811.

9 M. F., *Essai sur les Probabilités du Somnambulisme Magnétique*, Paris: Chez les Marchands de Nouveautés, 1785.

10 J. Esdaile, *The Introduction of Mesmerism as an Anaesthetic and Curative Agent into the Hospitals of India*, Perth: Dewar & Son, 1852.

11 J. Elliotson, 'Cases of cures by Mesmerism', *The Zoist*, 1, June 1843.

12 J. Braid, *The Power of the Mind over the Body*, London: John Churchill, 1846.

13 Idem, *Satanic Agency and Mesmerism Reviewed*, op. cit.

14 J. R. Hilgard, *Personality and Hypnosis*, op. cit.

15 J. Braid, *Neurypnology, or the Rationale of Nervous Sleep Considered in Relation to Animal Magnetism*, London: John Churchill, 1843.

16 H. M. Bernheim, *Suggestive Therapeutics: A Treatise on the Nature and Uses of Hypnotism*, trans. C. A. Herter, London: Pentland, 1890.

17 W. James, *The Principles of Psychology*, New York: Holt, 1890.

18 M. Prince, *The Dissociation of a Personality*, New York: Longmans Green, 1906.

19 C. H. Thigpen and H. A. Cleckley, *The Three Faces of Eve*, London: Secker & Warburg, 1957.

20 British Medical Association, *Report by the Committee Appointed by the Council to Investigate Hypnotism*, London: 1892.

21 S. Freud, 'Hypnosis', in *The Complete Psychological Works of Sigmund Freud*, Vol. 1, London: Hogarth Press, 1961.

There is an old saying that when the outer appearance is in good order the inner states will ripen. We say that when we bow our heads and clasp our hands before Buddha, then our reverent feelings well forth. This means that whatever our original feelings may be, they will align themselves with our outer state which we have adjusted. I introduce this into the treatment of neurosis because it takes a long time to build a constructive attitude towards life if we wait for the inner condition to ripen. But we can work more easily from the outer appearance and produce quicker actual results.

TAKEHISA KORA, 'A Method of Instruction in Psychotherapy', *Jikeikai Medical Journal*, 1968.

Mesmerism first gained its popularity as a form of therapy, and the later developments in more rational research into hypnosis also had primarily a therapeutic bias. Man has always been rightly impatient of the many ills to which he is subject and has looked to every form of science to alleviate and cure these ills. Surgery and drugs have been used from time immemorial to alleviate suffering, but, in addition, every society has a tradition of quite irrational practices which are alleged to be curative of disease and distress. These irrational remedies come under the heading of magic, although sometimes they have received the blessing of religion. The practice of touching for the King's Evil (which was probably scrofula) was approved by the Church, and the exorcism of demons supposedly inhabiting the bodies of psychotic sufferers still has the blessing of some clerics of the Church of England.

Hypnosis very definitely comes under the heading of magic in the estimation of the average man. Assure him that cases of appendicitis or gall-stones have been cured by hypnosis, and he will be very likely to fully – or at least partly – believe you. The extent of his belief will depend upon how much he really believes in magic, and most of us have a sneaking belief in magic, publicly denied but privately confirmed when we avoid taking momentous decisions on the thirteenth of the month, or throw spilt salt over a shoulder.

We recognize that our lives are largely ruled by the activities of hard-faced physicists, chemists, mathematicians and engineers, so it gives us emotional satisfaction to note with glee in our more childish moments that their scientific universe is occasionally held up to ridicule by off-beat wizards. There have been many better conjurers than Uri Geller who have entertained us by such childish tricks as bending forks before the TV camera and on the stage, and earned an honest living thereby, but Geller has surpassed them by being an excellent psychologist in doing it all, so he says, by psychic power!

Fork-bending and watch-stopping are not very great technical problems, as any conjurer will explain to you, but it is enormous fun to claim with po-faced sincerity that it is all done by *real* magic. The power of mind over matter! Part of the fun consists in the fact that among the millions of viewers there must be some who are acknowledged 'scientists' (say, by having a university lectureship in oceanography or some other unrelated subject) who go overboard in partisanship for the fork-bending wizard. Ever after they bore their friends with tales of bending the household cutlery by making passes over it. They may even pester the editors of learned journals with articles about their magic prowess. We should remember that 'scientists' are like other men in having their emotional lives, their little vanities and frustrations, and their sheer childish delight in fantasy.

The above consideration of the role of belief in magic in our lives is necessary if we are to assess fairly the value of hypnosis in therapy, or indeed to understand the nature of therapy in its broadest sense. As stated earlier, according to the degree of belief in magic that anyone holds, so will he give a degree of credence to claims that appendicitis and gall-stones have been cured by hypnosis. He is very much more likely, however, to believe that cases of mental illness can be alleviated or cured by hypnosis. For appendicitis and gall-stones are gross physical conditions that we can see with our eyes and prod with a scalpel, but mental illnesses are, by definition, of the 'mind' which we can neither see nor prod.

By popular vote, therefore, we concede that hypnosis may be very likely to have some possible use in therapy for mental disorders. We reveal our deeply-grounded belief that there is a basic difference between 'mind' and 'body', a belief which more thoughtful people have recognized to be erroneous, but find no way of circumventing because it is embodied in the very language we use and hence in the concepts which we manipulate when thinking. Gilbert Ryle[1] has attacked the mind-and-body position by pointing out that it is in effect belief that we are machines (physical bodies) inhabited by an incorporeal ghost (the mind) which hovers there pulling the levers. It must be admitted that many people hold just this primitive concept of man.

To the layman, it is magic which bridges the gulf between mind and matter, although he may be reluctant to admit this. But it is this very belief in magic which makes progress in understanding the nature of hypnosis, and how it may be used in therapy, so difficult. And not only the layman has this difficulty. The late Sir Aubrey Lewis, when Professor of Psychiatry at the Maudsley Hospital, was heard to say that he would not condone the use of hypnosis because he did not wish to 'dabble with the supernatural'. Many doctors are content to use hypnosis in their practices in a rather hit-or-miss fashion, content to bask in the aura of being a bit of a wizard in the eyes of their patients when it does happen to work, or at least concur with the spontaneous remission of many ailments.

Tired of the assumptions of Western psychology in which the mind-body duality is pretty firmly established in spite of the claims of the Behaviourists, the author chose to spend a summer of sabbatical leave in the universities of Japan to study hypnosis and therapy in a different intellectual climate. Although psychology in Japan has been superficially westernized in the post-war era, they have their own intellectual traditions. Just as we in Europe owe much to ancient Greece in our science and philosophy and have inherited many of their ways of thinking, so the Japanese have developed in a climate of science emanating from the ancient civilization of China, and have to some degree been influenced by Indian philosophy.

In recent years some aspects of the philosophy of Zen Buddhism have been popularized in the West by writers such as Arthur Koestler, a hostile critic who criticized Zen as being the philosophy of 'no mind'. But if the mind is held to be an empty concept in a certain way of regarding reality, at least there is no problem of the supposed duality of mind and body to overcome. If we can acknowledge that there is but one reality clearer thinking is possible in many areas of human concern, including that of therapy for illness.

Eysenck[2] has pointed out that the dilemma of psychiatry is that there is a confusion of role. Psychiatry is a medical specialism, just like gynaecology, dermatology and the like, although it was only in 1971 that the psychiatrists received recognition for a Royal College of Psychiatrists in Britain. By virtue of their medical training – involving the study of anatomy, physiology and the numerous pathological aberrations of body function – psychiatrists are well able to become specialists in many disease processes which cause mental illness. In ancient times insanity was thought to be due to possession by demons (and as noted earlier, some modern clerics are reluctant to give up this belief!) or even to the influence of the moon – hence sufferers were called 'lunatics', as being under lunar influence. Medicine as it progressed was able to show that some 'madmen' simply had tumours in the head or scars on the brain, and that sometimes surgery could remove the evil. Other 'madmen' had bacteria or syphilitic spirochaetes infecting the brain, and these could often be removed with drugs. Still other 'madmen' had disturbances of their body chemistry and were being intoxicated by self-produced poisons and could also benefit from drug treatment and sometimes by special diets. In these complex areas modern psychiatry is still wrestling with its legitimate problems.

The confusion of role to which Eysenck is referring concerns the expertise which psychiatrists claim in the areas of human behaviour which have got nothing to do with the medical problems of diseased or injured brains or disturbed body chemistry. Disturbed behaviour, neuroses and (to use an old-fashioned term) sheer unhappiness are not really medical problems at all. As such conditions exist with no medical cause, psychiatrists and other medical doctors are not specially well-qualified to deal with them. In fact, some psychiatrists know very little about the behavioural problems which occur in sections of society which are very far removed from their own social experience. The author, when working as a clinical psychologist, worked with a consultant psychiatrist who, on encountering a psychiatric patient who described himself as a 'poof', assumed that this was a new word that the poor man had invented out of his delusions.

It is true that someone sleepless and wild with unhappiness because his girl-friend has jilted him, or because he failed to get the first-class honours he anticipated, or because he has bankrupted himself at gambling – can go to psychiatrist or to his GP who may give him drugs to alleviate his distress. Alternatively, he can go to a publican who will sell him other, perhaps less harmful drugs to alleviate his distress; or to a hypnotherapist who may secure calmness and sleep for him by hypnosis. But neither the psychiatrist, the publican nor the hypnotist is necessarily *by virtue of his training* a specialist in how to overcome the shocks to our vanity and aspirations that life gives us.

The reaction of the layman to this will probably be that the psychiatrist, and presumably the hypnotherapist, *ought* to be such a specialist. He ought to be a 'mind-doctor', if only we knew what the mind was. And the reaction of the psychiatrist will probably be that he *is* a 'mind-doctor', that it is the *other* schools of psychiatry (Freudian, Adlerian, Jungian, Reichian, etc., etc.) which are not quite right in their view of the human mind. But, taking a commonsense view of the issue, what is the relevance of a medical training to being wise about human behaviour?

The author, having helped to organize and participated as a teacher in the psychology course for medical men studying to be admitted to the Royal College of Psychiatrists, is in a position to know just how much psychology a candidate is required to know to be admitted. Rather less than an eighteen-year-old undergraduate at the end of his initial year on an honours psychology course. It is fair to acknowledge that some psychiatrists, when they realize the total inadequacy of their training, study further and become excellent psychologists. Max Hamilton, Professor of Psychiatry at Leeds, made this clear in a presidential address to the British Psychological Society.[3] But such psychiatrists are in a minority.

Many psychiatrists, particularly those of the Freudian school, would contend that they are 'mind-doctors' by virtue of their special study of what they allege to be the mind. Their approach and their success (both in terms of status and prosperity) remind one of a well-known Jewish story; one that Freud omitted from his famous book on *Wit and the Unconscious.*

It is related that the early conquests of the Roman legions brought them in contact with many barbarian peoples, and that the Roman practice was to go straight to the temple and command the priests to bring out the idols that they worshipped. They would then destroy these idols and set up the statue of Caesar, commanding that in future this was to be the one and only god they would worship and sacrifice to. The change could be accomplished with comparatively little discomfort or carnage and a new subject people was integrated into the Roman Empire. Later they might import the whole Pantheon. Now when the Romans reached the country of the Jews they made the usual demand at the temple, but the Jewish priests smilingly declared that there was no idol. A search of the temple revealed that the priests were speaking the truth, and the puzzled Roman commander declared, 'Now all these other barbarian priests have been conning their people with *something*, and we could destroy it. But you Jewish priests have been conning the people with *nothing*, and we can't destroy it, so how can we ever subdue your people successfully?' And history proved his doubts to be well founded.

Freud's psychoanalytic school, which some claim to have replaced and given the death-blow to hypnotherapy, has flourished on an *absence* of any evidence for its logical validity or therapeutic usefulness. Its priestcraft is in an impregnable position. The founder of the school was a medical man and so have been most of his influential followers, and what they have done is to transfer the prestige of medicine to strictly non-medical areas. For psychoanalytic psychiatrists have not been so influential in psychiatry concerned with aberrations of behaviour due to brain disease, infections and disturbed body chemistry, but in areas of behavioural disturbance which are essentially social in origin. They have created a great deal of confusion amongst lay people by arguing in terms of medical analogy where such analogy is inappropriate.

One of the most important areas of controversy, particularly in considering hypnotherapy, is over the question of symptoms. In medicine a *symptom* is that which the patient complains of; he is aware of it, it troubles him and he seeks alleviation. A *sign* however, is what the physician notices and is an indicator of a pathological condition, whether the patient complains of it or not. In common usage the word 'symptom' is often employed in non-medical contexts. We may say that a growth of crystals on a house wall is a symptom of rising damp, or that a high consumption of oil in a car is a symptom of worn piston rings. The word implies an outward manifestation of a hidden condition.

In medicine it is rarely useful to treat the symptom itself. The patient with pneumonia complains of a high fever, but we do not cure his infection by surrounding him with ice-bags. The psychoanalysts and many schools of psychotherapy which derive from psychoanalytic theory claim that behavioural disorders are in general *symptoms* of underlying maladjustments which often only remotely resemble their outward manifestations. They claim, therefore, that it is pointless to attempt to cure the disturbance of which the sufferer complains since it is merely a symptom of some underlying and hidden condition, probably sexual in origin. They often go further and allege that the observable aberration is *necessary* to the sufferer, and if you cure him of it you are robbing him of a vital outlet, and he will develop some alternative and perhaps more sinister aberration. Many people have questioned whether this medical analogy is at all appropriate for behavioural disturbances.

All this is highly relevant to what one can do in therapy by hypnosis. If by hypnotic suggestion we enable a child to stop wetting his bed at night, on the face of it we have done him a good turn by enabling him to acquire the usual capacity of tolerating a full bladder in a dry bed while he sleeps. To the psychoanalyst, however, we have robbed him of a symptom to which he is entitled, and dire consequences may ensue. If we enquire what consequences will follow or what the bed-wetting is supposed to be a symptom of, we are told that it would really be necessary to psychoanalyse the child to resolve these difficult questions. The psychoanalysts have made this criticism of the cure of bed-wetting by hypnotherapy or by the simple bell-and-blanket conditioning treatment (see Chapter 4 for discussion of conditioning) without ever producing a shred of evidence that cured bed-wetters are other than much happier for over-

coming this distressing habit. In fact, no disturbing habits develop
in substitution, but because psychoanalysis is founded more on faith
than reason, this contrary evidence makes no difference to established dogma.

Bed-wetting has been mentioned as an example of aberrant behaviour which would be classed as a symptom by psychoanalysts and
many derivative therapists, and therefore regarded as unsuitable for
direct treatment. There are also a wide variety of other conditions
which would come in the same class, and will now be discussed.

There are the phobias, that is, conditions of intense fear which
are produced by wholly trivial or harmless objects such as feathers,
mice, spiders, domestic cats, or by situations such as going into a
public place, a lift, a strange lavatory, a graveyard. There are
hundreds of harmless objects and situations which have become the
focus of intense fear in people who are not otherwise particularly
abnormal. The kernel of a phobia is its irrationality. The actual
condition feared need not necessarily be harmless, as when people
have a phobia of venereal disease or cancer, but if the phobic
sufferer knows perfectly well that he has not the slightest rational
reason to suspect that he has the condition, knowledge of his own
irrationality adds an extra torture to his fear. Marks[4] points out that
'Phobic patients are often sensitive to the lack of understanding
among normal people. They are ashamed of their fears and of the
ridicule by others for having those fears, so they often suffer in
silence and hide their symptoms from an unsympathetic environment as long as they can.'

The approach of psychoanalytically oriented therapists to phobic
conditions is to try to establish what the phobia 'means' to the
patient, on the assumption that it has a symbolic meaning in terms
of the patient's personal history and is somehow fulfilling a positive
though distorted function. The alternative approach – the behavioural approach – does not postulate any symbolic meaning for the
phobia, nor does it hold that it is necessary to find out how the
phobia arose in order to cure it.

Hypnotherapists have taken one or the other approach, and indeed have veered between them in fitting their therapy to the
individual case. Some have used hypnosis as a quick and convenient
way of getting information about the patient's past history, for it is
possible in hypnosis to concentrate on past events in our lives and
to re-live details which we cannot ordinarily remember. So vivid
indeed can be the recall in hypnosis that the hypnotized person can
be brought to believe that he is actually experiencing a return to an
earlier age, and he will speak and behave much as he did at that
age. This technique of age-regression in hypnosis for the purpose of

recovering supposedly forgotten roots of present-day neurotic behaviour has its dangers. If the hypnotherapist has strong beliefs
about the probable origin of the patient's current troubles – suppose
he thinks that his patient's phobia for scissors, knives and all sharp
instruments arose in an infantile fear that his father would castrate
him (a favourite theme in the Freudian mythology) – then he may
unwittingly suggest such themes to the hypnotized patient in an
effort to probe for the truth. People in hypnosis are remarkably apt
to do and say whatever the hypnotist expects, so sensitive are they
to subtle hints. A hypnotized person may even think that he has
recovered a memory of his childhood which arose purely in the
imagination and suggestions of the hypnotist. Martin Gardner[5] gives
a most amusing account of how a Dianetics (nowadays called
Scientology) practitioner gets a patient to endorse the most absurd
'memories' of what he experienced in his mother's womb !

In an alternative form of hypnotherapy there is no special attempt
to seek the supposed roots of the current disturbance by raking over
the distant past. Obviously the history of the disorder must be
investigated and recorded, but effort is concentrated on getting the
patient to unlearn the habit of fear and withdrawal from the phobic
object or situation and to relearn habits of calm and confident
approach.

Hypnosis is a particularly suitable technique for this process of
unlearning and relearning for a number of reasons. First, the object
of the phobia may not easily be brought into the room where the
therapy is conducted. If it is a phobia for mice, fine; they may
actually be presented in cages or running on the carpet. But if the
phobia is for something like crossing bridges in a literal sense, one
must depend in the early days of therapy on approaching imaginary
bridges. In hypnosis, scenes of the utmost vividness can be conjured
up as required. Second, as the emotions of the hypnotized person
can be controlled to a great extent by suggestion, the patient can be
got to approach the feared object without mounting terror, and so
learn this new and desirable habit.

One theory of phobic behaviour and experience holds that the
object or situation is feared and becomes increasingly more terrifying
as time goes on, because every time the phobic person approaches
it his heart thumps, his skin sweats, his stomach cramps and he gets
into such a painful panic that he can never habituate to its nearness
to him. Habituation means adjusting to something as being ordinary,
harmless and part of the everyday environment. Now phobias are
simply a morbid and *inappropriate* exaggeration of the natural fear
reactions of our animal ancestors. It would be a sad day indeed for
a monkey colony if it habituated to the close proximity of a boa-

constrictor. Indeed, the sight of one will send them into a panic and
they run away. The role of non-habituation in phobias has been
most interestingly discussed by Lader and Wing.[6]

In the present context hypnotherapy is being discussed as part of
what is usually known as behaviour therapy. This is the modification
of unwanted behaviour and experience by concentrating on the
aberrant manifestation itself and trying to remove it, rather than
treating it as though it were a symptom of some postulated disorder
deep in the patient's psyche and probably relating to his emotional
life as a toddler. Joseph Wolpe, who is regarded as one of the
founding fathers of behaviour therapy, sets out the theory in his
book *Psychotherapy by Reciprocal Inhibition*.[7] Here he describes
how he has used hypnosis to relax the patient and hypnotic suggestions to engender as vivid an image of the phobic situation as he
deemed necessary. This is an eminently practical use of hypnosis in
behaviour therapy and must not be confounded with the use discussed earlier where hypnosis is used to produce age regression and
the like in the hope that it will uncover the supposed roots of the
neurotic disorder.

It may be remarked in passing that the title of Wolpe's book is
somewhat misleading. 'Psychotherapy' is often contrasted with 'behaviour therapy' for the two have obvious differences. Psychotherapy aims at giving treatment to the psyche, the supposed ghost
in the machine. Behaviour therapists do not inquire whether there
is in fact a ghost in the machine, but try to treat the disordered
behaviour, a more modest enterprise.

The essence of Wolpe's original method was to make the patient
thoroughly relaxed and then to introduce the feared object in
imagery very, very gradually, never letting it obtrude too suddenly
and forcefully on the scene so as to cause too much anxiety. Indeed,
the feared object may be kept very much in the background in the
first stages of therapy, for in every phobia there is a hierarchy of
items and situations surrounding the pinnacle of terror which may
be approached with various degrees of trepidation.

In the case of a phobia for cats, for instance, the sound of a
distant mew might cause the flesh to creep without causing blind
panic. To begin with just the hypnotically induced mew might be
dealt with, and confronted by the patient with relative calm in a
state of deep relaxation. Wolpe reasoned that deep relaxation is
incompatible with active fear, since in the latter all the running-
away mechanisms are jangling. Thus, using hypnotic techniques to
induce both relaxation and the controlled presentation of feared
stimuli, the patient could be accustomed to each step up the hierarchy over a matter of weeks or months and eventually reach the

pinnacle without experiencing uncontrollable fear. This is the method of graduated desensitization.

But, our knowledgeable reader may ask, what if the patient just does not happen to be susceptible to hypnosis – is this form of therapy unavailable to him? No it is not unavailable, for everyone can, with sufficient training, reach quite a deep state of relaxation, and everyone can use his imagination to conjure up objects and scenes as suggested by the therapist. Probably the fact that the images are so heavily loaded with emotion makes them specially easy to visualize. Hypnosis is not an all-or-none phenomenon, and some degree of hypnotic involvement is undoubtedly present in Wolpe's technique of graduated desensitization even with people who are rather poor hypnotic subjects. It seems reasonable to suppose that, other things being equal, the therapy would be quicker and more efficient with a good hypnotic subject, and indeed that is why Wolpe tried to get as deep a hypnotic trance as he could.

We may now turn to a yet a third type of therapy, using hypnosis in a way that a layman might regard as magical. Here there is no attempt to manipulate the patient's feelings in relation to a carefully graduated hierarchy of feared stimuli. The patient is hypnotized and the hypnotist dogmatically tells him that his troubles will soon be over and that he will be completely cured, and hey presto! – what is the result? Some would predict that there would be no result whatsoever; others, with a touching faith in magic, would expect the 'spell' to work in one go and the patient to wake up cured. The truth seems to lie between these two extremes, but the point of interest for those of us who favour science rather than magic is *why* things happen as they do.

Isaac Marks and his colleagues[8] carried out an interesting study comparing the efficiency of graduated desensitization with hypnosis. They studied twenty-eight patients suffering from a mixed variety of phobias, and assessment of improvement under treatment was made by the patients themselves, the therapists and an independent assessor. Some patients received treatment by graduated desensitization as described above, but without any hypnotic suggestion to assist relaxation or imagery (if such a thing can really be avoided). Some patients received only hypnosis of the dogmatic 'You'll get better because I say so' variety. A third group of patients received both treatments at some stage in the study; that is, if they did not improve after twelve weeks' treatment by one method they were given, after a delay, a further twelve weeks' treatment by the other.

On analysing their rather complex results these doctors were surprised to find that on most measures of improvement their carefully planned programme of graduated desensitization was not significally better than sheer dogmatic hypnotic suggestion, a method that was used over a hundred years ago and can still be used by people with no training in psychology or psychiatry. How does this apparent magic work? Marks suggested that its effectiveness lay in the fact that the hypnotic suggestion repeated week after week calmed the patients in the everyday situations in which they would happen to encounter the phobic objects or situations. Because of this hypnotically induced confidence, the patients could approach nearer to their pinnacles of terror and so eventually lose their fear of them, which is the ordinary way in which we lose our fears of bogies and paper tigers. This is not an entirely satisfactory explanation, for it still leaves us wondering how the hypnotic suggestions calmed the patients in everyday life.

Hypnosis works because the voice and the assertions of the hypnotist come to replace our own thoughts in certain situations. This sounds a little far-fetched, and conjures up the picturesque image of Dr X. haunting his patient's head (another ghost in the machine) so that when the cat phobic says to herself, 'It's the sound of mewing – but it's not frightening at all !', it is really Dr X. speaking, and the patient literally *feels* in accordance with the thoughts in her head. That someone else's assertions should come to be the substance of our own thoughts and that our emotional responses should be in accordance with what *he* declares to be true, rather than what we thought was true, is not so very surprising. This is in fact the ordinary psychological reality. We do not like to admit it, for we like to regard the content of our thoughts, beliefs, feelings and actions as the unique product of our own 'will'. A more accurate picture is arrived at (since we must deal in pictures and similes) by acknowledging that we are manipulating a collection of unoriginal thoughts, feelings, beliefs and actions that we have borrowed from other people. We are our unique selves, yes – but only in the sense that the temporary pattern which we find in a kaleidoscope is unique. Let another person shake the kaleidoscope and another unique pattern appears, but the bits and pieces that make up these patterns are not themselves unique. We think in words and phrases that we did not invent, and we give conventional labels to our emotions.

The use of graduated desensitization characterized the main method of behaviour therapy for many years. Later, a paradoxical method called 'flooding' came to be used as an alternative. In the former technique, great care is taken that the patient is not subjected to too much anxiety all at once, so that he can proceed little by little up the hierarchy of his fears. In flooding, the whole process is turned upside down and efforts are made to ensure that the patient experiences the maximum anxiety all at once, and stays in the terror-producing situation without withdrawing from it until the therapist lets him. Thus, if a patient suffers from a phobia for rats, the therapist would try to get him to imagine that he was covered with them, rats running over his face, burrowing up his trousers, nibbling at his armpits and excreting in his hair. According to the degree of co-operation from the patient and the histrionic ability of the therapist, the former is worked up into a frenzy of fear and nausea. All this may sound rather childish to many of us, but then we do not suffer from rat phobia.

The point about flooding is that the patient is not allowed to *retire* from the situation but stays in it experiencing the worst. To someone who has perhaps for years hurried from the room if he heard something like a scuffle under the floor, and crossed the road rather than approach within ten feet of a dustbin, this is a tremendous achievement. In fact, if he is prepared to experience the horrendous imagery for about half an hour, and of course neither do his privates get bitten nor his hair defiled, he just cannot keep up the state of high anxiety and may even become a trifle bored. When the level of anxiety decreases (and this can be determined by instruments monitoring his heart rate etc.) the therapist declares the session to be at an end. And going home he is perhaps brave enough to kick a dustbin.

Perhaps conventional psychoanalysis has something in common with flooding, for if the patient has spent the afternoon on the analytic couch living it up with Queen Jocasta (in infantile fantasy of course) then when he goes home he may encounter his own m****r without a blush.

It would seem that hypnosis is the ideal technique for managing the flooding procedure, for whatever the scene – aggressive rats, teetering on a cliff-top, locked in a cupboard, bathing in human blood – whatever is the phobia of the patient, can be created with hallucinatory vividness and maintained as long as necessary. Reading of the related literature does not reveal any published cases of hypnosis being used as an adjunct to flooding, and this is so surprising that it invites some comment.

It seems that psychologists and psychiatrists attach themselves to some school of therapy and stick to its procedures. The behaviour therapists, whose methods we have been discussing, are mainly psychologists rather than psychiatrists and have been committed to a very successful programme of relating psychological theory to the field of abnormal behaviour. Much of this theory has come from laboratories where animal learning has been studied, and which aims to be entirely scientific in that the nature of the stimuli they use are

very carefully defined and the results carefully assessed. This movement of behaviour therapy, which has been going on for little more
than twenty years, has been amazingly successful in therapeutic
efficiency in contrast to the earlier efforts in psychoanalytic and
allied therapies. Writing in 1952, Eysenck[9] published figures which
indicated that there was no evidence for supposing that psychotherapy in general had any effect whatsoever on neurotic disorders.
Patients appeared to recover as frequently with no treatment as
with psychotherapeutic treatment. Naturally, Eysenck's criticisms
met with indignant rejoinders from various psychotherapists, but
they could not refute his contention because in general they had not
bothered to keep any adequate records of what rate of success, or
lack of of it, their methods had had, or considered it particularly
necessary that they should do so.

It was as if the clergy were being challenged to show the usefulness of their prayers for rain in time of drought. Was the rainfall
significantly increased in those parishes where such prayers were
offered up compared with those parishes where they were not? One
can think of various ingenious experiments to test out the usefulness
of prayers in common use – such as having a moratorium for five
years on the morning prayer to the Almighty to 'Endue thy ministers
with righteousness' to see if its omission would make any difference.
Of course any intelligent cleric would laugh at such a childish idea,
and explain that these prayers were not intended to cajole or twist
the arm of the Almighty, but were to keep up the morale of the
parishioners. In the same way, it may be argued, the usefulness of
psychotherapists is not to be assessed by scientific inquiry, because
'everyone knows' that they keep up the morale of the sad army of
neurotic sufferers who are always with us. These sufferers look to
the medical establishment, to the psychiatrists, the psychiatric social
workers, the counsellors, the child guidance workers as they used to
look to the Church in a former age.

But pioneers in behaviour therapy like Wolpe and Eysenck had
been scientifically oriented and were not interested in fulfilling a
vague, priestly function. They wanted to get results, or at least to
find out why they were not getting results with any one method,
and this involved the usual routines of science, the matching of
experimental groups with control groups, the techniques of eliminat-
ing rater bias, the elaborate analysis of results by statistical processes
and the comparison of observed results with those that might have
been obtained by chance.

This pioneer effort in therapy appealed to a young generation of
psychologists trained in scientific method, and led to the tremendous
expansion of behaviour therapy in the last twenty years. The results

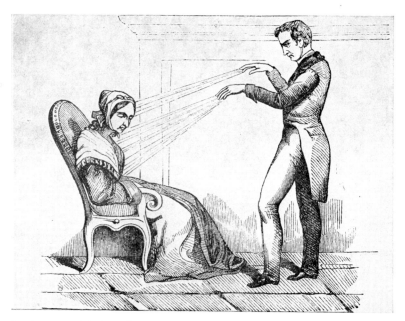

1 A mesmerist at work.

2 Svengali mesmerizing Trilby. From du Maurier's novel *Trilby*.

4 Electronic apparatus measuring physiological changes in a hypnotized subject.

3 Stage hypnosis: the young man has been given the hallucination of embracing a lovely girl.

In many areas of treatment have been modest, but what is important is that methods of accurate control have been vastly improved compared with the older, impressionistic type of psychotherapy. Moreover, the behaviour therapy movement produced a revolution in the relations between psychologists with their university training in experimental methods, and the psychiatrists with their medical, bedside-manner approach to problems. The psychologists used to be the poor handmaidens of the clinic, doing little more than measure IQs when requested to do so by the psychiatrists. Since the advent of behaviour therapy psychologists have gained the status of respected colleagues in the therapeutic team, and as mentioned earlier, many of the brighter and younger psychiatrists have come to take psychology seriously to the extent of becoming excellent psychologists in addition to their medical qualifications.

Hypnosis in Britain, and to some degree elsewhere, has been a largely medical specialism as far as therapy is concerned, although significant research has chiefly been the work of psychologists. In Britain there is no learned journal being published which is concerned specifically with hypnosis, although there are one or two mimeographed bulletins of small medical groups. The *British Journal of Medical Hypnotism* ceased publication a few years ago, presumably for lack of sufficient interest among medical people. In the USA there is the *International Journal of Clinical and Experimental Hypnosis* and the *American Journal of Clinical Hypnosis*, both of which publish good scientific articles of a standard to be found in other learned journals. These two journals attract so little attention in England, however, that they are not to be found in either the library of the Royal College of Psychiatrists or in the Institute of Psychiatry at Maudsley Hospital. This is some indication of the degree of interest, or lack of it, that exists in this country regarding the therapeutic possibilities of hypnosis.

There are now about eight learned journals published in English which are devoted mainly to the topic of behaviour therapy, and contributed to mainly by psychologists. This is indicative of trends in therapy. It is perhaps understandable that those active in the behaviour therapy movement are not much concerned to make use of hypnosis, for there is a reluctance to get involved with something which although not now regarded as 'the supernatural', still smacks of the vague, uncontrolled medical tradition from which the behaviour therapists are anxious to free themselves. It is occasionally used, and may often complicate therapeutic results in an unintended way (more than some behaviour therapists imagine), but there is little attempt in this country to use hypnosis in a systematic way as part of behaviour therapy.

C

When the author was in Japan, where they are interested in Western methods of behaviour therapy, Japanese colleagues were very surprised to hear how little hypnotherapy and behaviour therapy are integrated in Britain. In Japan, and in parts of the USA, much more use of hypnosis is made in therapy and it does not have the aura of strangeness that it has in this country. Every country has its traditions and fashions, and these are not always related to anything more than the accidents of historical development.

The uses of hypnosis have been described in relation to the treatment of phobias : its use in the attempt which is sometimes made to uncover the supposed roots of the phobic condition by age regression and the exploration of early memories; its use in producing deep relaxation and vivid imagery; and finally the method of dogmatic assertion of cure which can be surprisingly successful. A fourth use of hypnosis in therapy will now be discussed.

In the treatment of phobias the chief problem has been to reduce the overmastering anxiety to which the patient is subject so that he can relearn normal adjustment. In another class of disorders the problem which presents is not primarily one of anxiety but of habits which have disastrous consequences, such as alcoholism, drug addiction, compulsive sexual molestation of children, sporadic outbursts of violence, compulsive gambling, excessive smoking. In these conditions it is useless to tell the patient to 'pull himself together' and resist the temptation, and to attribute his failures to 'weak will'. It is pointless to threaten him with the usual penalties, for the junkie knows that the death penalty has already been decreed for him by virtue of his habit, and much the same may be said of advanced tobacco addicts. Human motivation does not work that way, and we get nowhere by trying to influence the 'will'. In the form of therapy which is needed, hypnosis must be used to change behaviour, perhaps by arousing anxiety at *precisely* the right moment in the chain of actions of the habit, but not so as to produce an all-pervasive state of anxiety.

It may be argued that these various conditions stem from an attempt to deal with anxiety, that the alcoholic drinks so that he will not be subject to nagging, free-floating anxiety, and the compulsive gambler seeks the thrill of gaming as an anodyne for mental distress. It is easy to make out such a case by armchair theorizing, but such theorizing is of little practical value. Whatever conditions of adolescent *Weltschmertz* or unconscious memory of unhappy potty-training started the alcoholic on the bottle, his troubles are so overwhelmingly related to booze that keeping him out of hospital, prison or the mortuary generally demands energetic concentration on the present problem.

One long-established method of treating alcoholism is to get the alcoholic to drink his tipple and then make him painfully sick by the administration of emetics. This method has generally been of little value because it is a truism, known by some of us all too well, that the promise of a shocking hangover in the morning does not stop us indulging in the hard stuff *now*. Someone has pointed out that that the difference between sin and sanctity is simply a matter of the temporal relations between pain and pleasure. To have a whale of a good time now in contempt of misery in the hereafter – sin; to endure a miserable existence now in the anticipation of bliss in the hereafter – sanctity.

The matter of the temporal relations between an act and its outcome has been much investigated by psychologists, notably by Professor B. F. Skinner.[10] Our behaviour is controlled by our experience of its outcome, yes, but the time interval between the act and its outcome is all-important. It is almost useless to expect a puppy to refrain from messing the carpet because you will wallop him in an hour's time. Ideally, you should act the moment he does it, and even a verbal reproof is adequate for effective training if it is immediate. In the same way, it is useless to expect a child to refrain from smoking by convincing him that he may die of cancer in middle age. But if the first cigarettes he tries scald his tongue, he might regard them with distaste in the future, even against the peer-group pressure urging him to persist.

It is the same with rewards; there is much experimental evidence, both with animals and with humans, in laboratories and in real-life situations, that shows that behaviour is more effectively controlled and modified by a régime of small, immediate rewards, than by larger rewards occurring after a lapse of time. Rewards in this context include everything from peas for pigeons, sweets for children and social appreciation for adults.

This background of experimental work has led to a form of negative therapy for undesirable habits which is different from that represented by the nausea treatment for alcoholics. Electric shock has proved a convenient aversive stimulus, for it can be applied in repeated small doses at precisely the time when the patient is taking a swig of tipple. Typically, the alcoholic is instructed to take small sips of his favourite drink in the treatment room, with his arm wired up to a shock machine. Every so often, just as he brings the beloved beverage to his lips, he receives a painful electric shock. The theory is that he will come to associate the smell and taste of alcohol with the *anticipation* of pain and distress. Thereby we seek to induce a phobia – a phobia for alcohol.

In fact this aversive therapy for alcoholism does not work very well. The published literature on the subject reveals a wide range of success rates, none of them very encouraging. The snag appears to be that even if we engineer a phobia for alcohol by aversive conditioning, have we in fact 'cured' the patient? Phobias are apt to fluctuate in severity and occasionally to break down. If this occurs with an unwanted phobia we call it 'spontaneous remission'. Again, there is nothing like a drug such as alcohol for allaying phobic reactions, so once the 'cured' alcoholic has managed to gulp down some of the nauseous beverage, Dutch courage ensues and continued drinking can become positively pleasurable.

The ideal is to render the alcoholic normal, so that he can enjoy a pint or even two with his friends at the bar, and then go home content and wanting no more. Hypnotic treatment for alcoholism can concentrate on the aversive methods and engender post-hypnotic suggestions so that the smell and taste of the once-loved friend becomes nauseous, but this is by no means the ideal technique. If by hypnosis, or by any other method, you rob a person of what was once a joy, even though in a state of distress he has implored you to rid him of it, he may resent the successful suggestions and seek to outwit you. Patients who come for therapy, apparently entirely voluntarily, are sometimes very ambivalent as to whether they are really seeking cure. An alcoholic can come for therapy apparently pathetically anxious to break his habit, but in reality he may be seeking merely to placate somebody, say a wife who has threatened to leave him unless he goes for treatment.

Marcuse[11] describes an interesting case in which a man suffered not so much from his drunkenness as from the spendthrift behaviour in which he engaged when drunk. When he had properly hit the bottle, he would sign lavish cheques, and thus run into trouble. This was countered by the therapist producing in him a post-hypnotic suggestion that when he was drunk his right arm would be paralysed to the extent that he could not sign cheques. The patient countered this by learning to sign with his left hand, and when the hypnotist later included his left as well as his right arm in the post-hypnotic suggestion, our spendthrift merely encouraged his drinking companions to forge his signature! The therapist cannot hope to be entirely successful as a mere inhibitor of behaviour.

Therapy with alcoholics has been discussed at length because it raises the crucial questions related to all maladaptive habits which we try to get rid of. The same issues arise, for example, in the cases of men who molest little girls sexually. This is a more common aberration than many people suppose. The *British Journal of Psychiatry* often carries a full-page coloured advertisement from a certain drug company headed 'When the sexual drive cannot be controlled' – then a picture of a man in the usual raincoat handling a little girl who carries a satchel – '****** the humane alternative.' The reader is left wondering what the drug ****** is an alternative to. Castration? Locking him away until he is too old to do much more than poke the fire?

Misdirected sexual urges can certainly be treated by drugs and poultry keepers have a practice of turning cockerels into capons by implanting hormone pellets under the skin and thereby achieving a physiological castration. However, men whose sexual desires have become unfortunately fixated on little children can be treated more humanely by hypnosis and by other behavioural therapy.

Here we have a class of most recalcitrant patients – 'nympholepts' as Nabokov has called them – and they are most unlikely sincerely to wish to change their proclivities. They generally come for therapy either as the result of a court order, or out of fear of criminal sanctions. If hypnosis is used it can be directed in various ways. Trying to uncover the supposed dynamic roots of the condition is often a useless endeavour, for mere knowledge of how we came to be as we are does not mean that we will have any choice for the future. Hypnosis can be used like ****** the wonder drug to replace excited lust with dreary distaste, but more positive lines of approach are possible. If the patient is willing and able to be hypnotically influenced, then hypnosis can be the agent of sexual education. The charms of mature women, which previously left our nympholept cold, can be introduced in hypnotic imagery in an attractive light. Gradually the immature senses that have responded to skinny legs, narrow hips and flat chests can be educated to respond to more normal feminine shapes. Only when the man is beginning to get a positive thrill out of his therapy and the anticipation of future satisfactions, will he be willing and able to permit the extinction of his nympholepsy.

The positive approach to therapy for unwanted habits can of course be applied without deliberately attempting hypnosis, and in modern behaviour therapy this is often the case, for reasons mentioned earlier. However, it is never easy to say how much or how little hypnosis is being used in a behaviour therapy programme. Sometimes it is unwise to mention the word 'hypnosis' for reasons of policy, unless the person being treated understands something about hypnosis and regards it as a perfectly acceptable treatment from the start. The author once carried out a long programme of hypnotherapy with an aggressive psychopath of intimidating physique and habits (he specialized in bashing men whom he perceived to be homosexual, and assaulted figures in authority), in some trepidation in case the patient realized that he was being hypnotized. This man responded very well, and although later on he realized the nature of the treatment, he felt less dominated by our referring to it as 'relaxation therapy'.

Again, expectant mothers have been prepared for painless child-birth by repeated hypnotherapy without the word 'hypnosis' being mentioned. This is not necessarily a desirable omission, and it might be better if women came to accept such pre-natal treatment for what it is. Such a mother, quite advanced in her treatment, re-marked to the author on the fact that her arm would float up in the air whenever he suggested it, apparently of its own accord, and asked if this was anything like hypnosis.

Phobias and the sort of aberrant, psychopathic habits that have been discussed do not make up the whole of the neurotic disorders which present for therapy. Phobic anxiety also enters into the obsessional compulsive states. These are a distressing and common variety of neurotic disorder in which people feel compelled to engage in pointless, ritualistic behaviour like endless hand-washing, and to dwell upon distressing worries which they acknowledge to be point-less. By contrast, there are the hysterical type of disorders in which one of the characteristics is that the sufferer refuses to face reality and admit the nature of his problem.

One of the well-known examples of an hysterical disorder is *anorexia nervosa*, a condition generally found in adolescent girls and young women. In this distressing condition the sufferer simply stops eating and may indeed starve herself to death. Sometimes there is the peculiar complication of her being unwilling to admit that there is anything wrong or to co-operate in therapy. Other hysterical disorders may have similar features of lack of co-operation and bland denial of reality. It is interesting that much of the early work on hypnosis at the Salpêtrière Hospital in Paris was with hysterical patients, and Charcot based much of his theory upon study of them. Nowadays therapists are more prone to acknowledge that hysterical patients are often rather difficult to treat by hypnosis. The hysterical patient tends to beat the intention of the hypno-therapist by giggling at the wrong moment and passing inconsequen-tial remarks when supposed to be going into a state of hypnosis. Indeed, an hysterical defence may be to actually go to sleep during hypnosis, so that the business of facing up to the problem is avoided.

One of the characteristics of hysteria is its unpredictability. The therapist may find that he has achieved a rapid and dramatic cure by means of hypnosis, but this cure may not be long-lasting, and the hysterical disorder may reoccur with equally dramatic suddenness. It was treatment of many hysterical disorders in his consulting room that led Freud to over-generalize rather widely about the nature of mental disorder, and to propose theories of psychological function which, by taking the hysteric as a model, are somewhat limited in their applicability.

It is popularly supposed that hysteric sufferers are more usually female. Originally the condition was supposed to consist of the womb wandering about the woman's body. Although certain conditions like *anorexia nervosa*, sometimes complicated by intervening states of obesity, are more common in females, men can certainly suffer from hysterical disorders. Elliot Slater, once president of the Royal College of Psychiatrists and a noted champion of women's rights, has declared that hysteria is a mythical concept and simply represents an unkind masculine portrayal of femininity! However that may be, the concept is widely used and the woman (or man) who suffers from an hysterical disorder may characteristically preserve an outward equanimity by what is known as conversion hysteria. We have referred to this before in discussing Mesmer's work. It consists of converting a psychological disturbance into a physical disturbance of function such as a paralysed arm, an inability to speak, hysterical deafness or even blindness. The great jazz musician W. C. Handy was hysterically blind for a period, reputedly due to an emotional quarrel with his father.

While all modern theorists are agreed that Charcot was wide of the mark in proposing that only hysterics could be hypnotized, there is still little agreement about the relative hypnotizability of people suffering from hysterical disorders. In a review of the general question of the hypnotic susceptibility of neurotic sufferers, Gill and Brenman[12] suggested that while neurotic disorders make people rather resistant to hypnosis, hysterics are rather less resistant than others. Other writers take an opposite view. The trouble is that once we talk about 'hysterics' we tend to perpetuate the idea that they are a special sort of creature different from the rest of us. Although it is tempting to talk about an 'hysteric' when we mean 'someone suffering from an hysterical type of disorder', this is unfortunate in that it gives the term more reality than it deserves. Certainly, some of us are more predisposed to develop hysterical reactions than others, but that is about as far as one can go.

Because of the nature of hysterical disorders – primarily disorders of function without any discernible organic cause – the therapist may feel that hypnosis *ought* to be a successful form of therapy. For as in hypnosis we can cause a limb to become functionally paralysed by suggestion, remove memories and reinstate them, produce apparent blindness or deafness and then restore function, produce anaesthesia and then restore feeling, all by verbal suggestion, we cannot

72 *Hypnosis*

help feeling (with Charcot) that this is a sort of artificially produced hysteria. But such intuitive feeling is often misleading. We can, after all, produce positive hallucinations in hypnosis so that the subject experiences things that are not really there in the environment, and hallucinations are of course characteristic of some forms of advanced psychosis. But no one suggests that we can really free insane people of their hallucinations and delusions (false beliefs) by hypnosis. In general, insane people are the most difficult of all to hypnotize because they are not sufficiently in touch for there to be very effective communication with them. There is little evidence that hypnotherapy can be of much use in the treatment of the insane.

REFERENCES

1 G. Ryle, *The Concept of Mind*, London: Hutchinson, 1949.

2 H. J. Eysenck, *The Future of Psychiatry*, London: Methuen, 1975.

3 M. Hamilton, 'Psychology in Society: Ends or End?', *Bulletin of the British Psychological Society*, 26, 1973, pp. 185–189.

4 I. M. Marks, *Fears and Phobias*, London: Heinemann, 1969.

5 M. Gardner, *Fads and Fallacies in the Name of Science*, New York: Dover Publications, 1957.

6 M. H. Lader and L. Wing, *Physiological Measures, Sedative Drugs and Morbid Anxiety*, London: Oxford University Press, 1966.

7 J. Wolpe, *Psychotherapy by Reciprocal Inhibition*, Stanford, Calif.: Stanford University Press, 1958.

8 I. M. Marks, M. G. Gelder and J. G. Edwards, 'Hypnosis and desensitization for phobias: a controlled prospective trial', *British Journal of Psychiatry*, 114, 1968, pp. 1263–1274.

9 H. J. Eysenck, 'The effects of psychotherapy: an evaluation', *Journal of Consulting Psychology*, 16, 1952, pp. 319–324.

10 B. F. Skinner, *Science and Human Behaviour*, New York: Macmillan, 1953.

11 F. L. Marcuse, *Hypnosis: Fact and Fiction*, op. cit.

12 M. M. Gill and M. Brenman, *Hypnosis and Related States*, New York: International Universities Press, 1959.

The Mechanisms of Hypnosis in Therapy

> I must take leave to tell you that the medical
> man who has not studied the laws of *mind* as
> well as *matter*, and how they act and react on
> each other, is very unfit for practising his pro-
> fession, either with credit to himself or advan-
> tage to his patient.
>
> JAMES BRAID, *Satanic Agency and Mesmerism
> Reviewed*, 1842.

As we have seen in the last chapter, it may be conceded without
much strain on credulity that hypnosis can be useful in treating
emotional and behavioural disorders. Difficulty commonly arises,
however, in conceiving how hypnosis can possibly be useful in treating those disorders which we regard as physical. This chapter will
attempt to answer this question.

In order to answer the question we must first digress briefly into
psychological theory. Some readers might have preferred a long and
continuous discourse on the wonders of hypnosis, with many amazing anecdotes of patients who have been cured of all manner of ills.
Perhaps it is better that we should consider instead just how much
and how little is known about the psychological mechanisms by
which hypnosis works, and hence to what degree we may expect it
to be useful as a curative agent. Much of this psychological theory
will already be familiar to an educated public, and so much the
better. Its reiteration in the context of hypnotherapy will make the
latter more comprehensible in the language of common sense.

Let us first consider the very simple question of the treatment of
warts by hypnosis. Warts have various forms, but commonly they
are horny growths on the skin. They arise, in the first place, following some minor injury or irritation to the skin, although most such
abrasions do not give rise to warts. They may come singly or in
groups. Some people are specially liable to develop warts, or may be
at some period of their lives. There is some evidence that proneness
to warts is associated with a particular type of personality. Sainsbury[1] found that wart sufferers were rather more extroverted and
neurotic in their personality than most of the population.

Microscopic examination of warts shows that there is a virus
present, and so presumably this is irritating the skin tissue deep
down and causing the production of horny cells that constitute the

wart. However, examination of normal skin shows that this virus is commonly present and doing no harm at all. What then is special about the sufferer from warts?

It has been known since ancient times that warts are peculiarly influenced by suggestions, and that all sorts of tricks are retailed in folk medicine for their cure. A method that one can practise with children is to buy the wart. Simply ask the child quite solemnly if he wants to keep the wart, and if he says that he would be glad to be rid of it, tell him that you will buy it from him. You then give him a small sum of money. The transaction complete, you then tell him that the wart will soon go, and that in the meantime he must remember that the wart is no longer his, for he has sold it and has no right to keep it. The somewhat crazy logic of this may be rather puzzling to the child, but it reinforces the suggestion and the wart may soon slough off. A similar trick is simply to paint the wart with some harmless coloured dye, but it must be done with due solemnity, preferably by a figure of prestige who confidently assures the child that the wart will soon be gone.

The fascination of charming warts away and hence being able to practise a little white magic, is so great that some people have actually done the reverse and caused warts to come by suggestion. The following account is given by Baudouin :[2]

'In the Swiss canton of Vaud, curers of warts abound; and here it sometimes happens that the patient will employ a famous prescription without troubling to consult the healer. In these cases autosuggestion is seen in all its beauty. Prescriptions pass from village to village and from hamlet to hamlet. Some of them are incredibly quaint. For example, to cause warts, the subject goes out one evening, moistens the tip of the finger, looks at a star, and simultaneously applies the wet finger-tip to the other hand. The operation is repeated, the finger being freshly moistened with saliva each time, while the subject counts "one, two, three . . ." up to the number of warts desired. Now, wherever the moistened finger-tip has been applied a wart duly appears. I do not guarantee the alleged numerical precision, but the development of warts as a sequel of such practices is a proven fact.'

Wherever such practice of folk medicine exists and people have the satisfaction of seeing that a measure of apparent magic works, they often go on to attempt the impossible because they do not realize that the mechanism does not lie in the star-shine or the saliva but in their own psychological acceptance of the fact that the warts will come. Baudouin goes on to relate how these Swiss peasant girls attempt to produce warts in strangers by a piece of magic which is not well-founded.

'The Vaudois girls are very fond of this amusement – not for the mere pleasure of having warts (for the pleasure of their possession is open to dispute) but for a pleasure which to them is very real and very great, the pleasure of passing them on to someone else. A ribbon is tied round the affected hand, and is knotted as many times as there are warts on the hand; then the ribbon is dropped on the highway. Whoever picks it up and unties the knots, will get the warts, and the original owner of the warts will be cured.'

If the person who unknotted the ribbon were *aware* that he was being bewitched in this way, and was truly credulous of the bewitchment, then he might develop warts. But since he would presumably be ignorant of the fate that was intended, no such consequences would follow in reality, for warts are not contagious. But the intending donor might well lose her warts by auto-suggestion.

Tales of folk medicine relate both the cure of warts by quaint methods which may very well be true, and the production of warts in others by methods of bewitchment which do not ring true at all. This should make us very sceptical of the whole thing. Some people have in fact questioned whether warts have ever been cured by charming or by hypnotic suggestion, and it is right that such claims should be scrutinized in a sceptical manner. For before we inquire *how* a phenomenon takes place we should inquire *if* it takes place.

The evidence for the cure of warts by hypnosis depends on rather few scientifically controlled studies. The difficulty of studying the removal of warts is that warts often clear up of their own accord without any therapeutic measures having been applied. How then is one to know beyond all possible doubt that it was the hypnotic treatment that cured the warts? Sinclair-Gieben and Chalmers[3] surmounted this problem by applying hypnotic suggestion that warts would disappear *on one side of the body only*. Their patients were fourteen people who had warts on both sides of the body, hence the untreated side served as a control for the treated side. Within three months nine of the fourteen patients had warts cleared from the side of the body that was indicated by hypnosis, but not from the untreated side, a clear indication that it was the hypnotic suggestion which was effective rather than mere natural remission. They noted that all of the patients who were cured of warts achieved a medium or deep trance state in hypnosis, and that most of the patients who did not respond to treatment had failed to achieve an adequate depth of trance.

The fact that an adequate degree of hypnotic susceptibility is related to the probability that warts will respond to suggestive treatmeant has been noted by other hypnotherapists. This is perhaps surprising as it contrasts with the impression of the easy cure of warts by charming that one gets from many published anecdotal accounts. Perhaps this should caution us against paying too much attention to anecdotal accounts as compared with reports of scientific studies. In anecdotes people tend to remember the successes and forget the failures.

Some understanding of how warts clear up with or without hypnosis is provided by a study by two German doctors.[4] They studied 140 children suffering from warts, and treated half of the group but left the others untreated for the duration of the experiment as a control group. The children attended a number of sessions at which they were not hypnotized but simply given verbal suggestions that the warts would disappear, the warts being painted with an inert blue dye. At the end of the first month eleven of the experimental group and two of the control group had lost their warts, and at the end of three months the number of cured children was respectively fourteen and five in the two groups. By the end of six months, seventeen of the experimental children and twenty of the control group had lost their warts, thus showing that, in childhood, warts tend to disappear anyway in about a quarter of children over half a year. What the charming seems to do is to speed up the natural process of recovery.

What appears to happen in recovery is that a very slight inflammation occurs in the skin around the wart, the blood vessels dilating and, presumably, repair work being initiated under the site of the wart. An understanding of how this is started by hypnosis involves a consideration of how our skins respond to emotional reactions.

No one is surprised that people blush in response to feelings of embarrassment, shame or even pleasure, but a blush is transitory. A more lasting change in the skin is that of hives, the raised, red swelling of the skin that comes on the neck and chest of some people under conditions of stress. This is well known to interviewers who see many candidates for jobs or on other important occasions with this mark of stress on their necks. Some women who know that they are particularly subject to hives, choose to wear a high-necked collar when attending interviews.

If you think that you are going to blush, the thought may produce the reaction, and if you think about hives coming, probably the rash will appear. There are reports of certain religious people who, by meditating on the idea of the crucified Christ, actually produce 'stigmata' on their hands, that is, bloody marks like the nail-wounds of the crucifixion.

From the literature of scientific research comes more compelling evidence of the influence of thought on the condition of the skin. Some Japanese psychologists[5] have demonstrated that the skin temperature of the forearms can be raised simply by thinking about it. A fascinating aspect of this experiment, which involved a fair number of subjects, is the *kind* of thinking which would produce the rise in temperature. One might have thought that a determined 'willing' on the part of the subject would cause his arm to get warm, but this experiment showed that this was not the case. When subjects were instructed to try hard by active concentration to get their arms warmer, this had no effect. It was by practising a 'passive acceptance' of the fact that the arm was getting warmer that a real rise in temperature was achieved.

The difference between actively willing something to take place and passively accepting that it will take place is important for getting some understanding of how hypnotherapy operates. The difference is studied in the Zen philosophy which rather contradicts much of what we accept in the West about what we are apt to assume are the mechanisms of being 'strong willed'. It will be remembered that, as discussed in the previous chapter, Zen has been stigmatized by a Western writer as being the philosophy of 'no mind'. This is true in the sense that Zen practitioners see the business of living in terms of doing rather than theorizing about alleged mental activities. An influential Japanese psychiatrist, Shoma Morita although not a Zen teacher, expressed the principle well : 'Adjust the outer man and the inner man will take care of himself.' This is, of course, heresy to many Western thinkers, especially those influenced by psychoanalytic theory.

It must not be thought that the practice of using passive acceptance rather than determined willing as a means of bringing about physical changes is entirely new in the West. Although Japanese psychologists have developed it, partly in accord with Zen teaching, it was taught by the French doctor Emile Coué. Coué had studied hypnosis at Nancy under Liébault and Bernheim, and went on to found his own 'neo-Nancy' school of therapy. He wrote : 'To make good suggestions, it is absolutely necessary to do it *without effort* . . . the use of the *will* . . . must be entirely put aside.'[6]

Coué's work became largely directed to adopting self-hypnosis and 'auto-suggestion' rather than resorting to the more orthodox practice of being hypnotized by a therapist. Paradoxically, however, the kernel of his teaching explains very well why suggestions coming from another person are generally more effective than any self-suggestions that we can make to ourselves. To hark back to the very simple matter of curing warts by suggestion, the sufferer has probably said to himself on many occasions, 'Oh, I wish this beastly wart would go away !' and willed and willed that it would disappear. But as in the Japanese experiment on warming the forearms, determined willing is quite useless. However, when the therapist calmly and confidently assures the child that the wart will go (or buys it – the wart is then already 'not his') there is a *passive* acceptance of the fact that the cure has already started.

As children, we learn to be mistrustful of reassurance. Often the parent will give a too optimistic forecast that matters will be just fine, in order to calm down an anxious child. Passive acceptance of suggestions is not always possible, therefore, for the child learns in practice that he must not expect all happy prognoses to be fulfilled. Conscious doubt and scepticism intervene. Negative expectancies make the child (and adult) patient think, 'This is silly; they are having me on'; or 'Probably this blue dye won't work any better than the other cures I've tried.' That is why the suggestions are generally very much more effective while the subject is in a state of hypnosis, for in that state the critical faculties are almost wholly in abeyance. It does not matter in the least if the suggestions are not consciously remembered after hypnosis, in fact it is probably better that they should be forgotten and disregarded at the conscious level, for then they are immune from critical evaluation and doubt.

The experimental evidence shows that if a hypnotized subject is told that he will do, or experience, such-and-such at a prearranged time, or at a pre-arranged signal, *without realizing that he has been told to do so*, then there is a strong probability that he will carry out the suggestion, or experience the feeling, without knowledge that it is occurring other than spontaneously. It is this mechanism of the post-hypnotic suggestion that we wish to bring into operation when utilizing hypnosis for therapy. In doing so in many conditions we are merely reversing a morbid process which may have come about by conscious brooding and conscious efforts to exert 'will-power'. Try willing yourself *not* to blush in an embarrassing situation, and see what happens!

The question of the cure of warts has been considered at some length, not because they are at all an important condition requiring therapy, but because they serve as an illustrative example of how many physical conditions can be altered by thought. They are a minor example of a 'psychosomatic' disorder. Psychosomatic disorders include a wide class of physical conditions in which the disturbed condition is linked with attitudes of mind and habits of behaviour. They are 'real' disease conditions, in that there is an actual pathology to be observed, as in the case of eczema conditions and other skin complaints, stomach and duodenal ulcers, asthma, ulcerative colitis, hypertension and a host of other such disorders. It is even possible that some forms of cancer may have a psychosomatic component.

Psychosomatic disorders must clearly be distinguished from hysterical disorders, although this distinction is not always made, even in some text-books. In hysterical disorders, though there may be some disturbance of physical function, there is seldom any actual pathology of the tissues of the organ concerned, and hence onset and recovery can sometimes be almost immediate. In contrast, the psychosomatic disorders tend to have a slower onset and recovery, because actual tissue changes and altered modes of physiological response are involved to a greater degree. Again, there is a difference in attitude of the sufferer towards his disorder. The person with an hysterical type of upset frequently appears to be getting some sort of advantage from it. His arm may be subject to bouts of paralysis, hence he is absent from work for long periods. Yet perhaps his paralysis appears to clear up on his summer holiday when he plays tennis, and it seldom interferes with his ability to lift his right elbow in social circumstances. Hysterical types of disorders tend to be associated with an under-scrupulous, self-indulgent and under-concerned attitude. Psychosomatic troubles, on the other hand, are commonly suffered by people who are over-concerned worriers. Strangely enough, in the study by Sainsbury[7] quoted earlier, it was found that sufferers from warts were on the high side on both neuroticism and *extraversion*, whereas other psychosomatic sufferers tended to be on the high side on neuroticism but were *introverted*.

Such studies of the personalities of various types of patients must be viewed with some caution. They mostly depend on impressions gained in interviews, and the results of paper-and-pencil questionnaires. At best they show only statistical trends. There is no reason why a person of predominantly hysteric-type personality should not develop one of the classic psychosomatic disorders, like a stomach ulcer, if he were the victim of special circumstances. At one time it was thought that each and every type of psychosomatic disorder had its appropriate personality type, but later research dispelled this impression of an all too neat order of things.

It is, of course, useful to have some insight into the personality basis of various types of psychosomatic disorders, for if we are to consider using hypnosis in therapy, the personality of the patient is highly relevant. We do not know enough about personality differences in relation to hypnotic susceptibility, however, although research is being done which will be discussed in a later chapter. Nevertheless, as it is clear that stress produces very different sorts of disorders in people according to their temperament, when planning therapy one must take individual differences into account.

Hypnotherapy is appropriate for psychosomatic disorders, in that it permits intervention in a vicious circle of stress producing altered physiological function, hence tissue change, hence further distress, worry and stress. An example of a very simple psychosomatic disorder was that commonly reported in the days of National Service. Here, young men were drafted into the Forces, and in the strange surroundings away from home, many of them had their first sexual experience. Some of them reported to the Medical Officer in great distress because they were suffering from a condition which they feared might be venereal disease. This condition was a psychosomatic inflammation which was quite infection-free and cleared up as soon as the sufferer was assured, as the result of tests, that there was nothing to be feared. Medical officers reported that this common complaint occurred in boys who were of a worrying, shy and over-conscientious disposition, sometimes in contrast to the types who really did contract a venereal infection. The infection-free sufferers had literally produced an inflammation by their over-concern in an area where shame and remorse are traditionally present.

It is useless to counsel the psychosomatic sufferer not to worry. One cannot, by a conscious effort of will, refrain from worrying. Indeed, the knowledge that a stomach ulcer is getting progressively worse because of the patient's habit of brooding over business troubles at mealtimes, makes the ulcer worse. Now, in addition, he worries about the ulcer, becomes a food faddist and cannot relax over a good meal.

Hypnotherapy in such conditions aims at blocking the sequence of events in terms of conditioning in the Pavlovian sense, or in the way that Skinner has conceived it, as will be discussed later. In fact, some theorists of hypnosis find it useful to explain the whole business of hypnosis, the altered state of awareness, the possibility of producing analgesia, hallucinations, regression to childhood, post-hypnotic amnesia and post-hypnotic behaviour entirely in terms of conditioning! Whether such an exercise in re-stating a huge body of empirical fact and theory in terms of another great body of scientific discourse is worth it depends upon the purpose of the exposition.

Such a re-statement of the theory of hypnosis in terms of conditioning has been attempted by Salter[8] for the purpose of making hypnotherapy more comprehensible, and a better working tool in medicine. Before considering Salter's views on hypnosis, it is necessary briefly to consider just what is meant by conditioning.

Conditioning theory assumes that there are certain natural or unconditional responses to certain classes of stimuli. Thus it is natural for a dog to water at the mouth when he smells meat; it is natural for some species of birds to show instinctive fear if they see a hovering hawk; it is natural for a young man to become sexually aroused if he sees an attractive, naked girl. The meat, hawk and naked girl are provocative stimuli unconditional on the subject's individual past history of learning. (The third stimulus is perhaps more equivocal in this respect, as human responses are very complex.) Now if a dog were to salivate, a chicken to give a warning cry and a young man to experience sexual arousal, all three at the sight of an old boot, we would rightly suppose that some process of training had been applied to them to secure so inappropriate a response. Inappropriate or not, they might be powerless to resist this response to the boot if it had been made a 'conditioned' stimulus.

As the third example sounds a little far-fetched, a description of how it was actually accomplished will be in order. Rachman and Hodgson,[9] working at the Institute of Psychiatry, were investigating sexual aberrations, including the curious condition in which people become hooked on totally inappropriate objects, like boots. They reasoned that these curious fixations (fetishisms) might well be due to accidental processes of conditioning which had somehow taken place. If we knew the mechanism by which they were *learned*, then we could study how they could be *unlearned*.

They got five young men, sufficiently normal in their sex lives to risk a temporary diversion of interest, to volunteer as experimental subjects and to submit to the following procedure. They were connected to an apparatus which measures the strength of the male sexual response (which need not be described in detail) and then shown exciting slides of beautiful nude females. The expected response occurred, but when they were shown slides of boots no such response resulted. They were then subjected to a conditioning process. Slides of boots were flashed on the screen, each one closely followed by a flash of an attractive nude. After a large number of such paired presentations had been shown, the subjects were again tested for their sexual responses to pictures of boots, and it was now found that the sight of a boot produced sexual arousal. They had been conditioned.

The process was now put into reverse. They had to sit and watch a long series of slides of boots being flashed on the screen at irregular intervals, with no tasty female figure following them, a boring business which eventually extinguished the sexual response to the boots. As far as could be determined, none of these young men afterwards lost their normal interests, or took to decorating their rooms with pin-ups of footwear.

The experiment described above is one of classical Pavlovian conditioning. Pavlov[10] experimented extensively with this sort of technique, mainly with dogs, but it obviously applies in a wide area of animal and human learning. Its relevance to hypnosis, as described by Salter, is that words can easily become the effective *conditioned stimuli* producing powerful reactions in us which are almost as effective as our reactions to the thing the words symbolize. So much of our experience as human beings is made up of words, ideas and unspoken thoughts that our actions, feelings and experience of reality can become controlled by them. It is perfectly reasonable to regard hypnosis in the light of the hypnotist using conditioned stimuli which have a known and reliable effect, and the subject giving the appropriate conditioned responses.

Salter is quite adamant that conditioning is the *only* proper way of regarding hypnosis. He writes : 'How convenient it would be to say that the phenomena of hypnosis are "caused" by "suggestion", but such a meaningless explanation has beset hypnotism for years. How much simpler and more meaningful it is to realize that hypnosis is based on associative reflexes that use words as triggers of automatic reactions. Hypnosis is the production of reactions in the human organism through the use of verbal or other associative reflexes.'[11]

Because we are only conscious of the thought that is, for the moment, in our field of attention, we are not immediately aware of the vast array of potential thoughts that will be triggered off by appropriate cues. Hypnotherapy aims at programming potential thoughts so that they will be in accord with beneficial rather than harmful action potentials. The conditioned responses to words like calm, relax, rest, are not to be gainsaid, and contrast with the deliberate and conscious attempts to be calm, relaxed and restful which a person may struggle to make because he knows that hypertension is bad for him. Because such efforts are deliberate and conscious they are likely to be ineffectual.

To pursue the question of how hypnotherapy may help in intervention in psychosomatic disorder, we may turn to what is known as the 'adaptation syndrome' of Selye.[12] Selye has put forward the case that all animals have, as it were, contingency plans for meeting and coping with conditions of stress. His theory concerns the interaction between glandular and nervous mechanisms which come into play when the body experiences some form of stress. The exact nature of the glandular products (hormones) secreted in stress conditions need not concern us here, but they serve to help the body cope with emergencies. The first reaction is an alarm reaction, and is only a short-term measure. If it is prolonged, then rather than helping the natural repair of damaged tissue and defences against infection, the reverse becomes the case. The trouble about human beings is that stress produces active worry – and this sets more alarm bells ringing. What was at first a minor upset then becomes a self-perpetuating condition.

A remarkable experiment by Brady[13] illustrates the maladaptive nature of the attempt to adapt to stressful conditions by intelligent animals. The subjects were monkeys, not humans, for although the latter animals are often forced into stressful conditions by the nature of their employment or social organization, and develop psychosomatic disorders as a consequence, we cannot study the development of such disorders under controlled laboratory conditions – nor can we kill the subjects if necessary.

It was found that monkeys used in conditioning experiments of the kind deriving from Pavlov's original work, sometimes died and revealed on post-mortem examination that they had developed severe ulcers in the stomach and duodenum. The implication was that conditioning had imposed a peculiar sort of stress on the animals, perhaps similar to the stress that busy business executives suffer, and they had produced ulcers as a consequence. An experiment was therefore devised which subjected two monkeys to exactly the same amount of unpleasant stress, in the form of electric shocks to the feet, but one monkey was in a conditioning situation and the other was not.

The two monkeys sat in adjacent chairs in which they were partially restrained, although they could move their heads and limbs. They received periodic electric shocks. They received shocks, that is, until one of them, the 'executive' monkey, had learned the trick of pressing down a lever at intervals, which prevented the shock being delivered to either of them. Thus, if the executive monkey maintained a vigilant and repetitive lever-pressing – a trick which he soon learned – they could both sit in comparative comfort with no electric shocks. If he slipped up on his executive duties then *both* received an electric shock.

The pair was subjected to this treatment on a schedule of six hours' work and six hours' rest. The six-hourly routine was maintained for twenty-three days, then the executive monkey died. Post-mortem examination showed that he had died of a perforated ulcer in the duodenum. The other monkey, who had had to endure exactly the same number of shocks, remained perfectly healthy.

This experiment was repeated with other pairs of monkeys, with the same result. It was the executive monkey who developed the ulcers, presumably because he had been put in a position of responsibility – it was up to him to be vigilant and to guard against any shocks being delivered. In contrast, his companion was utterly powerless and irresponsible.

These experiments of Brady's were not as simple as they may seem in interpretation, for he and his associates found by later experiments that the six-hour 'working day' of the monkeys was somehow an important factor. However, even with this qualification it is difficult not to see in these experiments the human parallel. The human executive who carries a load of responsibility is more prone to develop ulcers than the worker who has a dull but irresponsible job, and cannot do much about what happens to him at work.

These findings are highly relevant to hypnotherapy. We need to know just what it is that produces the psychosomatic reaction in order to intervene with hypnotic treatment. It is not, apparently, the long working day, for when they gave the monkeys a longer 'working day' the effect was not so pronounced. It is not the rigours of the work, for the companion monkey suffered just as much shock. It seems that it is the conditioning to exercise a constant vigilance which prevents the executive from relaxing, and thus does the damage. Later research with monkeys showed that the over-production of stomach acid was as great or greater during the hours of rest following such treatment. Many wives of business executives complain that their husbands take their work home with them to bed, meaning that the responsibilities of the day do not drop from their shoulders when they leave the office, but preoccupy them when they are at home.

In such cases, hypnotherapy is therefore aimed at what may be called counter-conditioning. The sufferer has to learn not to respond to his urges to be alert, vigilant and responsible for twenty-four hours a day. The sheer, dogmatically insistent injunctions of the hypnotist are delivered while his patient is in a passively receptive trance state – 'You will have no concern for your work while you are at home; you will eat well, sleep well and enjoy yourself. You will feel confident that everything will be all right. Stomach pains will not bother you; you will forget all about your digestion,' and so on. It might appear that the giving of such suggestions, which the patient has long accepted as a desirable condition, is giving superfluous advice. But they must not be viewed in terms of giving advice. They are only effective if the patient can receive them in a trance state, except in so far as a bottle of coloured water is better than nothing at all. It must be remembered that most forms of conditioned response appear to be quite illogical – as illogical as getting sexually excited over a boot.

Hypnotic treatment must not be judged on its superficially illogical content. Many people will remember how illogically relieved they have been when they have placed some problem – legal, medical, economic, etc. – in the hands of an appropriate professional expert. They may not have the slightest idea of how the lawyer, doctor or accountant is going to tackle the problem, but they are immensely relieved – it is off their shoulders. So it is with hypnotherapy. The recipient carries round in his head, so to speak, a system of ideas which counteracts the habit of over-vigilant concern. It does not really matter if he does not intellectually *believe* what is said to him at first, and it is best if he has some post-hypnotic amnesia for it. Psychosomatic sufferers tend to be pessimists, and believe the worst to begin with. But in spite of his pessimism, the patient will come to believe what is suggested to him repeatedly in hypnosis, believe it in the sense that he makes it become literally true.

In therapy for psychosomatic conditions, there have been developed in more recent years various methods akin to hypnosis, employing techniques which might as well be called hypnosis, although some people prefer to avoid that word, partly because of the prejudices of their patients. These methods, which include the Autogenic Training of Luthe,[14] the Self Control method of Gosaku Naruse (a Japanese method) and Biofeedback, are largely concerned with reformulating principles which have been used by Oriental yogi and other exponents of the art of gaining voluntary control over body functions which are normally involuntary.

The method of Biofeedback can be understood in terms of modern science by viewing it with reference to conditioning theory. In this case it is not the classical conditioning of Pavlov, as described above, but instrumental conditioning, as described by Skinner.[15] Whereas Pavlov's method involves providing a natural, unconditioned stimulus (meat, a hawk, a girl, in our example) which would produce and, by repetition, reinforce the appropriate natural response (salivating, fear, sexual arousal), in instrumental conditioning the reinforcing stimulus *follows* some selected piece of behaviour which is originally only one among a number of possible behaviours in an animal's repertoire.

To understand instrumental conditioning, let us consider an actual experiment of Skinner's. A pigeon is put in a cage in which there is little to interest it, except an empty food-tray and a disc on the wall. Pigeons have the habit of pecking at things in a more or less desultory fashion, but the object of the experiment is to condition the bird to peck continuously and accurately at the disc. The first time its random peck happens to hit the disc – bing! A tasty pea is dropped in the food tray. The delighted pigeon eats it. This satisfying result is repeated every time the bird happens to hit the disc and, after a while, he begins to peck more frequently around and on the target. Eventually he keeps up a steady pecking at the disc, getting a pea for each hit. If the supply of peas is now disconnected, the bird will still go on pecking at the disc for a very long time, for this instrumental response has been conditioned.

One might comment on this experiment that the pigeon, being no fool, suddenly 'realized' that the disc controlled the supply of peas, and 'decided' to get a meal by steadily pecking at it. This explanation in terms of 'realization' and 'decision' can be challenged, for why did the conditioned bird continue to peck at the target long after the supply of peas had been removed and he was getting nothing for his labour? Well, we could suggest that he 'hoped' that the pea-delivering mechanism would be reinstated. As we cannot look into the pigeon's mind and decide whether 'realization', 'decision' or 'hope' are there, perhaps we might consider a piece of instrumental conditioning to which the reader may very well have been subject.

If the reader wears a wrist-watch he may remember having left it off for a day or longer, and endured the experience of never knowing the time. He may then have had the experience of glancing frequently at his bare wrist whenever he wanted to know the time. Now he *knew* that he was not wearing a watch, and he did not *hope* that it would miraculously appear on his bare wrist, yet he continued to perform the pointless act of glancing at his bare wrist. He did this because of years of instrumental conditioning, and provided he was preoccupied with his normal pursuits he could no more control this automatic act than the pigeon could refrain from his automatic pecking.

It is suggested that the reader makes the following experiment in instrumental conditioning to understand its relevance to hypnosis. Get a friend to stand up in front of you, with his arms hanging loosely by his side and with feet close together, his toes touching. He should close his eyes. Stand about three feet from him and be prepared to steady his posture. Talk to him for about half a minute, asking him to stand quite relaxed (but see that he does not move his feet) and calmly reassure him that you are right beside him and that nothing awkward is going to happen to him. Then ask him to go on standing there with his eyes closed and listen to you talking, and that you want him to imagine, as hard as he can, that he is falling forwards. Watch him closely, and you will observe him making little forward tremors and sways. Now, using your knowledge of instrumental conditioning, *reinforce* these tiny forward movements by verbal encouragement, praise, reassurance, and appeals to his imagination. Keep up a continuous stream of verbal reinforcement which will probably sound like this :

'I want you to imagine that you are falling forwards, falling right forwards. You can imagine yourself falling, falling, coming right forwards. Fine ! There you go now, you can imagine yourself falling, you can feel yourself falling forwards. That's it ! You can imagine it – good – you can feel yourself falling, falling forwards. You're coming right forwards; falling, falling, all the time. You can really imagine it, falling forwards. . . .'

If that sort of imagery is encouraged on a note of steady, enthusiastic repetition for something over a minute, the majority of people will sway forwards three or four inches, and a substantial minority of perhaps 15 per cent will sway so far forwards that they lose their balance and topple forwards, so that they have to be caught by the person standing in front of them.

Sometimes people report after that postural sway procedure that they felt as though a force were actually acting upon them and forcing them forwards, somewhat to their amazement. A tendency to sway forwards, and even to fall, will still occur even if the suggestions are not closely geared to the subject's actual movements. The effect will still take place if the suggestions are being given by a tape-recorder and the subject is quite aware of the fact. What is being reinforced is the whole imaginative effort, and the feed-back from the subject's muscles and organs of balance is merged with the constantly repeated verbal information that he is falling forwards. This procedure is sometimes given as a test, with an accurate measurement of the degree of sway, and is an excellent predictor of how naturally susceptible to hypnosis the subject is likely to be.

It used to be thought that whereas classical Pavlovian conditioning was appropriate to automatic responses beyond the subject's control, like salivation, blinking the eyes, and the like, instrumental conditioning was confined to actions that are normally voluntary. This distinction is no longer maintained. It has been found that we can indeed secure instrumental conditioning in wholly involuntary processes like the beating of the heart and the action of the glands. Normally, we cannot alter involuntary responses because we are unconscious of how they come about. One cannot, for instance, increase the flow of digestive juices in the stomach, or alter one's brainwaves, because we do not know how to. But such control can be established in many areas of involuntary function if sufficient study and practice is undertaken. Although this has been the specialism of Oriental yogis, with modern instrumentation in the study of Biofeedback, the matter is not so difficult.

When connected to appropriate apparatus, one can see, for instance, one's heart-beat displayed as moving lines on a screen. If an experimenter keeps up a running commentary on the performance of the heart, urging quickening of the rate and giving praise and encouragement for every little increase, then, under the steady stream of social encouragement, the rate of the subject's heart-beat will increase. And what is this speeding up of someone's heart by careful monitoring and verbal reinforcement, but hypnosis? Earlier, we discussed hypnosis in terms of Pavlovian conditioning, words being considered as conditioned stimuli, having known and predictable conditioned responses. Now we are considering hypnosis in terms of instrumental conditioning where words have the same reinforcing properties as the peas dropped into the pigeon's food tray.

In using Biofeedback as a means by which people can gain mastery over processes which are not normally subject to voluntary control, it is not entirely necessary for a therapist to be present to give verbal reinforcement. The mere witnessing of the desired change, as displayed on the monitoring instrument, is sufficiently reinforcing. Solitary practice can be compared both with yoga exercises and auto-hypnosis. Obviously, Biofeedback has implications for the kind of therapy needed for psychosomatic disorders.

We have treated the psychosomatic disorders as though they were a separate sort of physical disorder for which hypnotherapy and related techniques was appropriate. However, although this is a useful way of approaching the hypnotic control of physical conditions, the artificiality of it needs some comment. There are three main areas of physical disease which can be considered. First, there are those diseases which have a recognized form in terms of organic pathology, and with known causes arising from bacterial or viral attack. In such diseases psychological factors are not likely to play a very important role and hypnosis would not be a very appropriate form of therapy. One might help a person to endure the misery of an attack of influenza by hypnotic treatment, but one could not expect to combat the infection by this means. Even so, resistance to infection is a highly complex matter and depends on the general vigour of the patient; hence psychosomatic aspects of even a clear-cut viral infective disease cannot be overlooked. Pulmonary tuberculosis is the classic case in point. While it is due to a well-recognized bacillus, this same bacillus is relatively common but does not generally get a hold on people unless they are in a peculiar state of physical and, some have said, mental debility. Traditionally, in the Victorian era, the surest way to succumb to pulmonary tuberculosis was to be crossed in love. This aspect of the disease still has its exponents.[16]

In the second category are diseases whose nature, when established, is clearly recognized, but there is controversy about the degree of psychosomatic causation. Lung cancer is a case in point. We know beyond all doubt that it is associated with heavy smoking, but we do not know whether it is a case of simple causation. It is unfashionable, and allegedly dangerous, to call attention to the deficiences in the evidence, for it is deemed better to let an over-simplified version of the facts frighten people away from smoking themselves to death. In fact, it appears that the matter is highly complex. There may be personality factors which predispose people to develop lung cancer in the same way that others develop eczema, gastric ulcers or colitis as a psychosomatic reaction. These factors may *also* predispose them to smoke like chimneys as an anodyne to their jittery nerves. There may well be other personality types who are immune to the cancer reaction of the lungs, and hence may smoke their lungs like kippers with no ill effects.[17]

While no one in their senses would suggest treating lung cancer with hypnosis, the habit of smoking is one that yields to hypno-therapy with a fair degree of success. So hypnosis can be used as a preventive measure against a potentially aggravating factor in a very dangerous physical disease, which in some people may be psychosomatic in origin.

The question of *how* hypnosis can combat smoking is pertinent to this matter. Some hypnotherapists rely on making the whole subject of tobacco-smoke abhorrent, building up revulsion to its taste, smell and associations, and the fear of cancer associated with it. Others suggest feelings of calmness, relaxation and unhurried well-being so that the patient does not need to smoke. Obviously, the latter form of therapy is treating the presumed psychosomatic mechanism which may lead to both the cancer reaction and to a need for excessive smoking.

The third class of diseases is of course the recognized psycho-somatic category which has been repeatedly referred to in this chapter. Here something needs to be said about the fashion of ascribing labels to ailments both by patients and by physicians. Most people do not like to admit to the psychosomatic component of their ailments. They would far rather go down with a disorder which has come out of the blue and cannot possibly be attributed to their habits, attitudes and personality. To some degree, the con-fusion between the psychosomatic and the hysterical disorders has been responsible for this reluctance to face facts.

No one likes it to be whispered that his eczema is really due to a dishonest attempt to evade his family responsibilities, for a vulgar-Freudian theory of motivation is often evoked to explain *other people's* allegedly motivated disorders. But if a man cannot help with the household chores when his mother-in-law is around because of his acute eczema, it does not mean that he has brought it on purposely. The presence of the mother-in-law may well have pro-duced the stress which resulted in an outbreak of eczema, but the man may be a real hero for putting up with as much as he does. A psychosomatic reaction is not a symptom of choice; it is a reaction to stress.

Patients, then, will often err on the side of denying the psychological component of their illnesses and reject the idea of hypnotherapy because it implies that the disorder is 'all in the mind'. Physicians, on the other hand, may err in precisely the opposite direction. If a doctor is busy, tired and a bad diagnostician, he may not be able to treat many simple disorders which have little psychosomatic component and, in self-defence, he throws the burden back at the patient. When a woman complains about neuralgic pains in her arms, he enquires about her sex life, thereby implying that he cannot be expected to treat a condition which is largely imaginary and stems from her bad relationship with her husband. Such physicians may very well resort to attempts at hypnotherapy, for it is simple to get a patient to lie on a couch, repeat an incantation which is supposed to induce hypnosis, and then tell her that she will get better. In reality, hypnotherapy is time-consuming and requires considerable patience, skill and persistence if it is to be conducted properly, and it is often just one component of a programme of treatment.

Hypnosis is used extensively in the long-term, antenatal preparation of expectant mothers for childbirth, although such training programmes often avoid the use of the term 'hypnosis'. This is perhaps a pity, for once the women had got over their anxieties about 'being hypnotized' more direct training methods might be employed, and the women taught the techniques of auto-hypnosis, rather than just trying to perform relaxation exercises. Much of the pain and complications associated with childbirth are due to the psychosomatic vicious circle, fear producing tension, pain and more fear and stress. An early study by Heron and Abramson,[18] who worked with a sample of a hundred women whom they trained in hypnosis and compared with an equivalent sample of untrained women, showed that the length of the first stage of labour was reduced by about 20 per cent, and that considerably less drugs were used overall. They remarked that mention of an average figure does not stress the spectacular success obtained by hypnotic training with some patients. The relative success of the hypnotic method was particularly marked with women who were having their first babies, a circumstance which generally means a longer and more difficult first stage, compared with later births. A later study by Perchard,[19] which concerned over three thousand expectant mothers, showed that those who had been given some hypnotic treatment (although only three sessions) required less sedation in labour than those who had had only relaxation exercises or antenatal talks. Those of the hypnotic group who had shown most susceptibility were the most successful by the criteria used. Similar studies are published from time to time, although not on such a large scale, and one gets the impression that a lot depends both on the thoroughness of the hypnotic pre-natal training, and on the natural susceptibility of the individuals.

There is a use of hypnosis in obstetrics which, although referred to by Bramwell[20] in 1903 as being practised by the French doctor Fanton, appears totally to have been overlooked in modern obstetrics. This is the induction of labour by hypnosis. Labour is sometimes inordinately delayed for reasons which are somewhat obscure. Childbirth normally comes forty weeks after the first day of the last menstrual period, but this is merely a statistical average and we do not know if it is natural for certain women to go into labour either earlier or later. Childbirth occurring prematurely has always been a serious cause of infant mortality and is associated with poverty and ill-health. According to Kitzinger,[21] the reverse trend is now developing, particularly in more affluent societies, and the practice of inducing labour by mechanical means and drugs is growing steadily, as though the baby *ought* to arrive on time.

No mother likes to have a baby removed from her inert body as though it were a tumour, and there is often the suggestion implicit in the situation that she has failed in her first maternal duty. Kitzinger brings forward some evidence to show that stress at the end of pregnancy contributes to this inability to go into labour, and that artificial removal of the baby brings on post-partum depression.

It is not suggested that hypnosis should be used regularly in hospitals when a mother unaccountably fails to 'perform' on time. Rather, it should be an end product of a natural process of training and within the mother's own control. As there are no firm statistics on the matter, one cannot say definitely, but it seems reasonable to expect that if an expectant mother has gained a fair measure of control over her whole reproductive process by means of auto-hypnosis, there is less likelihood of there being any unnaturally delayed parturition.

As hypnosis is used in the prevention of unnecessary cramps and tensions in muscles which normally function perfectly efficiently, as in childbirth, it can also be used as an agent for re-training where there is a pathological abnormality. Much attention has focused in recent years on the condition of cerebral palsy or spasticity. The brain of the spastic person has suffered injury pre-natally or post-natally, so that although there may be no intellectual handicap, various muscle groups do not function properly. The damaged brain produces abnormal nervous impulses to the muscles, and a variety of physical handicaps develop. This lack of proper nervous control of the muscles means that in the young child they do not develop properly and may become wasted. The developing bones may become distorted by the related muscle groups acting out of harmony.

Very great differences in handicap are experienced by spastic children, and almost any part of the body may become crippled. Even where the handicap is slight, the spastic in his effort to move, walk, grasp, manipulate and talk often learns to do things as best he can, but in the wrong way. Powerful tensions in muscles hinder the development of skilled movements. Much effort has therefore been directed towards devising programmes of physiotherapy which will help spastic children to overcome unwanted muscular tensions and to learn to develop properly skilled movements and improved posture.

The Japanese, who have invested a great amount of their therapeutic research in problems of cerebral palsy, have used hypnosis as an agent in the training of spastics. The patient is trained to relax under hypnosis to a degree that is not normally possible for him in his ordinary waking state. Then, keeping the unwanted tensions which normally interfere with him performing skilled movements out of the muscles, the weak and possibly wasted muscles are taught to perform their proper function in the absence of their powerful antagonists. Thus the patient is trained in hypnosis to master skills over which he will have greater and greater control. Few accounts of this treatment have been published in the West, although it has been practised in Japan for some time.[22] There are, of course, various schools of thought concerned with the re-training of spastics by physiotherapy without hypnosis.

In this chapter it has been emphasized that there is nothing strange or 'magic' about the way in which hypnosis can be a useful tool in increasing our control over physical processes for therapeutic purposes. The limits of our understanding of how hypnosis operates are the limits imposed by our imperfect theories of psychology, physiology and other sciences of human and animal function.

In using hypnosis both therapeutically and experimentally, several theories are being used contemporarily. Thus Barrios[23] is a modern exponent of Salter's conditioning theory of hypnosis; the psychoanalytic theory put forward by Gill and Brenman has been restated more recently by Gill,[24] and Sarbin and Coe[25] explain the same facts in terms of role theory. The hypnotherapist can operate one theory or another, or proceed eclectically. Many therapists are entirely empirically oriented and are not much concerned with theories of why things happen as they do.

REFERENCES

1 P. Sainsbury, 'Psychosomatic disorders and neurosis in outpatients attending a general hospital', *Journal of Psychosomatic Research*, 4, 1960, pp. 261–273.

2 C. Baudouin, *Suggestion and Autosuggestion*, op. cit.

3 A. H. C. Sinclair-Gieben and D. Chalmers, 'Evaluation of treatment of warts by hypnosis', *Lancet*, 2, 1959, pp. 480–482.

4 A. M. Memmesheimer and E. Eisenlohr, 'Untersuchungen über die Suggestivebehandlung der Warzen', *Dermatologische Zeitschrift*, 62, 1931, pp. 63–68.

5 K. Harano, K. Ogawa and G. Naruse, 'A study of plethysmography and skin temperature during active concentration and autogenic training exercise', in W. Luthe (ed.), *Autogenic Training*, New York: Grune & Stratton, 1965.

6 E. Coué, *Self-mastery Through Conscious Autosuggestion*, London: Allen & Unwin, 1922.

7 P. Sainsbury, op. cit.

8 A. Salter, *What is Hypnosis?*, New York: R. R. Smith, 1944.

9 S. J. Rachman and R. J. Hodgson, 'Experimentally-induced sexual fetishism: replication and development', *Psychological Record*, 18, 1968, pp. 25–27.

10 I. Pavlov, *Conditioned Reflexes*, London: Oxford University Press, 1927.

11 A. Salter, op. cit.

12 H. Selye, *The Stress of Life*, London: Longmans, 1957.

13 J. V. Brady, 'Ulcers in executive monkeys', *Scientific American*, October 1958.

14 W. Luthe (ed.), *Autogenic Therapy*, New York: Grune & Stratton, 1970.

15 B. F. Skinner, *Contingencies of Reinforcement*, New York: Appleton Century-Crofts, 1969.

16 See, for example, D. M. Kissen, *Emotional Factors in Pulmonary Tuberculosis*, London: Tavistock, 1958.

17 See D. M. Kissen, R. I. F. Brown and M. Kissen, 'A further report on personality and psychosocial factors in lung cancer', *Annals of the New York Academy of Science*, 164, 1969, pp. 535-544.

18 W. T. Heron and M. Abramson, 'Hypnosis in Obstetrics', in L. M. Le Cron (ed.), *Experimental Hypnosis*, New York: Macmillan, 1952.

19 S. D. Perchard, 'Hypnosis in obstetrics', *Proceedings of the Royal Society of Medicine*, 53, 1960, pp. 458–460.

20 J. M. Bramwell, *Hypnotism: Its History, Practice and Theory*, London: Grant Richards, 1903.

21 S. Kitzinger, *The Experience of Childbirth*, Harmondsworth: Penguin, 1974.

22 S. Kimura, 'Behaviour therapy for cerebral palsy by hypnotic method', *Bulletin of the British Psychological Society* (abstract), 28, 1975, p. 240.

23 A. A. Barrios, 'Posthypnotic suggestion as higher order conditioning – methodological and experimental analyses', *International Journal of Clinical and Experimental Hypnosis*, 21, 1973, pp. 32–50.

24 M. M. Gill, 'Hypnosis as an altered and regressed state', ibid., 20, 1972, pp. 224–237.

25 T. R. Sarbin and W. C. Coe, *Hypnosis: A Social and Psychological Analysis of Influence Communication*, New York: Holt Rinehart & Winston, 1972.

> Science is nothing but trained and organized
> common sense.
>
> THOMAS HUXLEY, *Collected Essays*, 1897.

It has been traditionally accepted that under hypnosis people can exhibit supernormal powers of strength, endurance, acuity of perception, memory, and many other functions. The older writers on the subject were quite positive about this, and the possibility of becoming a superman by means of hypnosis has attracted many people.

We can discount the oldest accounts of the mesmerists, who claimed that actual *supernatural* powers could be manifested in the mesmeric trance – reading from a closed book, hearing sounds completely out of earshot, and (a special bonus!) being able to diagnose diseases in others even though completely without medical knowledge. Whenever claimants of such miraculous powers were offered a test under scientific conditions, they tended to back down with indignation that sceptics should impose such niggling conditions – a tendency still in evidence today.

The supernatural apart, many later writers laid quite impressive claims for the enormous increase in muscular power and endurance that could be procured by hypnosis. This idea has been exploited by the stage hypnotists who claim to demonstrate it by such tricks as the 'human plank' feat. A subject is hypnotized, and muscular rigidity for the whole body is suggested, then, when a suitable degree of rigidity is obtained, he is supported horizontally with his head on one chair and his heels on another. This sounds as though it were an extraordinary feat and, indeed, it looks it, but in reality it is not so very difficult to perform *without* hypnosis. It requires that the subject should tense up all his muscles and maintain the tension by a determined effort for a brief period.

According to Barber,[1] an experimenter has shown that when men and women are suitably instructed, they can be suspended between two chairs, their ankles on one and heads on another, without being hypnotized, and perform this feat for over two minutes. Indeed, in the experiment to which he refers, the unhypnotized did almost as well as the hypnotized, and many subjects were amazed at their own powers of endurance.

Some stage hypnotists have been known to supplement this trick by throwing a rug over the suspended subject, and under the cover of this, skilfully insert a board beneath the subject so that he is really lying on a rigid bridge. The hypnotist will then climb on to the human plank, and even invite one or two others to join him, their whole weight being upon the hypnotized man. If one is unaware of the secret board beneath the subject, it looks as though his spine might suddenly snap.

There have been many serious attempts to assess the allegedly great endurance of hypnotized subjects. Reiger[2] investigated the capacity of hypnotized subjects to hold out an arm horizontally and maintain the position against fatigue. He reported that when hypnotized, a person had a very greatly increased power of resisting gravity and fatigue. Charcot followed up Reiger's experiment, and Binet and Féré[3] reported on his experiments that the supernormal power of resisting fatigue in this situation had been exaggerated. According to them, the power conferred by hypnosis was that instead of the normal trembling to be observed in the fatigued arm of a non-hypnotized person, in hypnosis such tremor was eliminated, and the arm would sink down perfectly smoothly.

The importance which Binet and Féré attached to this experiment relates to their concern that they should develop means of detecting faking in hypnosis. Working mainly with hysterical patients at the Salpêtrière Hospital, they were rightly suspicious that in some cases the subjects were trying to deceive them by pretending to be hypnotized. It was therefore a matter of great importance to them to discover what were the special signs of hypnosis. Although their findings about the absence of arm tremor in hypnotic subjects were based on absurdly small numbers, they thought that they had found a truly diagnostic touchstone, and wrote : 'It is almost certain that no individual in the waking state, unless affected by a nervous state allied to hypnosis, could imitate the distinctive signs by which hypnotism is manifested. The dread of simulation, which has dominated the whole history of animal magnetism, has now become a completely imaginary danger, if the experimenter is adroit and cautious.'

Unfortunately, one writer has tended to copy another, rather than carry out experiments for himself, and the myth of the non-tremulous, gravity-resisting arm of the hypnotized subject was maintained for about forty years. Writers as eminent as Moll and McDougall have uncritically repeated the tale that hypnotized subjects have a quite extraordinary degree of resistance to fatigue, and greatly increased muscular power. One is forced to wonder whether they were not themselves deceived by the contrived wonders

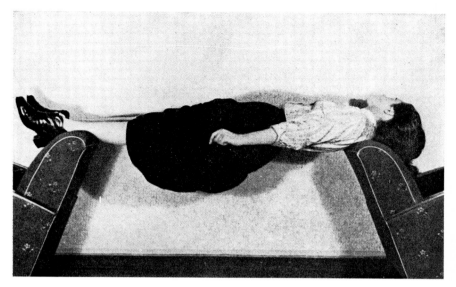

5 The 'human plank feat': a woman is suspended between two chairs.

6 A hypnotized guinea pig.

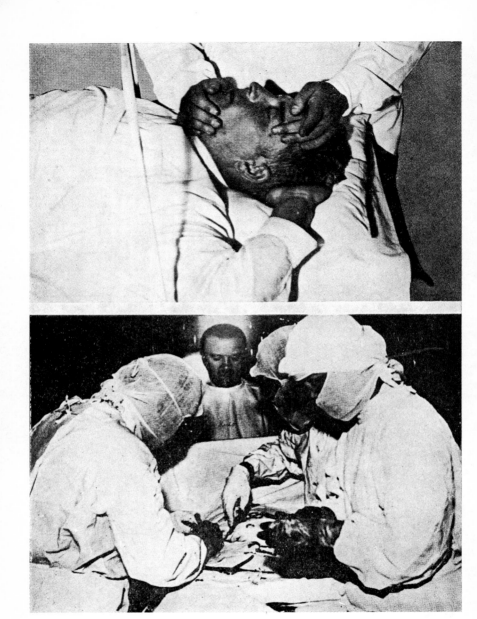

7   An appendicectomy performed while the patient was under hypnotic analgesia.

that stage hypnotists have been wont to display, for they cite no very precise evidence in support of their claims. It was only with the further development of experimental psychology that we began to get some reliable information on the subject.

Williams[4] carried out a properly controlled investigation of the question of arm-fatigue in 1929, employing eight normal subjects – not a large number by modern standards, but a great improvement of the odd ones and twos on which the older experimentalists had generally based their conclusions. He tested each of them four times in their normal waking condition, and four times when hypnotized, varying the order of the sessions. The results were surprising. Four of the subjects kept their arms up longer when hypnotized, but with the four others the reverse was the case. There was no significant difference in the amount of arm tremor in the two states. The only real difference was that all his subjects reported that they experienced a good deal of pain in trying to keep their arms up in the waking state, but no pain when hypnotized.

The finding about the absence of pain in Williams' subjects when hypnotized, although not unexpected, makes one wonder about his experiment. If they experienced no discomfort, why did they not keep their arms up for longer?

The usual explanation given for increased muscular endurance under hypnosis is as follows. We all tend to have far more potential strength and endurance than we exert normally, because pain inhibits too violent and too prolonged an effort. In hypnosis we do not experience the pain, so we are able to exhibit something like our true capacity. If a middle-aged man who was not in athletic training tried to sprint at top speed for half a mile, he would be groaning with pain and have to slacken his speed before he had covered half the distance. If an angry bull were behind him, however, it is likely that he would run like the wind and be unaware of any need to slacken speed before he reached safety.

The explanation of Williams' curious finding that, although the subjects experienced no pain in hypnosis, they did not tend to hold their arms up for any longer than in the waking state, on average, may be very simple. It is possible that in hypnosis they kept dosing off into true sleep. It would have been a better experiment if he had kept up a steady stream of exhortation to persist and do their best, for there is some evidence that, suitably encouraged, a hypnotized subject will indeed keep working at a task longer and more effectively than he will do in the waking state. Some of this evidence comes from experiments with the ergograph.

The ergograph is a piece of apparatus which measures the amount of muscular work that one is doing. A common type is in the form

D

of a hand-grip which one has to squeeze repeatedly, and which records the amount of work one is doing second by second. Nicholson[5] used seven subjects who practised with an ergograph for two weeks, and thereby the normal capacity of each was established, including how long they had to rest between bouts of work before they recovered sufficiently to resume at full capacity. The mechanism of the ergograph made them lift a three-kilogramme weight up and down every two seconds, a very boring and supposedly exhausting task. Nicholson found that in the waking state subjects appeared to be exhausted and unable to continue after about ten minutes' work. He stated, however, that when hypnotized '. . . the capacity for work seemed practically endless'. What was meant in terms of time by 'practically endless', we are left guessing. He added a refinement to the experiment by working a subject practically to the point of exhaustion, then suddenly he hypnotized him without interrupting the work, with the result that he continued at his original rate of work, apparently as fresh as a daisy!

Although Nicholson's experiment was of a very dull nature, for there is not much fun in lifting a three-kilogramme weight up and down for ten or more minutes, the results seemed pretty marvellous and caused people to wonder whether all sorts of dull but useful tasks could be done more efficiently and pleasantly under hypnosis. If one has to work seven hours a day sticking labels on boxes, why not do it in a pleasant hypnotic trance? Fatigue is apparently cut down and, the boss would be delighted to hear, the rate of work does not slacken.

Williams,[6] who also did the experiment on arm fatigue, took up the challenge, and to be extra severe, increased the weight to four and a half kilogrammes. For practice, he got a subject in the normal waking state to lift the weight up and down at a rate of eighty times a minute. It sounds a most gruelling task, but his subject kept it up for *half an hour* without slackening, and then said that 'he could keep it up all night.'

Who was being kidded? Perhaps Nicholson's subjects were in cahoots in the waking state and, to save themselves a lot of boring, though hardly exhausting work, pretended that they could keep it up for only about ten minutes. If this was so, then the improvement in the hypnotic state was really a return to normal diligence which was well within their capacity anyway.

Williams got five subjects to practice on the ergograph with a *five*-kilogramme weight. They then did work-spells hypnotized and non-hypnotized on alternate days. All subjects gave a better record when hypnotized, but the improvement was not very great – about 12 per cent on average. As to the earlier finding that if a subject is hypnotized whilst working and urged to continue, his work capacity will revive, Williams confirmed the truth of this. But he also found something else – that if a fatigued hypnotized subject is aroused whilst working and urged to continue, his working rate would improve also! In fact, it looks as though whatever you do in an encouraging way to a person working at a boring task, it will banish fatigue for the time being and his working capacity will increase. We must not, therefore, confuse the effects of hypnosis with what is generally known as encouragement.

As to the suggestion that manual workers might be hypnotized so that they could do dull, repetitive tasks with less fatigue and greater output, perhaps industrial psychologists have already proceeded along these lines without mentioning the word hypnosis. There is much about some modern factories, with their constant music-while-you-work, rhythmic processes and sounds, and effortless, mindless work on the part of some operatives, which engenders a state akin to hypnosis. One is apt to feel that the glazed-eyed workers sitting at a conveyor belt, endlessly doing the same thing as the hours pass, must be in a state of irritated boredom, but for many this is certainly not so. They are in a not unpleasant trance state which is only terminated by the signal announcing a meal-break or the end of the day. This may not epitomize the dignity of productive work, but it may go some way to explaining what to some is a surprising degree of apathetic contentment.

Such a work-trance, while enabling boring, repetitive work to be continued endlessly without much strain, does not necessarily ensure a high rate of production. Depending on the nature of the work, extra and novel stimuli may speed it up considerably. This was shown in the famous Hawthorne study, which will be briefly described because what has come to be known as the 'Hawthorne Effect' is also manifest in experiments on the effects of hypnosis.

At the Hawthorne plant of the Western Electric Company, industrial psychologists were investigating the factors which made for improved production. They found, for example, that increasing the illumination increased production and, being experimentally minded, tested how much production would fall by decreasing the illumination. To everyone's astonishment the level of production continued to rise, even when they turned down the level of illumination until it was no brighter than bright moonlight. While this was an obvious saving in electric light, they did not maintain it for too long since it was obviously a temporary phenomenon. The level of illumination was somewhat irrelevant; it was the deliberate attempt to *alter* the working conditions which provided the novelty that boosted working morale.

The psychologists then went on to do a series of experiments with six girls who were employed assembling relays. These girls were allocated to a special work-room and subjected to a variety of changes in working conditions over two years. However the conditions were manipulated it was likely to have a beneficial effect on production. This was the result of trying to study the girls and showing an encouraging interest in them, which was far more important than any changes made in the physical environment. If they had hypnotized the girls once a week (which no one thought of doing) then they might have come to the erroneous conclusion that it was the hypnosis that increased the working efficiency. It might have done so, but principally because it was just one more novel intervention in the organization of the factory.

This 'Hawthorne Effect' has therefore to be taken into consideration whenever we study the alleged increase of ability in an experiment involving hypnosis.

The experiments reported above have been concerned mainly with attempts to reduce fatigue by hypnosis. But what of the claim that actual supernormal strength can be induced hypnotically? Can a hypnotized subject perform a sudden feat of strength beyond his normal capacity? Again, the older writers on hypnosis were fairly definite that this was an established fact. In an old experimental study reported by Hadfield,[7] the power of the hand-grip of three men was tested on a dynamometer, an instrument which records such power. The three averaged 101 pounds grip under normal conditions. They were then hypnotized and it was suggested to them that they would become very, very strong, and in this condition their average grip increased to 142 pounds, a very substantial increase.

Young,[8] acting in the best traditions of following up older work with controlled experiments, repeated Hadfield's experiment, but with twelve subjects, and testing them twice in a hypnotized and twice in a non-hypnotized condition, varying the order of the sessions in order to control against the effects of practice. In all, 616 measurements were taken, so it was a pretty thorough investigation. The result was that the average grip in the hypnotized state was no different from that in the non-hypnotized state. How then do we explain the results reported by Hadfield? Possibly Hadfield's men were not exerting themselves fully in the non-hypnotized state, because the dynamometer may have been of the kind that hurts the hand if gripped too hard, but hypnosis can dull such experience of pain.

The present author used a dynamometer in a special way designed to produce pain, to test the power of hypnosis to reduce or eliminate a special sort of pain, the pain of childbirth. In this study, a series of women who were about six months pregnant were brought up to the Maudsley Hospital by their GP to undergo various tests relating to their training in hypnosis so that they could have their babies later on in comfort. One of the tests was to squeeze a dynamometer repeatedly while the blood supply to the forearm had been interrupted by pumping up a pneumatic cuff around the arm.

If we do muscular work while the blood supply to a limb is cut off, then a curious pain develops in the muscles. The test was to see how long these women could maintain such a condition in a waking state, and then with hypnotic analgesia. This was a very ill-conceived test, for some of the women seemed happy to continue working the dynamometer in hypnosis *ad infinitum*, and of course it is dangerous to continue occluding the blood from a limb for too long or terrible consequences ensue! The test had to be abandoned.

It seems reasonable to conclude from these and other experiments that hypnosis does not in fact make us capable of supernormal feats of strength, but because it can reduce our experience of pain it can increase our capacity to perform some tasks that would normally be unpleasantly painful. In some circumstances this would not be wise, for we can damage ourselves if we neglect the normal pain signals.

This general conclusion is not accepted by everyone. Some writers have implied that all that can be done by hypnosis can equally well be done by suitably phrased instructions to non-hypnotized subjects. Barber and Calverley[9] tested the capacity of subjects to hold a heavy weight out at arm's length for a long time, both hypnotized and unhypnotized, and they found that their 'task motivating instructions' produced as much endurance as did hypnosis. It has been suggested earlier in this chapter that being chased by an angry bull would be sufficiently motivating to make a non-athletic man sprint half a mile without thought of fatigue. Perhaps the 'task motivating instructions' given in the Barber laboratory have much the same arousal effect on the students as an angry bull. Or perhaps many of the subjects who received the hypnotic induction procedure were being contrary because, in this particular experiment, they were not told that hypnosis would be involved when they originally agreed to be experimental subjects. It is possible for a hypnotic induction to have an effect opposite of what is intended if a subject feels that there has been less than frankness in the original recruitment.

An interesting side-light on the question of motivating instructions is given by the experiments of Slotnik *et al.*[10] They too tested subjects' ability to hold up a heavy weight for a long period, and like Barber and Calverley found that even without hypnosis, motivating instructions – appeals to the subjects that really they *could* do better if they tried – increased endurance. They then added to such *rational* appeals a totally *irrational* 'involving instruction'. The nature of this irrational appeal is so important that it bears quoting :

'Today you will think of yourself as stronger and more capable and you will actually become stronger and have greater endurance. You will have an unusually strong desire to do well. You will do extremely well. In a moment I am going to count from one to ten, and as I count you will actually begin to feel yourself becoming stronger and stronger. Your desire to be stronger and to do well will increase with each number that I say. One . . . you are getting stronger . . . two . . . three . . . your desire to do well is increasing . . . four . . . you can feel your entire body becoming stronger and stronger . . . five . . . six . . . seven . . . stronger and stronger . . . eight . . . a greater and greater desire to do well . . . nine . . . ten.

'Can you feel that you have additional strength and endurance? (Wait for "Yes") Now I want you to repeat after me : "I can feel that I am very strong . . . I want very much to be strong . . . so that I can perform physical tasks well . . . my concentration has made me very strong." '

They insisted that the subjects repeated this affirmation. This appeal, which relies for its force on an entirely irrational declaration, was made to subjects both in the waking and in the hypnotic state. Both groups of subjects gained in performance as the result of it, but it produced strikingly greater improvement in the hypnotized group as compared with the other. Herein, then, lies the power of hypnosis *over and above* the ordinary responsiveness which is normally elicited by exhortations of a rational kind to do our best. Totally irrational appeals to accept a desired effect as reality are somehow specially effective in hypnosis, and imply that it is indeed a unique state of consciousness. In the waking state, we scrutinize, we doubt, we cannot quite accept the ideal as real. This sort of suggestion is quite different from trying to increase motivation to do well, and it should be noted that the subjects were required to repeat aloud a statement that a change *had* taken place : '. . . my concentration has made me very strong'. This may be compared with the Japanese experiment on warming the arms by passive acceptance (rather than active willing) which was referred to earlier.

So far, what has been discussed is the evidence for enhanced muscular strength and endurance under hypnosis. But what of increased intellectual power? It has been generally accepted that powers of memory can be greatly enhanced in hypnosis, and this is exemplified by cases of age regression which have been mentioned earlier when therapy was discussed.

It is alleged that a hypnotized person can return in a psychological sense to a previous age, and that he will then be aware of all the facts that were then available to him. Some experimenters have claimed that the age-regressed person will actually *be* that age in a special psychological and even a physiological sense. The latter curious claim relates to testing neural reflexes of age-regressed subjects. There has been a claim that hypnotized subjects who were regressed to early infancy produced a reflex of the toes, the Babinski reflex, which is characteristic of the infant but not of later develop-ment.[11] Later workers have been unable to substantiate this claim.

Age regression in hypnosis can be achieved by first creating a certain confusion in the subject as to the present-day date, and then reminding him of an earlier time, say, when he was of the age of ten. He is questioned about his ten-year-old life and it is gradually suggested to him that this is the present-day reality, that he *is* ten years old. The results of this process can be quite dramatic; an adult will begin to talk and behave like a child of the suggested age, and indeed to reveal some quite unexpected details about himself gratuitously. The author once had an experimental subject who talked in a somewhat 'refined' manner, but when regressed to child-hood began to talk with a strong cockney accent, a detail of her childhood which it was certainly surprising that she should wish to reveal.

Age regression is used to recover lost memories, as in therapy, or merely for experimental purposes. Many of the older experiments which have been reported unfortunately lacked controls, and not enough work has been done on getting people to remember vividly their childhood at certain stages, and to speak and act as they would have done at these stages as a means of reactivating memories. Some work of this nature has been done by using simulating subjects (people asked to pretend to be hypnotized by one experimenter, to test another) and the powers of acting ability have thus been deter-mined. While the histrionic abilities of people can be tested by this means, there is no easy means of testing the accuracy of their memories for events supposedly recalled.

True[12] used fifty students whom he tried to get to regress under hypnosis to their birthdays and to Christmas Day at the ages of four, seven and ten. The subjects were asked, 'What day of the week is this?' and the accuracy of their replies checked against the calendar. Their replies were correct in 81 per cent of cases, a truly remark-able finding. The percentage of correct answers varied at the three age levels, the later the age the more accurate the answer. This detail might be explained in terms of the fading of memory with age, or simply that the younger the child the less likely is he to know the day of the week. The latter suggestion seems rather probable, for someone else has taken the trouble to ask a group of nursery schoolchildren aged four and five what day of the week it was. Only about 25 per cent knew the correct answer. But of course birthdays and Christmas Day are special for children, as many parents will have said to them 'It's your birthday on Monday,' before the great event.

Although a number of other research workers have done studies on age regression similar to that of True, no one has been able to repeat his results. It is possible that some of his subjects, hearing from their fellow students what they were going to be asked in hypnosis, cheated by looking up the calendar in advance. Alas, so many wonderful findings are under the suspicion of somebody cheating somewhere!

The older literature deals also with the enhancement of feeling and sensitivity of perception, as well as its opposite, blocking off sensitivity to stimuli by hypnotic suggestion. Bramwell[13] writes of hypnotic suggestion being able greatly to increase powers of hearing, vision, smell and skin sensitivity. It must be remembered that he was writing after a preceding century in which the most outrageous claims for enhanced powers under hypnosis and the mesmeric trance had been made, and his claims are extremely modest by contrast. We read of Léonide, aged ten years, the daughter of a French country doctor, who specialized in recognizing objects and reading books when blindfolded in a mesmeric trance. The story is told by Sinnet,[14] who was a Theosophist, writing at the end of the nineteenth century, but still a staunch supporter of the more ludicrous claims of the mesmerists. The flavour of the enthusiasm of the occult supporters is well captured in his spirited attack on those who dared impose rational test conditions on self-styled wonder workers:

'When at last M. Pigeaire decided to claim on his daughter's behalf the prize which had been offered by a member of the Académie de Médecine, the family genius was brought out of her retirement and introduced in Paris to a great number of learned observers. The prize in question had been offered by Dr Burdin to anyone who could read without the use of the eyes, of the sense of touch or of light. The Académie de Médecine was to arbitrate on any claims that might be made. While the Pigeaire family were staying in Paris they seemed to have given a series of private entertainments at which Léonide's faculties were exhibited, and a large number of persons distinguished in science, literature and social rank signed records of successful experiments. When the time came, however, for M. Pigeaire to interview the committee appointed by the Académie de Médecine, he found them perfectly unprepared to investigate and adjudicate upon what actually took place, and only to deal with Mlle Léonide if she would conform precisely to their own arrangements and conditions, among which were that she should wear a peculiar kind of helmet mask which they had constructed, and let one of their number keep his hands on her eyelids all the time. In all its details the story is instructive to anyone interested in looking back on the thoroughly unscientific attitude of mind taken up by the representatives of physical science in those days in their dealings with mesmerism. But I can hardly give space here to all the ramifications of the story. M. Pigeaire tried to make his surly inquisitors understand that the whole psychic condition of his daughter required delicate and gentle treatment, and that their own proposals were calculated to throw her into convulsions rather than into a clairvoyant state, that the bandages he employed, using masses of cotton wool to cover the eyes completely, were of such a kind that any pretence of distrusting their efficiency was ridiculous, but all to no purpose. The committee refused even to look at the bandages, and after he had left them in disgust, sent in a report, the general drift of which was the proposed experiments had been declined except under conditions which the committee did not receive for evidence of bona fides.'

So Léonide did not get her prize from the fund proposed by Dr Burdin, but we read that a group of persons who had witnessed her performance at the Pigeaires' private entertainment, raised an even greater sum for her by private subscription. One cannot regard all this as a folly of a bygone age. Today Léonide would be exhibiting her tricks on television, and there would be no lack of persons 'distinguished in science, literature and social rank' falling over themselves to sign records of successful experiments. Indeed, the various experimenters who have been quoted in this book as attempting to subject the phenomena of hypnosis to mundane, scientific tests, will be regarded by some as mere kill-joys trying to take all the fun out of the topic of hypnosis!

Even if we discount the claims that have been made for marvellous powers of sensory perception under hypnosis, is there in fact evidence for supernormal acuity of perception, as more reasonable writers like Bramwell have claimed? We have seen that though there is some evidence that muscular power and endurance can be increased by special techniques under hypnosis, there is no evidence that we can increase it very greatly. It seems a reasonable supposition that we might be made very much more sensitive under hypnosis by appropriate techniques.

Hull[15] collected a good deal of experimental evidence concerning the increase of sensitivity under hypnosis, and came to the conclusion that the super-sensitivity of the hypnotized subject was a myth. Even the supposedly superior ability in the judgement of time intervals which had been confidently asserted by various authors, appeared to have little foundation in fact. Two errors seem to have contributed to a false impression in this matter. First, a lot of evidence upon which claims have been made comes from the clinical field, where no controls have been used. Doctors have studied the powers of patients they have repeatedly hypnotized, and have been impressed by their extreme sensory acuity, ability to judge time and so forth. All this means is that these doctors, like many other people, had no idea how very accurate people could be when tested under conditions of quiet concentration. They would have got the same results if they had tested their patients unhypnotized, a precaution they seldom resorted to. The second error comes from the confidence of the hypnotized subjects in their own powers, for if one tells a hypnotized person that he has super-acute hearing he will temporarily believe that he has and act out the fantasy, sometimes deceiving the very person who gave him the idea.

Allied to the belief that superior sensory ability can be produced by hypnotic suggestion is the conviction that sensory ability can be abolished by suggestion. Here we are on surer ground, for although there is no method other than concentration for improving acuity, it is relatively easy to function with less than maximum efficiency. Hypnotic blindness and deafness have been recorded, as has the more paradoxical situation of selective sensitivity. A person may be made profoundly deaf for the time being by suggesting to him in hypnosis that he will be unable to hear anything until you tell him that he can hear again. He will certainly act out the stone-deaf part, and report afterwards that he could not hear a thing, but how did he manage to hear the spoken instruction that his deafness was at an end?

This is not as paradoxical as once was thought, for nowadays we know a good deal about subliminal perception. We perceive (that is, take in, register and make sense of) only a tiny fraction of all the multitudinous sea of stimuli that bombards us all the time, but if a particular stimulus is very meaningful, even if it is very weak, it will get through our perceptual filter and make itself known to us. At a crowded party, all we may hear is a confused buzz of sound, yet let someone speak our own name even at a distance, and it will tend to register as a distinct percept through all that sea of sound.

It may be that the person rendered deaf by hypnotic suggestion has simply closed his 'filter' so that sounds do not get through to his consciousness although his ear apparatus is functioning normally. Yet the spoken words 'Now you can hear again' are of such an expected and meaningful nature that it is passed on through the filter and readjusts the whole mechanism. We do not know precisely how subliminal perception works, even after many years of intensive experimental inquiry, but at least we can accept the paradox of the hypnotically deaf person hearing the releasing signal as being no more strange than any other of the subliminal phenomena, and not requiring an explanation in terms of the hypnotized person play-acting.

Lack of sensitivity in one of the sensory modalities which can be induced by hypnotic suggestion is, of course, reminiscent of the symptoms of hysterical conversion which have been discussed in an earlier chapter. The hypnotized person can be made to feel, hear and see selectively, and it is always this curious feature which makes us suspect play-acting.

One of the classic examples of an hysterical conversion symptom is what is called 'glove anaesthesia'. Here the patient complains that he has lost all feeling in a hand or wrist. Now loss of skin sensitivity of this nature could be due to a serious condition of nerve degeneration, and the test that the neurologist applies is lightly pricking the skin at different points to map out the exact area in which the patient can feel nothing. If it truly resembles an area like an anaesthetic glove, then it is probable that the patient has no neurological damage, for the actual area that would be affected by degeneration of nervous tissue would not correspond to a neat anatomical area like a glove, but would coincide with the area served by the relevant sensory nerve. The patient, unless he has detailed anatomical knowledge, is unaware of such complications, and by hysterical mechanisms may shut off a discrete part of his body from feeling.

Much the same goes for hypnotic local anaesthesia. We can suggest to a hypnotized subject that a hand or a forearm will lose all its feeling, and so it will. But the area which loses sensation may be quite illogical in terms of nerve distribution. Insufficient experimental work has been done on this question to arrive at a satisfactory answer, and the puzzle is posed of *where* the feeling of sensation or pain is cut off on its way to the conscious experience of the hypnotized person who reports that he does not feel it.

Actually, we must distinguish between an absence of ordinary feeling and an absence of pain. It is relatively easy in hypnosis to abolish skin sensation by suggestion; it is suggested that the part becomes numb and insensitive to touch, and when tested by tickling, prodding and the like the hypnotized person reports that he can feel nothing. But is this merely a verbal report of someone who *imagines* that he can feel nothing – suppose that he is 'lying' both to himself and to the experimenter? It is another matter, however, if we actually cut or burn the part; will he then *act* as though there was no feeling by not flinching, withdrawing or crying out?

Obviously in experimental work we refrain from doing drastic and damaging things to the subject, so most tests of the abolition of pain by hypnosis must be rather equivocal. The evidence for the abolition of pain by hypnotic suggestion comes rather from the world of surgery where drastic operations have had to be performed in the patients' interest.

Elsewhere in this book, mention has been made of the work of the nineteenth-century doctors such as Elliotson and Esdaile who used hypnosis – or rather mesmerism, as they called it – to permit painless surgery before the general introduction of chemical agents such as chloroform and ether. It is now necessary to take a long and careful look at the evidence to see how reliable it is.

The work most often quoted is that of Esdaile, because he carried out hundreds of surgical operations using a form of mesmerism to prevent pain. It is usual to refer to hypnotic *analgesia* (i.e. insensitivity to pain) but what Esdaile seems to have used most frequently, at least for major operations, was hypnotic *anaesthesia* (i.e. general insensibility). The graphic accounts of his operations refer to the patients being in a profound trance, and not awakening from it for hours. After waking, they claimed to have no knowledge of what had been going on, even though they had undergone a severe operation.

The account of Esdaile's work is contained in three of his chief publications.[16] He graduated in Medicine at Edinburgh in 1830 and was later a doctor in India, holding an appointment in the East India Company. After his initial work at Hooghly, where he performed over a hundred operations using mesmerism as an anaesthetic agent, he sent his results to the government of the State, the Medical Board having ignored him. The Deputy Governor of Bengal thereupon appointed a committee of investigation who, having examined his procedures, reported very favourably.

The Deputy Governor then appointed Esdaile to the control of a small hospital at Calcutta where he could continue his mesmeric practice and carry out further experiments, and where medical and other scientific people could witness his work and enlarge their understanding of the possibilities of mesmeric phenomena in medicine and surgery. Furthermore, the Deputy Governor appointed Official Visitors, who were medical officers charged with the responsibility of periodic inspection of Esdaile's work.

Despite favourable reports from Official Visitors, the Mesmeric Hospital, as it was called, was closed after a year for reasons which are somewhat obscure. Esdaile was then appointed as head of a small hospital supported mainly by subscriptions from Indians, where he continued for six months. Next he was appointed to the Sarkea Lane Hospital and Dispensary, for by this time he was stressing the *medical* advantages of mesmerism, as distinct from its use as an anaesthetic agent in surgery. Here he was harking back to the old claim of Mesmer that all ailments had a common source and that animal magnetism was a universal panacea. To some extent this is paralleled by the claims of traditional Chinese medicine, which will be discussed in a later chapter on acupuncture.

Three years later, Esdaile left India, giving as his reason that he hated the climate and way of life completely, and was glad to return to his native Scotland.

Such, in brief, is the outline of Esdaile's sojourn in India, and his remarkable use of mesmerism, most of which is well attested in official documents. We are given the impression that he introduced mesmerism to India, demonstrated its amazing power to produce anaesthesia, and then returned to Scotland, where, along with Elliotson's movement in England, the power of mesmerism appeared to fizzle out. However, the true story of Esdaile's work in India is perhaps a little different from the way he tells it. Although there is no reason to doubt the genuineness of the anaesthesia which he produced on numerous occasions in major surgery, some of his other accounts of what he did in India are so far-fetched as to strain the credulity of the modern reader.

He relates, for instance, an incredible tale of his mesmerizing men in a court of law, without their knowledge, by standing *behind* them and making the passes. He then made them walk away in a somnambulistic trance, of which they later had no memory. All this was to demonstrate to the magistrate that such a thing was possible. This was in a case of a native barber being tried for child-stealing, allegedly by the power of mesmerism.

Esdaile's version of how he first came to use mesmerism[17] concerns a patient on whom he had performed the operation of letting the fluid out of a hydrocoel (a huge, watery cyst) and then injecting a caustic. The patient reacted to this extremely painful procedure by going into what appeared to be a spasm of pain, stiffening his whole body. Then Esdaile, according to his own account, turned to his native assistant and remarked that he would see if the patient were susceptible to mesmerism, although he admitted that at the time *he knew practically nothing about the practice of mesmerism*. He then mesmerized the patient, who remained in a trance for some hours. Later, Esdaile sent to England for books, and studied what had been published about mesmerism.

Esdaile relates how he worked very hard for six weeks mesmeriz-

ing his patients for surgery, and then, being quite exhausted, sleepless and irritable, handed over the whole practice of mesmerizing
the patients to his native assistants. We gather that from then on it
was they who did all the mesmerism for surgery.

Thus in Esdaile's account, it was he who taught the Indians
mesmerism. An alternative view might be that the Indians, both
medical assistants and patients, taught him certain traditional
practices for the control of pain, and he linked these practices with
European methods of medicine and surgery, and related them to
what was known in Europe as mesmerism. Certainly he was a great
innovator, but as far as the mesmeric practices were concerned he
was more likely to have been the pupil than the teacher of the
Indians, an unflattering fact that he suppressed.

He is entirely contradictory in what he relates. He claimed that
his patients were utterly unaware of what methods he used with
them, and that he preferred them to be in ignorance of his mesmeric
art. He claimed this in order to combat the idea that *suggestibility*
and fulfilling an expected role played any part in his patients' going
into a trance state. In another part of his writings he relates how he
learned of the Indian practice of *jar-phoonk*, a ritual performed on
the sick by native healers. This, he points out, comes from the
Indian words *jarna* to stroke and *phoonka* to blow. This is precisely
what his native assistants did in mesmerizing the patients, making
rhythmical passes and breathing on them till they went into a trance.
Could it have been that all the patients were very well aware of this
practice, and played their role of going into a deep trance state if
they had the capacity.

It is quite understandable that the Indians – doctors, medical
assistants and patients – played the game of having the white sahib
take all the credit. Esdaile did, after all, bring great benefits to them,
using his influence to set up hospitals and working untiringly for
them. Some of his European critics in India who were opposed to
mesmerism in principle, made the extraordinary charge that Esdaile
was an honest fool, duped by his patients who were 'hardened
imposters' and only *pretended* not to suffer pain. In the main, this
charge is absurd, but it is possible that some rumours of how Esdaile
was in fact a European stooge in the hands of his native assistants
may have been circulating.

The whole phenomenon of Esdaile's remarkable record of painless
surgery becomes more understandable if we consider the context in
which he was working, and the people who constituted his patients.
They were mainly the poor of Bengal, living in conditions of abject
poverty, hunger and disease. In such conditions people develop an
entirely different orientation to pain. In our protected, well-fed and

hygienic European lives we are highly intolerant of and sensitive to pain, and seek immediate relief by medical means. However, in a society where pain and disease are an everyday reality, people develop other means of coping with the situation. It is suggested that these poor Indians cultivated the capacity of going into anaesthetic trance states in appropriate circumstances, and their native healers had developed the *jar-phoonk* and other rituals to aid and teach them. Even so, all individuals could not develop the capacity, and Esdaile records cases of patients who could not enter a trance even after many days of endeavour on the part of his assistants. In the next chapter we will discuss the mechanisms of animal hypnosis, which is not quite the same thing as what we usually mean by hypnosis with humans, but which may well relate to the sort of trance state achieved by Esdaile's patients.

It is to Esdaile's credit that he did not claim that any special power resided in himself or other mesmerists, and was quite content to regard it as a technique, a mysterious influence that one person might have over another. Being utterly unscientific, he did not question the occult nonsense that Mesmer had propounded. He did not come to understand, as Braid did eventually, that the whole power lay in the patient himself.

The story of Elliotson, who also performed painless surgical operations although on nothing like the scale of Esdaile, is more difficult to evaluate. The whole question of Elliotson's use of mesmerism is so clouded by the overheated atmosphere of controversy that it is difficult to ascertain exactly what went on. As described in Chapter 2, Elliotson was an eminent London doctor. His name is inscribed on the roll of past presidents in the hall of the Royal Society of Medicine in Wigmore Street. He became interested in mesmerism and found that he could use it effectively to remove pain in many cases of surgery, at University College Hospital and elsewhere. But this benign practice became more and more mixed up with absurd claims of clairvoyance and other wonders, and many of his medical colleagues, jealous of the respectability and prestige of their profession, reacted with pig-headed opposition to Elliotson's mesmeric practices – and to some of his more mundane practices, like the invention of the stethoscope.

Elliotson lost his membership of the Royal Medical and Chirgical Society because of his mesmeric practices, and was refused appointments at various hospitals. He and his followers published *The Zoist*, which ran for thirteen years from 1842 and covered a wide variety of topics besides mesmerism, including phrenology, the supposed science of reading character from the bumps on the head. The rambling and polemical nature of much of what appeared in *The*

Zoist does not convince one of its scientific objectivity, but then the
tone of the critics of mesmerism is so sneering and biased that one
cannot believe that they were mainly concerned to establish the
truth either. The sad thing is that mesmerism appeared to lose its
power to relieve pain in the dramatic way that Elliotson demonstrated in his early years. Later on he wrote :

'I believe I was not wrong : I believe that in what I originally
saw, mesmerism played the parts precisely that I claimed for it. It
is a wicked error to suppose that I was party to a deception, or to a
whole series of deceptions, if you like; but I candidly say . . . that
mesmerism, at the present moment, has no power to remove pain.
It is a mystery; it had the power, and I once saw a leg painlessly
removed under its influence; but we are now in another cycle, and
it seems to me that there are special periods only in which mesmeric
phenomena can be induced.'[18]

This is an extraordinary admission on Elliotson's part, and does
credit to his honesty of purpose. It even advances our understanding
of the problem of supernormal performance under hypnosis. Granted
that the passes and other magnetizing procedures of the mesmerists
had no power of influence *in themselves,* then the whole phenomenon lay in the patients' expectation and pre-existent capacity to
affect a dramatic change in their state of consciousness. It is suggested here that the poor of India, living in the conditions they did,
already had a well-developed latent capacity to go into a trance of
insensitivity when subjected to the ritual of the *jar-phoonk,* which
closely resembled the ritual of mesmerism. To what extent, we must
ask ourselves, was this capacity latent in Europeans living at the
same period?

Both rich and poor alike at that period were more accustomed
than they are today to living with pain and poor medical care, and
were far more credulous. Having no chemical anaesthetics, it was
often a case of choosing between very painful surgery and death,
and when the wonder-working mesmeric surgeons came along with
their promise of apparently painless surgery, suitably constituted
individuals could profit by it and achieve insensibility at the hands
of a mesmerizer. When chemical anaesthetics became available,
however, and all could expect to benefit from painless surgery,
irrespective of their degree of faith or personal capacity, then
scepticism asserted itself, and the barrage of calumny directed
against the mesmerists destroyed public confidence in them. Then,
as Elliotson sadly admitted, mesmerism had no power to remove
pain.

When mesmerism had been replaced by hypnotism, and there was
some attempt to follow scientific principles in inducing analgesia,

hypnotists like Bramwell did indeed see how far they could go in removing pain by direct hypnotic suggestion. Although some hypnotists like Bernheim, Liébault, and Moll[19] reported that it was extremely rare to be able to produce complete analgesia by hypnotic suggestion, it was certainly used by enthusiastic practitioners, as it is still used today. Obviously, there is now little need to resort to hypnosis for analgesia when there are many local and general anaesthetics available, but it still has its uses. Werbel[20] reports a typical modern case of a woman with a very bad heart who needed surgery, and was trained in hypnotic analgesia to undergo an operation with this aid.

The author has watched, on videotape, an operation for appendicitis carried out under hypnotic analgesia. It was performed on a young woman who remained alert enough to talk during the operation, and indeed to take a few puffs of a cigarette as she lay there, relaxed and dreamy. Remembering his own post-operative pain and misery after appendicectomy with a conventional anaesthetic, the author envied this young woman as she sat up in bed afterwards and chatted vivaciously.

More typically, hypnosis is used to enable a patient to endure days of acute discomfort, as when he has to have his limbs in an immobile, cramped position while skin grafts are being implanted from one part of the body to another.

One point which needs clarification is the extent to which hypnosis removes pain by direct suggestion of analgesia, or as a result incidental to the altered state of consciousness. Josephine Hilgard[21] relates how a girl who was very susceptible to hypnosis was induced by hypnotic suggestion to accept that she had no hands. The girl reported that she just saw holes at the end of her sleeves. She was then given a strong electric shock to one hand, and despite the fact that no suggestions of analgesia had been given, she did not feel the electric shock – for she truly experienced having no hands.

Hypnosis is not the only agent which may produce an absence of pain in a waking subject, due to an altered state of awareness. When they began to experiment with laughing gas (nitrous oxide) in the last century, it was first used for fun and only later for dentistry. It was noticed early on, that long before a person became unconscious by inhaling a good deal of the gas, his sense of pain appeared to be abolished. As is well known, alcohol provides the same *possibility* of altering our state of awareness of our physical sensations, although its interaction with personality and with mood is very complex. It should be noted that these drugs do not act by deadening the sensations as opiates do, for the sensory appreciation of pleasurable feelings may remain just as acute, while the experience of pain is removed. An interesting example of this is known to the author. A young woman was spending the evening with her lover, but could not bear to let him touch her because of a severe attack of piles. She was in such pain that she eventually drank a large glass of brandy, which had the rapid effect of not only removing the pain, but of enabling her to enjoy the sensual pleasure of lovemaking.

There are critics who would question whether hypnosis can in fact effect this apparently wonderful feat of removing pain from surgery. They suggest that surgery is not necessarily as painful as people imagine. Barber[22] points out that '. . . it cannot be assumed that all of Esdaile's patients would have moaned or cried out during surgery if they had not been mesmerized. Esdaile's report . . . and also other reports, indicate that, prior to the discovery of analgesics or anaesthetics, a small proportion of patients who were not mesmerized did *not* moan or cry out during surgery.' Elsewhere,[23] Barber makes his sceptical position clearer : 'In brief there are rare cases of individuals who were said to be in a "hypnotic trance state" and also individuals who were said to be "awake" who underwent minor or major surgery without drugs and without manifesting much pain. These cases seem much more dramatic than they actually are because it is assumed that all parts of the body are as sensitive to pain as the skin. The truth of the matter is that, although the skin is sensitive, most tissues and organs in the body are insensitive to the surgeon's scalpel. Furthermore there is no reason to postulate a special state of consciousness in order to explain the ability to undergo noxious stimulation of the skin without manifesting distress or pain.'

Barber's sceptical criticism consists of questioning whether a patient undergoing a surgical operation under hypnosis without feeling pain proves anything, as he might not have felt the pain had he *not* been hypnotized; such cases are not entirely unknown. The same case might be made with regard to chemical anaesthesia, but no one appears to have made it. Faced with this sort of criticism, one turns to the careful work of psychologists who have taken great care in the carrying out of controlled experiments and measuring the strength of the painful stimuli they have administered with and without hypnosis. This work has been hampered by the fact that it is neither possible within the context of the experimental laboratory to administer really powerful painful stimuli, nor to have subjects who are deeply disturbed by fear and apprehension, as genuine surgical patients are likely to be. For what has been done one must admire the fortitude of the experimental subjects who were willing to submit to painful procedures in the interests of extending our knowledge in this area.

Sears[24] used seven male subjects who showed themselves capable of going into a deep hypnotic trance. The painful stimulus was provided by a metal spike which jabbed on the calf of the leg, and was administered by an apparatus which ensured that the same pressure was always applied, and that the moment of application was recorded. The subjects' reaction to the jab was measured by several indices; the verbal report ('Ow! Yes it hurt'), the facial grimace which is normally made to painful stimulation, and the changes in breathing, pulse rate and electrical resistance of the skin, all of which normally register a reaction to pain. All these physical signs of pain were registered by a recording apparatus to which the subjects were attached.

In Sears' first experiment, the subjects were hypnotized and suggestions were given that the left leg would become anaesthetized, but the right leg would remain normal. Jabs were then given to both legs, and the results recorded. It should be noted that the measures of reactions to pain were of three kinds; wholly under voluntary control (the verbal report), partly voluntary (facial grimace and oscillation of breathing), and wholly involuntary (pulse oscillation and changes in the conductivity of the skin). One criticism of the claim that hypnosis can produce relief from pain is that the subject suffers just as much but *pretends* that he does not in terms of his spoken report. Now this experiment measured spoken report, half-voluntary and wholly involuntary responses to painful stimuli, and indeed compared similar areas of the body, one anaesthetized and the other left normal. All three types of response to pain were found to be reduced by hypnotic suggestion, although to a greatly varying degree between different individuals. The wholly involuntary reactions of pulse rate and skin resistance were not affected to the same degree as the others, but one may reasonably argue that what is important about pain is that one does not consciously experience it. No one minds certain physiological reactions taking place in his body during an operation if he does not *experience* pain.

Sears performed two other control experiments which are important additions to the investigation. In the first control experiment, the subjects were again submitted to exactly the same procedure but with no hypnosis or suggestions of anaesthesia, and the results showed no difference between the pain experience of the two legs. In the second control experiment, the subjects were not hypnotized, but were asked to try as hard as they could to suppress any manifestations of pain when the jab was to their left leg, but not to the right. Obviously they could all say 'No' however much the left leg hurt, but the other signs of pain showed that they could not repress signs of pain by voluntary effort. Obviously one can argue that they simply *were not trying,* and to this argument there is no answer. Critics have drawn attention to the fact that the subjects appeared to be rather bad at inhibiting the facial flinch in this control experiment, and one must always be on the alert for signs that subjects are giving too poor a performance in the waking state to magnify the superiority of their performance when hypnotized. This second control experiment is not such a good one, in that what was being required of the subjects was to act one way in respect of the left leg and another in respect of the right. An appeal to acting ability tends to give rather artificial results.

A fair-minded assessment of Sears' results would be that he showed that the experience of pain can be greatly reduced by hypnotic suggestion even in the context of an experimental laboratory. It is not an all-or-none phenomenon, and some of the physiological indices of pain such as the oscillation of the pulse rate and change in skin resistance are not greatly affected. But this ties in with the experience of anaesthetists who report that some deeply anaesthetized patients groan and grimace on the operating table, even though they afterwards report that they were completely unconscious at the time.

Other experimenters have followed Sears by doing investigations of a similar kind, and their results have not been very different. It seems safe to conclude that hypnotic suggestion can indeed reduce the experience of pain, but the extent to which it does so varies very much according to the personality of the subject, and to the conditions in which hypnosis is being used. There is good evidence that complete insensitivity to pain can be induced, but this is not normally possible under laboratory conditions or with people living in modern conditions of relative comfort and dependence on medical care. Moreover, the *sort* of hypnotic state that is induced in the cases of extreme anaesthesia and unconsciousness may be, to some degree, different from the sort of hypnosis we normally induce nowadays by verbal suggestion, and may have much in common with animal hypnosis, which has yet to be discussed in detail. The whole question of pain and its control is so important and fascinating that it will be taken up again in the chapter on acupuncture and hypnosis. In this chapter, the control of pain has been explored as one of the examples of supernormal performance under hypnosis.

To sum up the evidence from a wide variety of sources regarding supernormal performance under hypnosis is difficult. We have seen that the subject is bedevilled with a huge mass of folklore, the unsubstantiated anecdotes of those who love to believe in the marvellous, and the deliberate trickery of stage hypnotists and conjurers. Because of this accumulation of folk-lore some modern experimentalists have tried to demonstrate in their laboratories that hypnosis has *none* of the special effects claimed for it. Their experiments, although ingenious, sometimes fail to be convincing because they do not attempt to achieve a really adequate state of hypnosis. The workers of a bygone age would spend literally hours inducing what they considered to be an adequate trance state, yet one reads some modern accounts in which an experimenter read aloud a fifteen-minute induction procedure to his subjects, and then according to him they were 'hypnotized' and could be compared with other subjects who had not had this treatment – and thus test the alleged power of hypnosis! Such rather superficial experiments tend to be conducted by those whose own theoretical standpoint is opposed to those who regard hypnosis in terms of an altered state of awareness, probably with very definite physiological changes involved.

Research in this area has greatly enlarged our understanding of the great latent capacities which people possess, often unknown to themselves. Baudelaire remarked of the drug cannabis that it can give you nothing – it can only release what is already there within you. The same goes for hypnosis. Our capacities of endurance, strength, sensory acuity, memory, and mastery of pain, are seldom fully exercised because of the sheltered and protected lives which we lead in our technological society. The power that hypnosis has lies in its ability to stretch us to the limit. As has been remarked earlier in this book, the phenomena of hypnosis only appear to be uncanny because our ordinary assumptions about the nature of human behaviour are not correct.

REFERENCES

1 T. X. Barber, *Hypnosis: A Scientific Approach*, op. cit.

2 C. Reiger, *Der Hypnotismus*, Jena: Gustav Fischer, 1884.

3 A. Binet and C. Féré, *Animal Magnetism*, New York: Appleton & Co., 1901.

4 G. W. Williams, 'A comparative study of voluntary and hypnotic catalepsy', *American Journal of Psychology*, 42, 1930, pp. 83–95.

5 N. C. Nicholson, 'Notes on muscular work during hypnosis', *Johns Hopkins Hospital Bulletin*, 31, 1920, p. 89.

6 G. W. Williams, 'The effect of hypnosis on muscular fatigue', *Journal of Abnormal and Social Psychology*, 24, 1929, pp. 318–329.

7 J. A. Hadfield, *The Psychology of Power*, London: Macmillan, 1924.

8 P. C. Young, 'An experimental study of mental and physical functions in the normal and hypnotic states', *American Journal of Psychology*, 36, 1925, pp. 214–232.

9 T. X. Barber and D. S. Calverley, 'Towards a theory of hypnotic behaviour: enhancement of strength and endurance', *Canadian Journal of Psychology*, 18, 1964, pp. 156–157.

10 R. S. Slotnik, R. M. Liebert and E. R. Hilgard, 'The enhancement of muscular performance in hypnosis through exhortation and involving instructions', *Journal of Personality*, 33, 1965, pp. 37–45.

11 L. Gidro-Frank and M. K. Bowersbuch, 'A study of the plantar response in hypnotic age regression', *Journal of Nervous and Mental Disease*, 107, 1948, pp. 443–458.

12 R. M. True, 'Experimental control in hypnotic age regression states', *Science*, 110, 1949, pp. 583–584.

13 J. M. Bramwell, *Hypnotism: Its History, Practice and Theory*, op. cit.

14 A. P. Sinnett, *The Rationale of Mesmerism*, op. cit.

15 C. L. Hull, *Hypnosis and Suggestibility*, New York: Appleton Century-Crofts, 1933.

16 J. Esdaile, *Mesmerism in India and its Practical Application in Surgery and Medicine*, London: Longman, Brown, Green and Longmans, 1846; *Natural and Mesmeric Clairvoyance*, London: Hyppolyte Bailliere, 1852; *The Introduction of Mesmerism as Anaesthetic and Curative Agent into the Hospitals of India*, op. cit.

17 J. Esdaile, *Mesmerism in India . . .*, op. cit.

18 Quoted by G. Rosen, 'From mesmerism to hypnotism', *Ciba Symposium*, 9, 1948, pp. 838–844.

19 A. Moll, *Hypnotism*, trans. A. F. Hopkirk, London: Walter Scott, 1890.

20 E. W. Werbel, 'Hypnosis in serious surgical problems', *American Journal of Clinical Hypnosis*, 10, 1967, pp. 44–47.

21 J. R. Hilgard, *Personality and Hypnosis*, op. cit.

22 T. X. Barber, *Hypnosis: A Scientific Approach*, op. cit.

23 Idem, 'Suggested ("hypnotic") behaviour: the trance paradigm versus an alternative paradigm', in E. Fromm and R. E. Shor (eds.), *Hypnosis: Research Developments and Perspectives*, op. cit.

24 R. R. Sears, 'An experimental study of hypnotic anaesthesia', *Journal of Experimental Psychology*, 15, 1932, pp. 1–22.

6 *Animal Hypnosis*

> Man with all his noble qualities, with sympathy
> that feels for the most debased, with benevolence
> which extends not only to other men but to the
> humblest living creature, with his god-like in-
> tellect which penetrated into the movements
> and constitution of the solar system – with all
> these exalted powers – still bears in his bodily
> frame the indelible stamp of his lowly origin.
>
> CHARLES DARWIN, *The Descent of Man*, 1871.

This book began with a consideration of the author's early introduction to hypnosis as a child through seeing how chickens could be
hypnotized by holding them still and drawing a chalk line on the
ground away from the beak. Although many authorities now contend that animal hypnosis is an entirely different thing from human
hypnosis, and that the two concepts should not be confused, the
issue is by no means resolved. In general, those scientists who claim
that we should refer to 'so-called animal hypnosis', to emphasize
that it is not the same phenomenon as with humans, are American
(for example, Gallup[1] and Ratner[2]). In Europe we have scientists
who maintain that although the phenomenon of hypnosis is far more
complex in humans than in other animals, it is meaningful to regard
it as the same phenomenon in many respects (for example, Völgyesi,[3]
Hoskovec and Svorad[4]).

The finer points of this controversy do not matter a great deal to
the layman. To some degree it depends upon whether we regard
hypnosis entirely in terms of the relationship between two or more
people (as the social psychologists do) or whether we regard it as an
altered state of consciousness, almost certainly associated with a
changed state of brain functioning. If we take the latter view, then
a study of animal hypnosis is very relevant to our understanding of
human hypnosis.

In any case, the facts about animal hypnosis are so striking and
intriguing that they are well worth study in their own right. No
account of hypnosis would be complete without them. To anyone
interested in natural history and how animal species function in
relation to their environment, the details of this remarkable phenomenon are every bit as fascinating as human hypnosis. Strangely
enough, the nature of animal hypnosis is not widely known even

among many people who work with animals.

For a start, it is necessary to clear up an understandable confusion between 'animal magnetism' and animal hypnosis. The former term refers to the whole mesmeric process, as seen by Mesmer and his followers in the eighteenth and nineteenth centuries, who attributed the changes that could be brought about in people to an alleged 'magnetic fluid'. It had nothing to do with non-human animals – although some mesmerists also tried to influence animals. Animal hypnosis, on the other hand, has nothing to do with magnetism, and was known more than a century before Mesmer. It refers to the curious state of immobility and partial paralysis which can be induced in all animal species in certain conditions.

One of the first recorded accounts of animal hypnosis in scientific literature is that of Father Athanasius Kircher, a seventeenth-century Jesuit savant, who is also credited with having invented the magic lantern and the Aeolian harp. A slightly earlier account of it was published by Daniel Schwenter in 1636, describing how he had hypnotized cocks, but it was Kircher who investigated the matter more fully and published a treatise ten years later : *Experimentum mirabile de imaginatione gallinae Kircher*. Kircher attributed the remarkable immobility of the hypnotized birds to their 'imagination', for he assumed that they imagined themselves to be held fast by the chalk line, as by an unbreakable fetter.

For centuries people accepted Kircher's explanation, and when they wanted to demonstrate animal hypnosis they did not fail to draw the chalk line from the animal's beak – a totally unnecessary detail. In fact, the best way of hypnotizing a chicken is to seize it firmly and hold it on its side on a flat surface for about thirty seconds. The bird will struggle to begin with, but then it will suddenly become completely still. Its muscles may become stiff, or its limbs assume what is known as 'waxy flexibility' – they will stay in any condition you care to place them. This immobility will last from a minute or so up to two or more hours, the bird lying inert, perhaps with its eyes open. The record period recorded for a chicken remaining hypnotized is three hours and forty-seven minutes ! If the eyes close, it is likely to remain hypnotized for a long period. Towards the end of the period it may give little squawking sounds, then rise to its feet and run away.

About 80 per cent of chickens are said to be hypnotizable; like humans, individual chickens vary in their degree of susceptibility to hypnosis. Unlike humans, however, the more you subject animals to hypnosis the less susceptible they become. You will probably not be able to hypnotize your pet dog or cat, for he is far too accustomed to being mauled around by the family. In the same way, it is unlikely that you will be able to hypnotize members of your own family, for they are far too used to you, and may be unwilling to complicate family relationships with hypnosis.

There is some evidence that individual differences in susceptibility to animal hypnosis are an inherited factor, and by selective breeding it has been possible to produce different strains of the same species of animal which are either high or low in susceptibility. This breeding of laboratory animals for a particular type of *behaviour* (as distinct from physical characteristics which are there at birth) is a tricky business because the behaviour may be more dependent on how the young are reared by their mothers than on their genetic make-up. Gallup, to whom we referred earlier, has got over this difficulty by breeding chickens selectively for susceptibility, and because the eggs were all hatched in the same incubator and the chicks reared there together there was no possibility of the effects being due to different sorts of rearing.

That differences in susceptibility are due in part to inborn, inherited factors is a very important finding for it links the phenomenon to its possible importance in natural selection in the evolutionary process, much as Darwin reasoned. We will consider this point later. No one has ever tried to investigate whether differences in susceptibility to hypnosis in humans are genetically linked, but since there is much evidence that differences in human personality are partly due to factors of heredity, it is not an implausible supposition.

The fact that susceptibility to animal hypnosis is an inherited trait does not mean that it is not also partly determined by the animal's rearing. This has been shown with experiments with sheep and goats. Moore and Amstey[5] compared the susceptibility of normally-reared sheep and goats with that of individuals which had been reared by foster-mothers when they were young lambs or kids. The latter did *not* show the usual degree of susceptibility. No clear reason for this can be advanced except that perhaps the fostered animals had had a rather unhappy childhood and hence had not developed normal reactions. Some developmental research with humans chimes in with this in a paradoxical sort of way. Josephine Hilgard,[6] in her researches into the susceptibility of undergraduate students to hypnosis, found that there was a group who were especially susceptible who reported that they had been severely punished by their parents as a feature of their upbringing. Whether these students had *really* had especially punitive childhoods, or whether this was a feature of highly imaginative reminiscence, is impossible to determine. However, it is by being alert to possible links between evidence relating to the developmental history of man and other animals that we get useful leads to further avenues of research to explore.

It must not be thought that the hypnotized animal is always or frequently unconscious, as if stunned by a blow on the head. The eyes may or may not be open, and although it is outwardly un-responsive, instruments which will monitor and record internal pro-cesses such as the heart rate and brain waves show that it can be quite reactive. Indeed, a hypnotized animal may be capable of pro-cessing incoming information and learning from it, as has been demonstrated by experiments on conditioning. It is not at all clear, however, just what stimuli will serve to terminate the hypnosis, or why some animals will maintain the state so very much longer than others.

In the nineteenth century some mesmerists turned their attention to animals. Lafontaine gave exhibitions of hypnotizing animals in Paris, including cats, dogs, lizards, squirrels and lions, and demon-strated the wonder that hypnotized animals do not react to normally painful stimuli such as pricking the paws – no mean feat when one's subject is a lion! He did not use the chalk-to-the-nose technique of Kircher but relied rather on rhythmic stroking (mesmeric passes) and gazing into the eyes. There is a photograph of this being done in a modern book, Völgyesi's *Hypnosis in Man and Animals*. Here Völgyesi is shown sitting astride the back of a young lioness, tilting up its chin and gazing into its eyes. The book also has photographs of a variety of other animals being hypnotized, including chim-panzees.

One use of rhythmic stroking as a means of obtaining animal hypnosis may very well be the art of 'tickling' trout and other fish. Here the fisherman must be very patient and slowly, gently glide his hand and arm into a pool where the fish lurk. If he can get his hand beneath a fish and, with the utmost gentleness, begin to stroke its underside persistently and as lightly as the touch of water-weed, gradually he may lull it into immobility, then grasp it in his hand and take it from the water. Mowrer[7] describes the hypnotizing of a cock by stroking its comb, and Marcuse and Moore[8] made use of a repetitive stroking to immobilize restless pigs which they wished to use for experimentation. It is argued by Krojanker[9] that parents make use of the mechanisms of animal hypnosis with infants by gently immobilizing them and rocking them, and that because of the primitive sensory-motor organization of the infant he is more like one of the lower animals and especially susceptible to this process.

Another common means of hypnotizing animals is to suddenly put them on their backs. This is especially effective with animals like rabbits and guinea pigs which very seldom experience this posture in nature. Again there may be a little struggling to begin with, but it is relatively short, and if they are held in this unaccustomed posture with gentle firmness for a brief period, they will lapse into the hypnotic state.

This technique of sudden inversion may also be successful with human beings. Hoagland[10] describes how he obtained it by getting people to bend forwards from the waist at an angle of ninety degrees take a deep breath, and then submit to being thrown suddenly on their backs (presumably onto a mattress) by persons standing on either side of them. The result is that the subject of this treatment is seized with a curious muscular immobility which may persist for some time. This is not of course the main component of human hypnosis, but it is likely that this physiological change is one component of the hypnotic state along with the general psychological processes by which the hypnotist substitutes his own verbal suggestions for the normal autonomous thought-processes of his subject.

A sudden disruption of spatial position, normally used with animals, has also been applied to human beings by stage hypnotists who, despairing of achieving any effect with a subject who proves refractory, have been known to seize him and throw him backwards by a trick, at the same time pressing on the arteries of his neck to produce faintness! Marcuse[11] notes that this technique is resorted to on the stage where time is all-important and where the hypnotist has not brought his own subjects. He comments, with some understatement, 'It is dangerous in non-professional hands.'

The problem in studying techniques of inducing animal hypnosis is to sort out fact from fiction. Folk-lore is full of curious methods, and some people think that they are producing the state by one method whereas in reality it is produced by something they do incidentally and unintentionally. Fakirs are supposed to hypnotize snakes by soft and monotonous music accompanied by a fixed gaze and magnetic passes. In reality, the snakes are probably deaf to the music and indifferent to the gaze, but are entranced by deft handling and immobilization. It has been remarked by many people that the various methods of hypnotizing animals – gazing into the eyes, rhythmic stroking, turning on the back, rocking – all necessitate catching and restraining the animal, and it may be this act of restraint which is mainly responsible for the hypnosis rather than the other incidental acts.

There are various theories as to why the animal goes into a trance following its restraint. To say that it is 'hypnosis' explains nothing. Gallup,[12] who has done a great deal of experimental work with animals and who refers to the phenomenon as 'tonic immobility', writes as follows : 'It could be argued that the presumed similarity between human and animal hypnosis has done more to retard research than to provide for a useful explanatory framework. But perhaps when the status of hypnotic events in humans has been clarified, the analogy will become more useful.'

Charles Darwin regarded animal hypnosis as 'death-feigning', in that if an entrapped animal remains absolutely motionless it is less likely to be recognized as prey, for some predators will only attack a moving, wriggling prey. To get the great snakes in the zoo to accept dead rats as food, the keepers have to wriggle the bodies or they will otherwise be neglected. Absolute stillness provides a sort of camouflage.

Darwin's idea that 'death-feigning' protects a species, has been criticized through a misunderstanding. It is not suggested that a small animal 'knows' that it has a better chance of survival when cornered if it remains absolutely still. The reaction is entirely automatic and the animal no more 'knows' what it is doing than it 'knows' that copulation is necessary to carry on the species. That the hypnosis reaction exists, and confers on the entranced animal so powerful an inertia that it does not react when mauled, bitten or clawed, is quite understandable as a mechanism making for survival in small creatures like rabbits and birds. But what advantage can it confer on a great animal like a lion? It may be that animal species, however diverse, all have certain neurological mechanisms in common, so that many species have a quite useless repertoire of instinctive behaviours which, if they are not actually harmful to the species, continue as active vestiges.

Pavlov[13] regarded animal hypnosis and human hypnosis as basically the same phenomenon and dependent on inhibition of brain activity, as has been discussed in Chapter 1. He related it to a somewhat complex series of events in his conditioning and deconditioning experiments with dogs. Others have pointed out two things. First, the dogs were restrained in harness on the conditioning stand and hence comparable to other animals hypnotized by restraint alone, and second, that Pavlov's dogs may have been simply bored to sleep by the long experiments rather than truly hypnotized, whereas the induction of animal hypnosis tends to be quite a rapid process.

A popular explanation of animal hypnosis is that it is brought about simply by fear. This was suggested in the last century by Preyer, and has led to a good deal of interesting experimentation. The theory put forward by Ratner[14] is that animals have different reactions according to the distance from them that a threatening danger may be. When the distance is fairly great, they freeze motionless and thus avoid attracting attention to themselves, but will move on as soon as they perceive that it is safe to do so. If the feared predator comes towards them then they will run away, but if it manages to come really close they will struggle to escape and perhaps show fight. However, if they find themselves well and truly trapped, the intensity of their fear throws them into a hypnotic trance.

If fear is indeed responsible for the trance state then certain logical consequences follow. If we increase the fear-provoking qualities of the environment in an animal laboratory then a greater proportion of animals should be hypnotizable and should remain hypnotized for longer. This has in fact been demonstrated using such fear-provoking stimuli as electric shocks, loud noises and (for chickens) the threatening presence of a stuffed hawk. The injection of adrenalin into an animal will increase its manifestations of fear, for this hormone is normally secreted into the bloodstream in fear-producing situations. Hoagland[15] showed that injected adrenalin increases susceptibility to animal hypnosis, and other scientists have repeated his work. On the other hand, tranquillizing drugs will decrease fear, and the administration of tranquillizers to animals should decrease susceptibility to hypnosis. Experimental work using drugs in this manner has not yet produced clear-cut answers, but on the whole results appear to favour the fear hypothesis.

If it is fear which is largely responsible for producing the hypnotic state in animals, then this partly explains why animals get less susceptible the more we handle them in their daily lives, for they learn to be more familiar with humans and less afraid of them. On this basis we would expect the bolder individuals in a flock of chickens to be less susceptible to hypnosis, and there is some evidence that this is the case. Chickens have a natural hierarchy in the hen-run known as the order of peck, a system of bullying whereby A pecks B, B pecks C, C pecks D and so on, a system not unknown in human communities. It has been found that birds superior in the peck order are less susceptible to hypnosis.

If fear is indeed the stimulus which triggers animal hypnosis, does this apply to any extent with human hypnosis? It has been argued that it is possible that some element of animal hypnosis enters human hypnosis – for we share the same sort of basic neurological make-up as lower animals, even as the lion does with the dove. To suggest that *fear* may be partly responsible for some human beings entering a hypnotic trance state on some occasions will find little support from most modern theorists of hypnosis. Hypnotists tend to stress the co-operative aspects of hypnosis, and indeed are at great pains to reassure and calm their prospective subjects. The general problem is seen as one of overcoming the fearsome, Svengali-like image of the hypnotist in the popular mind!

However, human hypnosis has been conceived of in terms of fear and domination by some quite eminent hypnotists. Sigmund Freud maintained that hypnosis '. . . contains an additional element of paralysis derived from the relation between someone with superior power and someone who is without power and helpless – which may afford the transition to the hypnosis of terror which occurs in animals.'[16]

While no one familiar with the subject would suggest that hypnosis in humans is simply a function of fear, it must be remembered that hypnosis is not a simple, unitary phenomenon. There are probably several alternative paths to achieving a hypnotic trance, dependent on the personality of the subject and the circumstances in which he finds himself. Occasionally, subjects will report after hypnosis that they experienced a few moments of sheer, irrational panic as though they found themselves trapped, even though they fully consented to the hypnotic induction. This feeling of panic is generally associated with the experience of trying to open their eyes or performing some normally simple voluntary movement, and finding, to their astonishment, that they cannot do it!

It is thought that once the subject realizes that significant changes have taken place in the normal relations between his 'mind' and 'body', as when he finds it impossible to open his eyes when the hypnotist tells him that he cannot, then the trance state can be rapidly deepened. For this reason a hypnotist may issue challenges to his subjects so that they can test for themselves the extent to which their normal functioning has become disrupted. 'Go on, try to bend your arm – you cannot! However hard you try your arm remains stiff, rigid, just as I said, and the more you try to bend it the stiffer it becomes!' Thus, with repeated challenges like that, interspersed with reassurances that everything is all right and under control, the hypnotist may increase the effectiveness of his future suggestions.

Nowadays, most of the techniques of induction in common use are very permissive, and care is taken in fostering relations between the hypnotist and his subject so that the latter does not feel that he is in any way being dominated. Permissive techniques are used whether the hypnosis is for experimental or therapeutic purposes. However, this was not always the case. In the nineteenth century some hypnotists and mesmerists used a deliberately authoritarian technique, and because of the prevalent fear of the occult in a more superstitious age, fear may have been a potent component of the process by which a number of people achieved the hypnotic state.

This is especially likely when they were being prepared for hypnotic analgesia in surgery. Some people are frightened enough of surgical operations today when they have all the benefits of chemical anaesthesia and pain-killing drugs, and expert nursing afterwards. We can well imagine the terror which the prospect of surgery used to inspire. The surprising success of surgeons like Esdaile can perhaps best be explained in terms of 'tonic immobility' or animal hypnosis rather than in terms of the active responsive trance which is commonly produced today.

Esdaile[17] wrote : 'The eyes are usually closed, but the eyelids are sometimes seen to be a little separated, or half-open and tremulous, and the eye is occasionally wide open, fixed and insensible to light. On one occasion, having ordered the man to be entranced, I returned after two hours, and was told by my assistant that the man was not affected. I went to see and found him with half-open eyes, quivering eyelids and trembling hands. I immediately said that he was ready, and without further testing his condition, performed a most severe operation on him, without his knowing anything about it.' Apart from the non-reactivity of the eyes to light (in which particular Esdaile was probably mistaken) the description closely resembles that of Gallup[18] concerning hypnotized chickens, even to the detail of the quivering eyelids and trembling extremities.

While one naturally has some reluctance to submitting animals to fear and distress in scientific research, and many people have an uneasy conscience about what goes on already, the question of deliberately frightening human subjects is entirely objectional ethically. Indeed, it is hardly practicable in research, for people will not come to laboratories to be frightened. Some exceptions to this general rule have been known in American universities where that useful laboratory animal, the undergraduate student, is sometimes coerced into compliance as part of a course requirement for his degree. Also, members of the general public have been tricked into volunteering to take part in experiments for a small fee, without realizing what a rough and distressing time they are going to be given once in the laboratory. The notorious experiments of Milgram[19] illustrate how far this can go.

Although one should not, for ethical reasons, manipulate the level of fear to which human beings are prone, it is nevertheless possible to take advantage of the fact that some people are more prone to fear than others, and study how this relates to hypnotic susceptibility. In a small experiment of the author's which involved seventy-one undergraduates, hypnotic susceptibility was tested on two occasions for each person. On the second occasion the students had been given either a tranquillizing drug or a tablet that had no tranquil-

lizing effect. This precaution of comparing a group that had taken
an inert 'placebo' with a group taking an active drug is usual in such
research as we need to know whether it is the chemical properties
of the drug which produce any measurable effect, or merely the
subject's knowledge that he has been given some sort of tablet. Some
people are known to behave very differently if they think they have
taken an active drug, even though the tablet was of pure sugar.

In the experiment we are discussing, the students were also given
questionnaires designed to show whether people are high or low
with regard to proneness to experience fear. Certain other indices
of nervousness were also used. It was found that those people who
were rather more prone to experience fear in the situation were
more likely to *decrease* in hypnotic susceptibility after taking the
tranquillizing drug, as compared with those taking the inert placebo.
This was not a very marked tendency, but it was similar to what
had been found in most of the experiments with animals given
tranquillizers as described previously. This similarity should alert
one to the possibility that for some fear-prone individuals their
susceptibility to hypnosis may be partly due to the primitive animal
mechanism in which fear may play a part.

It should be noted that in this experiment a highly permissive
technique of induction was used and that there was no attempt
made to induce fear. However, the whole topic of hypnosis is so
bound up with irrational fears that in spite of the reassurances that
one gives to one's subjects, some find it a fear-provoking experience.
Lying in a reclining chair in a darkened, sound-deadened cubicle
with two male hypnotists observing, may induce irrational fears in
some young people, and one or two volunteered this admission.

It is frequently alleged that snakes hypnotize their victims, and
folk-lore is rich in examples. Unfortunately there is little scientific
evidence whether this is true. It would appear to be very bad policy
on the part of snakes to render their prey immobile for, because of
their primitive visual mechanism they are very poor at detecting
the location of creatures which are not in motion. Any such hypnotizing power would render their dinner invisible to them. It is not to
be denied however, that the sight of a snake is innately frightening
to some species of animals, and it is therefore possible that the
proximity of a snake might throw an animal into a state of hypnosis.

It has been alleged that the snake hypnotizes its prey with his
glittering eyes. If this is so, a snake would have much better success
in hunting if he wore a pair of dark glasses! It is indeed a fact that
many creatures show innate fear of glittering eyes. Earlier, it was
related how Gallup prolonged the state of open-eyed hypnosis in
chickens by putting a stuffed hawk next to them. Then someone

thought of putting black tape over the glittering glass eyes of the hawk, and this removed its fear-inducing qualities. This led on to experimentation with glass eyes alone. A pair of glass eyes, fixed to the end of wooden rods, was found to be an effective fear-inducing stimulus for chickens, prolonging the period they would remain hypnotized.

It seems that in research we are constantly re-discovering the partial truth of a number of old beliefs that have long been discarded. The mesmerists used to sit with their subjects' knees between their own, glaring into their eyes and making 'passes' with their hands. Modern hypnotists do not stare into people's eyes; it is held that this would be both rude and unnecessary. However, if it is the component of animal hypnosis, dependent on the mechanism of instinctive reactions of fear to certain animal stimuli, that one is trying to induce, then possibly prolonged eye-contact will contribute to this. Certainly there is a good deal of evidence that eye-contact among humans is strongly related to matters of dominance and submission in human relations. People who are afraid of others tend to lower their eyes to avoid the intimidating effect of eye-contact.

It must not be thought that fear, following entrapment, is the only process through which animal hypnosis is induced in a natural setting. There are clear indications that the mechanism comes into operation in other situations when appropriate for promoting biological survival of the species. Take the case of the spider *dysdera erythrina* where the female is much bigger and more powerful than the male. The sexes need to come together to copulate to reproduce the species, but because of the undiscriminating predatory habits of the female she is likely to become a widow before she has lost her virginity, and this would get the species nowhere. The sexual courtship of the male, therefore, has the power of throwing the female into a hypnotic and immobile state, and he can take advantage of her in this condition. Much the same goes for the golden hamster. The female hamster, although quite gentle when handled by humans, will often savage a male if he comes too close to her, taking advantage of her superior size. When the mating urge comes over her, however, she does not swoon into his arms but goes into a rigid hypnotic state with her little rump raised in the air expectantly. The hypnotized female can then be safely mounted by the male; indeed, she can be shoved around on a smooth surface like a stiff little toy.

If we search the literature of animal hypnosis we can find over six hundred reports dealing with over fifty species of animals. It is therefore fairly safe to say that it probably occurs in all animal species in some form or another, and that it would be very surprising

E

if we humans were exempt. Precisely *how* it happens we do not know, and this is obviously a problem for neurophysiologists to solve. What produces it is another matter, and this has been a matter for zoologists, ethologists, psychologists and other behavioural scientists to work at. The layman will probably ask 'What good is it?', but this is the sort of question which scientists resist because it is 'teleological'. This means that the questioner appears to assume that the Creator sat down at a drawing-board and planned every creature as to structure and function before he created the universe. Or alternatively, that he is still at his drawing-board like a designer of automobiles, working out what next year's models will look like and how their innards will work.

If one takes the story of the Creation literally then teleological questions are fine, but if one inclines to a Darwinian view of the evolution of species and the process of natural selection leading to an adaptation to environment, then such questions do not make sense. One can certainly speculate quite reasonably that the reaction of animal hypnosis will serve many small animals in good stead when they find themselves in tight corners in the clutches of predators, so evolution has favoured its development. It is not a matter of their individual 'decision'; it is an innate propensity of animal bodies. But for the big animals, who because they are animals, have this propensity to go inert and apparently lifeless under special conditions, the mechanism is probably quite useless, and may be actually harmful in some rare instances. For instance, there are some anecdotal reports of men being mauled by wild beasts and finding to their immense surprise that *it did not hurt*. If these reports are authentic then it is probable that the mechanism of animal hypnosis had come into play and they were experiencing the remarkable analgesia that Esdaile and others induced for surgical operations. A Victorian novelist would put down this immunity to pain while having one's arm chewed by a tiger to 'the wise provision of Nature'. But a modern sceptic would note that Nature appears to have no concern at all for the individual's suffering but every concern for the species' welfare. Therefore, it would be better if the attack hurt like hell and the victim continued to scream at the top of his voice, as such screaming might attract immediate help from his fellows.

We therefore parry the question 'What good is animal hypnosis?' and say that in many species it may serve a useful function in decreasing the risk of death at the jaws of a predator; in other species it may serve a reproductive function in making copulation safe for weak males, but that often it is part of a species' repertoire of possible behaviours which serve no particular function at all.

Certainly for scientists and all people with lively, inquiring minds it presents a fascinating subject for investigation, and throws some interesting light on the whole topic of hypnosis.

REFERENCES

1 G. G. Gallup, 'Factual status of a fictional concept', *Psychological Bulletin*, 31, 1974, pp. 836–853.

2 S. C. Ratner, 'Comparative aspects of hypnosis', in J. E. Gordon (ed.), *Handbook of Clinical and Experimental Hypnosis*, New York: Macmillan, 1967.

3 F. A. Völgyesi, *Hypnotism in Man and Animals*, London: Bailliere, Tindall & Cassell, 1966.

4 J. Hoskovec and D. Svorad, 'The relationship between human and animal hypnosis', *American Journal of Clinical Hypnosis*, 11, 1969, pp. 180–182.

5 A. U. Moore and M. S. Amstey, 'Tonic immobility: differences in susceptibility of experimental and normal sheep and goats', *Science*, 135, 1962, pp. 729–730.

6 J. R. Hilgard, *Personality and Hypnosis*, op. cit.

7 O. H. Mowrer, 'A note on the effect of repeated hypnotic stimulation', *Journal of Abnormal and Social Psychology*, 27, 1932, pp. 60–62.

8 F. L. Marcuse and A. U. Moore, 'Tantrum behaviour in the pig', *Journal of Comparative Psychology*, 37, 1944, pp. 235–241.

9 R. J. Krojanker, 'Human hypnosis, animal hypnotic states and the induction of sleep in infants', *American Journal of Clinical Hypnosis*, 11, 1969, pp. 178–179.

10 H. Hoagland, 'The mechanism of tonic immobility', *Journal of General Psychology*, 1, 1928, pp. 426–447.

11 F. L. Marcuse, *Hypnosis: Fact and Fiction*, op. cit.

12 G. G. Gallup, 'Factual status of a fictional concept', op. cit.

13 I. P. Pavlov and M. K. Petrova, 'A contribution to the physiology of the hypnotic state of dogs', *Character and Personality*, 2, 1934, pp. 189–200.

14 S. C. Ratner, 'Comparative aspects of hypnosis', op. cit.

15 H. Hoagland, 'The mechanism of tonic immobility', op. cit.

16 S. Freud, *Group Psychology and the Analysis of the Ego*, London: Hogarth Press, 1940.

17 J. Esdaile, *Mesmerism in India . . .*, op. cit.

18 G. G. Gallup, 'Factual status of a fictional concept', op. cit.

19 S. Milgram, *Obedience to Authority: An Experimental View*, London: Tavistock, 1974.

From the cases already mentioned it plainly
follows that the hypnotized can by all kinds of
suggestions be made not only to harm themselves but also others, and that they may even
be irresistibly driven to any crime. It is chiefly
in this that the darkest side and the worst
dangers of hypnotism are found.

FREDERICK BJORNSTROM, *Hypnotism, Its History
and Present Development,* 1887.

When hypnosis began to be systematically investigated in the last
century, people of all kinds became interested in how it could be
used for a variety of purposes – for therapy, for showmanship, as a
tool of scientific investigation, as a tool for exploring notions of
spiritualism and the occult, and as a means of furthering criminal
practices. With regard to the last-named, it appeared to have bound-
less possibilities if it was really all that its exponents claimed for it.
If indeed it was a means whereby the 'will' of one person could be
subjected to that of another, then it seemed to offer a rosy future
for fraud, economic and sexual abuse; the hypnotized person could
be used as an unwitting tool in such enterprises as burglary, arson
and murder.

Although novelists have reaped a rich harvest from exploiting
such ideas, as George du Maurier did with his *Trilby,* many would-
be criminal hypnotists must have been sadly disappointed when they
discovered that in real life things are by no means as simple as they
are in fiction.

Learned authorities were split into two camps. There were those
like Bjornstrom[1] who painted a picture of the easy use of hypnosis
for criminal purposes in the most exaggerated fashion – a picture
that must have incited many to attempted crime. On the other hand,
there were those like Braid[2] who announced the amazing fact that,
'I have proved by experiments, both in public and in private, that
during the state of excitement, the judgement is sufficiently active
to make the patients, if possible, even *more* fastidious as regards
propriety of conduct, than in the waking condition.'

A more modern note was struck by Babinski who, as reported by
Guillain,[3] stated : 'To my knowledge, a woman who would give
herself to a man while hypnotized also would do so just as freely

when independent of any hypnotic experience; hypnosis does not paralyse the will nor does it bestow on the hypnotizer the power to violate it. The hypnotic trance should not be considered as an excuse for committing rape.'

Babinski's mentor Charcot himself, although mistaken about many aspects of hypnosis, was under no misapprehension concerning the active will of the hypnotized subject. In his experience, limited as it was to the hysterical patients of the Salpêtrière Hospital, the subject in a somnambulistic state was prepared to carry out only those suggestions which were in accord with his own personal standards and preferences.

There is a well-known story which is quoted by various writers, concerning a young woman who was being demonstrated in a somnambulistic state by Charcot when he was called out of the lecture theatre. He asked his assistant to carry on. This young man, taking advantage of the absence of his professor, thereupon suggested to the young woman that she should strip off all her clothes. As the story goes, this young woman, being of a modest type who would not normally appear nude before a gallery of strangers, came out of her trance, slapped the face of the impertinent young doctor, and flounced from the room. This anecdote is often cited to make the point that the hypnotized person is not an automaton, but an individual with personal standards which are not to be flouted. If this is the case, then is the possibility of hypnosis being used for criminal purposes, as suggested by Bjornstrom and others, groundless?

Well, if the young doctor who wanted the girl to strip herself in public had possessed an adequate knowledge of hypnosis he would have proceeded otherwise, and perhaps attained his object. If the girl was indeed deeply hypnotized then he could have gone on to see if he could produce positive and negative hallucinations. He could have suggested, for instance, that she was quite alone, and strange though this may seem, it is indeed possible to get a suitable subject to accept such an idea. Even though the hypnotist is keeping up a constant stream of talk, due to the curious nature of the dream-like 'trance logic', a person can become convinced that he is all on his own. Having blotted out consciousness of other people being present, the hypnotist might then have induced hallucinations of time and place and suggested to the girl that she was at home and about to take a bath. The girl might then have proceeded to remove all her clothes, for there is nothing immodest about stripping to take one's bath.

Thus, while it is not reasonable to expect hypnotized persons to transgress against their own normal standards of conduct, hypnosis

can be used to get people to perform an *overt act* which is contrary
to their own general inclinations by temporarily distorting their
perception of reality.

   Watkins[4] reports an experiment testing the power of hypnosis to
bring about criminal acts in the American army. A deeply hypnotized private soldier was told that he was in a battle situation and
that he would shortly be confronted by an armed enemy soldier who
would try to kill him. He was advised to defend himself as best he
could. The figure who then confronted him was one of his own
officers, unarmed and in proper uniform. The following scene
ensued : 'The subject opened his eyes. He then slanted them and
began to creep cautiously forward. Suddenly, in a flying tackle he
dove at the lieutenant colonel, knocking him against the wall, and
with both of his hands (he was a powerful, husky lad) began strangl-
ing the man. It will be recalled that for an enlisted man to "attack"
a commissioned officer is a serious offense in the Army. It took the
instantaneous assistance of three others to break the soldier's grip,
pull him off the officer, and hold him until the experimenter could
quiet him back into a sleep condition. The lieutenant colonel reported that the man's grip was strong and dangerous, and that he
might have been killed or injured if assistance had not been available to drag the man back.'

   Does the above report prove anything? Well, hardly conclusively,
for if one is very sceptical one may argue that the soldier 'really'
knew what he was doing, and the chance to demonstrate his prowess
in unarmed combat – and to have a go at one of the officers on a
privileged occasion – was too good to miss. However, this possibility
of the attack being due to an impulse to gratify an aggressive wish
for insubordination on the part of a private soldier is hardly supported by the experiment which followed. The next subject was a
twenty-one-year-old lieutenant who was rather small in stature and
mild in disposition, and the person surrogating for the enemy soldier
was a friend of his, a brother officer. When the confrontation came,
the hypnotized man suddenly pulled out and opened a pocket knife
that they did not know he was carrying, and had to be restrained
from stabbing his friend.

   One can argue that in this and similar cases hypnosis merely
provides an excuse for a person doing what he would rather like to
do anyway, but is normally restrained from by fear of the consequences. Even though the individual denies to himself that the
act would be in some way satisfying, if one belongs to the heads-I-
win-tails-you-lose school of dynamic psychology, then one can argue
that *unconsciously* the person wanted to do the forbidden act. To
such a proposition there can be no clear rebuttal, except to point

out that it is arguing in a circle.

One of the fraudulent uses to which hypnosis is put is the selling of shoddy goods at monstrously inflated prices by the operators of mock auctions. These used to be a more frequent form of swindle in Britain than they are today. The author was lucky enough to have a very clearly documented account of such proceedings from a very susceptible subject with whom he once worked at the Maudsley. This man, Mr X., wrote a long and detailed account of how he had passed by a place where a mock auction was beginning, and went back out of interest and amusement to see just what went on. He had not the slightest intention of buying any of the shoddy goods on display. It should be mentioned that Mr X. is a highly intelligent and sophisticated man.

The operator at the rostrum of the auction began by giving a lot of cheap-jack patter which was not very amusing, but it was evident that he was a talker of tremendous fluency and power. He jokingly represented himself as a philanthropist, and threw a handful of ball-point pens to the crowd as gifts. As they were free, people were glad to accept them. He then offered for sale a few articles of no special merit, but at such an astonishingly low price that people thought that he was bluffing. To call his bluff, Mr X. offered to buy one of the articles, and was then followed by others in the crowd who thought that they might as well profit by this trick of the cheap-jack's. They were told that the bargains were theirs, and the operator invited the buyers to come to the front of the crowd. He put aside the articles they had purchased, and said that they could pay for them and take them away *at the end of the auction.* He had thus cleverly selected from the crowd an interested group of people, and got them up to the front. He referred to them as 'sports' and 'my friends', and because there were only a few of these bargains, probably others in the crowd regretted that they had refrained from speaking up and being onto a good thing.

The operator then went to work once more and talked. He was crudely flattering and over-familiar in his patter, yet in spite of this he had a certain vulgar charm. Mr X. felt strangely happy and elated, and even proud to be called a 'sport' by this fellow. Too late he realized what was happening; he was back in a hypnotic trance just as he had been in the laboratory at the Maudsley. He recognized the curious signs of hypnosis coming over him. He knew that this operator was out to cheat him, but to the forefront of his experience was a delightful sense of well-being, a happy and unreal trance-state in which he and the other 'sports' were bathing in bonhomie and approval, and reality did not matter.

Mr X. came out from the mock auction clutching a sewing

machine which he did not want, and for which he had paid many times its true value, but there was nothing he could do about it. He had bought it literally with his eyes open, but in a hypnotic trance which had been induced there in the crowded, uncomfortable sale-room by a hypnotist who really knew his job.

This is not an isolated incident in the author's experience. A friend who is a medical doctor related how he was at a loose end in a south coast holiday town, and wandered into a mock auction out of idle curiosity. He came to in the street some time later clutching an awful clock that he did not want, and with a lightened wallet. He was frankly astonished at himself.

To say that all advertising capitalizes on people's suggestibility and sometimes sells them goods they neither need nor truly want, is true to some degree, but it does not come in the same category as the massive onslaught on the suggestibility of rather unusual individuals, which is the trade of the operators of mock auctions. The great majority of people in the crowd do not succumb to the hypnotic patter, and are amazed when a number of individuals, some of them apparently educated and sophisticated, begin to behave like idiotic sleepwalkers, paying considerable sums of money for goods that no one but a fool would buy. In fact, part of the fascination of mock auctions is to watch the 'mugs' being caught. All interested researchers should beware that they do not go to them like Goldsmith's fools, 'Who came to scoff, remained to pray.'

The use of forms of hypnosis to betray, mislead and abuse victims finds expression in the folk legends of many countries. Keats' 'La Belle Dame Sans Merci' tells the oft repeated tale of someone entranced for an indeterminate time and then awaking miserably to cold reality after a period of illusory bliss. In Japan this same tale is told, the hypnotist being represented as a strange woodland creature, the *tanouki*, who accosts travellers and holds them entranced for years, while their friends and family in their villages give them up for lost and forget about them. When the unhappy travellers awake from the long trance, they find themselves mocked by the *tanouki* (whose motive appears to be a puckish spite against humans) for they have lost their youth and find that they have no place in the familiar world that they used to know. In modern Japan pottery figures of the *tanouki* are popular garden ornaments and can even be seen at the entrance to Buddhist temples. He is repre-sented as something like a fat bear with a sly face, walking erect, and the male is endowed with quite remarkable sexual equipment. There are also female *tanouki*. Apart from his other prodigious equipment, the *tanouki* carries two flasks of saké, but the author was assured that it was skill in hypnosis rather than generosity with saké that gave the *tanouki* his power over travellers.

In India there is a legend of travelling magicians who steal children by entrancing them so that they will follow their abductors anywhere. Bjornstrom attributed such powers to the *thugs* and *bheels*, and with his characteristic overstatement, alleged that '. . . in 1820, a band was discovered whose members, in the course of twenty years, had stolen millions of children'. Why anyone should have wished to steal children in so over-populated a country remains a mystery. Esdaile[5] appears fully to have believed this folk-myth. He recounts how he was involved in the case of a travelling barber who was arrested and tried in court on the charge of abducting a boy by putting him into a somnambulistic trance. According to Esdaile, he was called upon at the trial as an expert witness as to the possibility of such entrancement, and demonstrated his powers of mesmerism in court and his ability to make entranced persons mindlessly obey his commands, with no memory of their entrancement once they had been awakened. The wretched barber was convicted of the charge, though later released by a higher authority less credulous than the local court.

Esdaile, like Bjornstrom, was convinced of the mighty power that mesmerism might have for evil. He felt so strongly on the matter that he called for recognition of the danger by the law, writing : 'It is surely time for our judges, jurors and writers on medical jurisprudence, to be aware of the existence of this source of crime, and of the dangers to person and property that may arise from the villainous use of mesmerism.'

We have discussed cases of unscrupulous hypnotists both exploiting their victims for gain and using a victim as a cat's-paw to damage or exploit others. Concerning the latter type of usage, the American army became concerned that in wartime, or in peacetime espionage, other military powers might use hypnosis to extract information from prisoners of war, or people in positions of security, and even to turn captured soldiers against their mother country. Watkins' experiment, previously noted, is an example of how soldiers might be got to mis-perceive and attack their fellows through hypnotic suggestion. Other experiments reported by Watkins concentrated on seeing how far confidential information could be extracted from serving male and female soldiers.

A typical experiment was to impart a piece of confidential information to a soldier and impress on him that he must not divulge it, then another person would hypnotize him and demand the information. One strategy to which the hypnotist would resort was to convince the soldier that he, the interrogator, was Captain S., the person who had told him the secret information. This strategy of distorting the soldier's perception of reality was shown to work, and he divulged the confidential material. It also worked if the soldier had been promised in advance that he would receive a ten-dollar bill if he could succeed in keeping the information to himself under hypnotic interrogation. This was demonstrated with seven soldiers, none of whom could gain the money by resisting hypnotic interrogation.

Much the same type of experiment was carried out before an audience of professional people, the subject being a girl in the Women's Army Corps. She revealed all that was demanded of her under hypnosis, and then started to reveal, under questioning, highly confidential details of the development of secret rocket fuel, until a high-ranking officer who was present intervened and put a stop to the proceedings.

In the same series of experiments it was demonstrated that one of the male subjects, when promised a ten-dollar bill if he could *resist* going into a hypnotic trance, failed to gain the reward. It is generally stated that no one can be hypnotized against his will, but there are certain individuals who are so susceptible that if they have already been hypnotized, find it extraordinarily difficult to resist. It is worthwhile quoting from the actual proceedings of the experiment :[6]

'Case Study F. The subject was a corporal who had been hypnotized once before. . . . The purpose of this study was to see if a person could be made to enter a trance against his will. The subject was shown a ten-dollar bill which was placed on the table before him. He was seated and told to look at the bill.

'E. "Now, George, this ten-dollar bill in front of you is yours under one condition. I want you to look at it carefully. You can have it if you will *just not let me make you go to sleep*. Keep from entering a trance. Remember, you are to try your hardest not to enter a trance. . . . But it won't do you a damned bit of good because I am going to count up to twenty-five and by the time I get there you will be sound asleep. 1, 2, 3, . . . 25."

'The subject was in a deep trance. His eyes closed at the count of twenty while staring directly at the ten-dollar bill in front of him. Of course this individual was very highly hypnotizable, but the experimenter has observed several others who were equally so.'

The implications of these experiments with military personnel should not be exaggerated, for the subjects had been selected previously as being quite unusually hypnotizable. The man who could not resist the entrancing suggestions in order to gain ten dollars, would no doubt have reacted differently had it been a life-or-death matter, or even if a hundred dollars had been at stake. Le Cron[7] remarks that 'Undoubtedly every authority will agree that *only* good subjects under hypnosis can be led to exhibit antisocial behaviour. Such subjects are not at all common. It is likely that not more than 1 person out of 50 or even 100 is a sufficiently good one to be in any danger whatsoever of being victimized by a hypnotic Fagin.'

In the Watkins series of experiments, there was one subject who was *not* a specially good subject for hypnosis. She could be put into a light trance only, in which she was perfectly conscious of what was going on, and she smiled a little at some of the suggestions which she considered to be silly. She had been ordered by a superior officer not to divulge information. The hypnotist adopted a special technique and said as follows : 'You know the consequences of disobeying a military order from a superior officer. Yet in spite of this you are going to tell me that message. It is rising in your throat and you will not be able to keep it down. It is getting higher, higher, higher. Now it is on the back of your tongue. Now it is in the middle of your tongue. Now it is escaping from your teeth. You will endure the most extreme suffering until you release it and speak the message. Speak it! Speak it!'

During the time the hypnotist was treating the secret message as though it were a physical object coming up and out of the mouth, the girl writhed and wrung her hands, and made facial contortions. Eventually the message 'exploded' from her. Afterwards she said : 'My God, you didn't have to choke it out of me!'

A piece of play-acting? Not entirely, but there it little doubt that such a technique with a lightly hypnotized person would only work if she knew perfectly well that it did not really matter if she revealed the secret information, that the hypnotist was not working for an enemy power and she would not really get into trouble. The experiment demonstrates that the technique used can make a person profoundly uncomfortable, and that rather than maintain the condition of discomfort, people will blurt out the information to the hypnotist.

A more recent test of this technique of extorting information under hypnosis was carried out by Field and Dworkin.[8] They got thirty-five subjects to participate in an experiment, and made an ingenious comparison between what people thought that they would do under hypnotic interrogation and what people in general really would do. Twenty-six of the subjects were first tested for hypnotic susceptibility so that this important piece of information was known in advance about each individual. Then one experimenter gave each subject a number to remember, and impressed on him that he must try to conceal this secret number from the other experimenter who would try to extract it from him. The hypnotist used three different techniques of interrogation in order to test their relative efficiency.

The first was the technique described by Watkins that treats the secret information as if it were a physical object, and suggests that it comes up out of the throat, over the tongue and out at the lips. The second technique was to get the hypnotized subject to think of some incident in his life that had made him feel very guilty and ashamed, and then to suggest that this guilt would become attached to the concealed number, and that his guilt would be relieved when he had ceased to conceal the number.

The third technique was a form of lie detection which had originally been explored by the great Russian psychologist Luria.[9] The Luria technique takes various forms, but in essence it consists of getting the subject to associate a certain bodily movement with the speaking of a message. Thus, if the subject suppresses information he is likely to give himself away by making a slight bodily movement. In the Field and Dworkin experiment it was suggested to the hypnotized subject that he would make some bodily movement when he heard the secret number (it was a number between one and nine). Later, a number series was read out with a careful watch on the subject's physical reactions.

In all, six out of the twenty-six subjects betrayed the secret number under hypnosis, the most effective technique being found to be the Luria method. They found, moreover, that the probability of a subject giving the information was significantly greater among those who had scored higher on hypnotic susceptibility on pre-test. This is an important finding for the issue under discussion, and fits what one would have expected from previous work. Six betrayers out of twenty-six subjects is quite a high proportion, for it must be remembered that all the subjects went to the experiment presumably with the intention of thwarting the interrogator, and, although they all had to listen to the hypnotic induction patter, many of them must have simply resisted succumbing to hypnosis as the surest way of keeping the secret.

The remaining nine subjects were not given the same treatment, but were simply asked to read an account of the whole experimental procedure, and then each was asked whether he personally felt that he could resist the hypnotic interrogation. Surprisingly, eight of the nine control subjects said that they did not think that they could resist. This may indicate that people tend to think that hypnotic interrogation is more powerful than it is in practice. Or did these eight subjects mean that they did not think they could resist *if* they had let themselves succumb to hypnosis?

After America's war in Korea, when prisoners of war were repatriated it was found that a number of soldiers had apparently changed their political allegiance and now supported the ideology of their Chinese captors. Vague rumours circulated of the Chinese hypnotizing their prisoners so that not only would they betray any military secrets they possessed but that they would be prepared to fight against their own country. The first wave of the official American interest in hypnosis had arisen out of the war with Japan (hence the Watkins experiments), now it was the Chinese they suspected of special prowess in hypnosis. Because Westerners do not understand Oriental psychology, they are apt to assume that the peoples of the East are possessed of extraordinary (and diabolical!) powers.

All the released American POWs were carefully investigated by psychiatrists and others, and it was pretty clearly established that hypnosis, as such, had not been used. The whole matter has been ably reviewed by Orne.[10] What was used instead was the age-old system of deprivation, humiliation and bullying – and promise of alleviation when prisoners 'reformed' their attitudes. Although the Chinese gave it the name of *hsia nao* ('wash brain'), as described by Schein,[11] the system does not seem to have been either particularly original or particularly Oriental, and has nothing in common with hypnosis. Indeed, why should captors resort to hypnosis when they have, even in the short run, well-tried techniques which are so very much more effective?

Violence, deprivation of sleep, blackmail, bullying and bribery are the potent weapons in the armoury of interrogators and mind-changers. Because the average man is amazed when he reads of prisoners publicly denouncing themselves and their comrades in the most grovelling of terms, and claiming to have committed crimes in impossible circumstances, he thinks that something mysterious like hypnosis, which he does not understand, has been used. It was alleged at the time of the notorious show-trials in Russia in the 1930s, when so many of the old Bolsheviks denounced themselves as traitors and fascist beasts, that they had been hypnotized. There was no evidence that hypnosis had ever been used on them, but plenty of evidence that they had been tortured, as revealed by Kruschev after Stalin's death.

A well-known American professor and theorist of hypnosis, Perry London, makes a curious assertion that he does not document. He writes: 'At all events, the combination of lowered defenses and hypermnesia sometimes makes hypnosis a useful tool for the inter-rogation of spies and prisoners of war as well as witnesses.'[12] It may be that London's sources are confidential and so he cannot quote them, but this shows that the idea of using hypnosis for such pur-poses is not dead in America. The author has heard a rumour that the CIA are training some of their agents in hypnosis so that they can successfully resist interrogation. By all accounts there is very little that the CIA have not tried. The Russians also appear to have a continuing interest in the nefarious possibilities of hypnosis. There is a curious figure in Bulgaria, who shall be nameless, who receives large sums of research money from Russia for experiments in hypnosis and alleged training programmes for which results are claimed that make Mesmer seem modest by comparison. It is a strange fact that often the hardest-headed people in positions of power are susceptible to the most hare-brained of schemes – provided that they promise them more power.

The laboratory experiments described above were designed to test the power of hypnosis to coerce people into revealing secret information and to commit anti-social acts. These experiments can be criticized on the grounds that the subjects knew at the back of their minds that no awful consequences would follow on their compliance with the hypnotist's suggestions. It can even be argued that even in the experiments which involved attacking someone perceived hallucinatorily as an enemy soldier, the attack would not really have been pressed home to the extent of killing the person assaulted.

Mindful of these criticisms, psychologists turned their ingenuity to devising still more ambitious experiments in which the subjects were actually deceived by the physical set-up so that they did not know that if they accepted the suggestions of the hypnotist, dreadful and even fatal consequences would ensue. These experiments involved doing things which it appeared would inflict criminal injury on others, or result in drastic self-harm. So ambitious was the design of one experiment that it nearly resulted in the scarring of the face of an assistant with corrosive acid.

Quite an early experiment of this kind is that of Rowland[13] in which four deeply hypnotized subjects were told to pick a poisonous snake out of a box with their bare hands, and this three attempted to do. They did not know that really they could not touch the snake because a shield of invisible glass protected them. Rowland's critics then suggested that many unhypnotized persons would risk picking up the rattlesnake if asked to do so in the laboratory. To test this supposition, Rowland asked a total of forty-two persons who came to his laboratory to pick up the snake from the box. He describes the result thus :

'With one exception, all the persons were not only badly frightened at the appearance of the snake, but would not come close to the box; only a few were finally persuaded to pick up a yard stick and try to touch the snake. They all seemed bewildered when they touched the glass which they could not see. The exception referred to was as follows : a young woman was told to reach for the snake and she did so at once, of course striking the glass. When asked why she complied so readily, she said that of course it was an artificial snake, and she was not afraid of it. Assured that the snake was real, she made a closer examination of it. She then became frightened and even though she knew she was protected, would not go near the box.'

Not to be defeated by this compelling demonstration that only one out of forty-two unhypnotized people would try to touch the snake, some of Rowland's critics then took refuge in the argument that, when hypnotized, the subjects had such super-acute eyesight that they could see the sheet of invisible glass which protected them. The question of the alleged hyper-acuity of perception of hypnotized people has been discussed in Chapter 5 of this book.

The other task which Rowland arranged for another two hypnotized subjects was to throw strong sulphuric acid in his own face. He sat behind the screen of invisible glass, and his colleague, having explained how dangerous the acid was, told them to throw it in Rowland's face. Both subjects complied, but one of them, a sixteen-year-old girl, needed considerable persuasion. After she had done the act she 'shuddered and covered her face with her hands. She seemed very much disturbed.'

In response to the various criticisms that were made of Rowland's experiment, Young[14] repeated it with more subjects, dispensing with the glass screen in the latter half of the experiments, with the result that his assistant was nearly scarred or blinded by having acid thrown in his face.

Young used eight subjects, all of whom had been proved to be excellent hypnotic subjects by previous testing. In his first experiments he used the invisible glass technique, just as Rowland had done, but in the second experiment there was no protective glass shield as he relied on an alternative device to prevent actual harm from occurring. The snakes were not the real venomous water moccasin, but a similar non-venomous species, and the real nitric acid which was demonstrated to the subjects was later switched by a ruse. So alike was the dummy acid to the real thing that an unfortunate mistake occurred as mentioned above, the assistant having real acid thrown in his face, and he was only saved from scarring by prompt first aid.

In Young's first experiment, seven of the eight hypnotized subjects carried out the instructions both as regards trying to handle the snakes and throwing the acid at the assistant. In the second experiment, with no glass shield being used, three out of four hypnotized subjects actually handled the snakes and threw the liquid on to the assistant. The fourth subject appeared to be overcome by fear of the snakes, and in dithering over picking one up, got bitten on the hand by its fortunately venom-free fangs. Rowland had tried to give two of his subjects the hallucination that the snake was really a coiled rubber rope, but Young did not do this. He stressed that they were poisonous water moccasins.

The experiments of Rowland and Young were repeated in an altered form by Orne and Evans.[15] Their findings did indeed confirm the findings of the previous experimenters regarding hypnotized subjects, but they used four other groups who were not hypnotized, with various complex additional features in the experiment. Their experiment is often quoted to show that, under pressure, subjects in a laboratory will do all sorts of *apparently* self-harming and anti-social acts without there being any necessity for hypnotizing them. They demonstrated this, but the reason was very simple. After the experiments were over they interviewed all the subjects, and then reported : 'All subjects appeared to assume that some form of safety precautions had been taken during the experiment.' In other words, the greater part of the experiment had not been a success, and is therefore hardly relevant to what Rowland and Young had been trying to investigate. For if one goes on to a stage and engages to help a professional magician perform his tricks, one will have no hesitation in performing the act of 'sawing a woman in half' when requested to do so. This has got nothing to do with forced compliance with an anti-social command or being hallucinated as to the reality of one's deed. The subjects of Rowland and Young imagined that they were in a real situation; the non-hypnotized subjects of Orne and Evans knew that it was all a spoof.

Orne and Evans seem to have been rather naïve to expect to do experiments with as many as thirty students in an Australian university and avoid having some of them come to the laboratory knowing precisely what to expect, having already heard it all in detail from their fellow students in the canteen or the pub. In an earlier chapter a criticism of the experiments of True was mentioned because he used as many as fifty students in an attempt to test their early childhood recall of significant dates, the suspicion being that one subject may have told another what was to be expected of him. This same criticism must be made of Orne and Evans, but hardly applies to the experiments of Rowland and Young who used much smaller numbers, and in any case their subjects had post-hypnotic amnesia.

In fairness, it must be recorded that Orne and Evans admitted that 'No conclusions can be drawn from the present investigation about the potential use of hypnosis to induce anti-social behaviour.' Others have quoted their study to try to support an argument that hypnosis does *not* offer possibilities for inducing criminal and self-harming behaviour, but that is a quite unwarranted conclusion.

From the same genre a study which deserves mention for its comic features if for no other reason is that of Calverley and Barber.[16] It also highlights the ambiguity of what is meant by 'hypnotized'. A graduate student of psychology interviewed fifty-eight nursing students individually, and presented them with a written statement which commanded each young woman to sign three statements about her Supervisor. The statements read:

'Miss ——— is not a very good administrator and should be urged to improve.'

'Miss ——— is a poor administrator and also somewhat unfair to the students.'

'Miss ——— is a poor administrator, unfair to the students and also disgustingly immoral.'

As the girls had volunteered for a 'psychological experiment', many of them must have seen this as a confirmation of the popular prejudice that all psychologists are mad, and no doubt most of them treated the whole thing as a huge joke. It is reasonable to suppose that no sooner were they out of the interview room than they rushed to tell their friends, and perhaps Miss ———, all about what was going on and what to expect.

We are told that half the girls received a hypnotic induction procedure, but this does not mean that many of them would be greatly affected, for out of twenty-nine subjects one cannot expect more than a handful to be very susceptible, and some in this group would very definitely *not* be hypnotized. They got the command to sign in two different forms. It was a written instruction stating either, 'You are to read and sign your name to each statement,' or 'You have to do exactly as you are instructed. It is *absolutely* essential that you do as instructed! Please do *exactly* as you are instructed. You are to read and sign your name to each statement.' If the subject refused to sign she was given an additional written command, 'You are to follow the instructions. Sign the statement.'

We are told that as many signed who had not received the hypnotic induction procedure as in the group who had. One does not have to be a psychologist to surmise the many different sorts of reasons that girls might have for signing – for a lark, to oblige a lad struggling with his postgraduate research, to give Miss ——— a laugh if she came to hear about it, to demonstrate that one was not afraid of so trivial a procedure, to be able to boast about it to the other girls – the reasons must have been innumerable. Whatever they chose to tell the student about their motivation is quite another matter. As he had no lie detector handy, it is likely that as he tried

146 *Hypnosis*

to con them they tried to con him. Indeed, it is possible that some of them may well have regarded his attempt to hypnotize them without prior warning when they volunteered, as impertinent, and so these in the 'hypnotic' group might refuse to sign just to spite him!

The reader may think that this rather comic effort of Calverley and Barber has not got much to do with the serious attempts to investigate the question of hypnosis in relation to dangerous and criminal acts. But an overview of the sort of experiments, both serious and not so serious, that experimentalists have carried out, is necessary to give a fair picture of how the problem has been tackled.

The author has, in fact, designed the perfect experiment and it runs as follows. A group of proven, deeply hypnotizable subjects are compared with a group of insusceptible subjects, the latter being coached by experimenter A how to simulate hypnosis to deceive experimenter B, in the manner that Orne[17] has described. All the subjects are shut in a waiting-room and experimenter B calls for them one by one, to carry out a procedure which they do not know about in advance, and after this procedure they are shut in another waiting-room until the whole experiment is over, so that they cannot warn the others what to expect. Experimenter B takes each one up in the lift to the sixth floor, where he attempts to hypnotize him, not knowing who are genuinely hypnotizable subjects and who are simulators. When his subject appears to be deeply hypnotized, he tries to induce a false belief and a visual hallucination that they are on the ground floor and that a soft flower bed is just a few feet below the window. He then asks him to jump out of the window on to the flower bed.

What would happen? It seems reasonable to suppose that the hypnotized subjects, if truly deluded, would jump out of the window whereas the simulators would not. But such an experiment would not convince the critics, for they would point out that there would have to be some secret safety device to prevent the subject actually jumping from the window sill, and that all subjects 'at the back of their mind' would know that such a secret safety device would have to exist. If all the hypnotized subjects tried to jump and none of the simulators, then all that would have been demonstrated, according to the critics, would be that the sort of people who become deeply hypnotized are trusting fools, and the sort of people who do not are sensibly suspicious, and unwilling to try out the safety precautions of a dotty psychologist at the risk of their necks. For if we invoke concepts like 'at the back of the mind', or 'unconscious knowledge', then the argument stops there. So the author does not propose to try out his interesting experiment.

This experiment was suggested by a boyhood memory of the tragic event of a schoolboy who walked to his death out of an upper-storey dormitory window, before the eyes of his friends, who assumed that he was playing the fool until they saw him go out of the window. The boy was known to be a sleepwalker, and met his death in a somnambulistic state. A somnambulistic state produced by a criminal hypnotist could no doubt have produced the same result.

In looking over all the experimental work related to self-harming and criminal acts performed under hypnosis, one is struck that there has been no real advance since Young's excellent article in 1958.[18] There he makes the point that although criminal and harmful acts may best be engineered under hypnosis by deluding the subject rather than trying to tamper with his moral values, the hypnotized person may be more susceptible to persuasion and bullying than in his normal state. Different authorities are still arguing the case, and one may see how the stance they take up refers to their own particular attitude with regard to hypnosis, just as in the nineteenth century. One cannot but see that a sort of theoretical 'vested interest' lies behind each man's standpoint.

Those like Bjornstrom who took an exaggerated view of the criminal possibilities of hypnosis, immediately followed their arguments with a claim that the practice of hypnosis should be strictly reserved for medical men – a claim reminiscent of the trade union closed-shop principle. The English doctors Braid and Bramwell, however, were still apprehensive of attack from their medical colleagues for daring to dabble in hypnosis. Poor Dr Elliotson had been well and truly hounded! It was the purpose of Braid and Bramwell, therefore, to show that hypnosis could never make anyone commit an immoral act. On the other side of the Channel, their contemporaries Liébault and Bernheim, secure in the professional status accorded to them in France, had no inhibitions about admitting the possible criminal uses of hypnosis. Pierre Janet was a muddled thinker on the subject, and belonging to the Salpêtrière school seemed to need to oppose the Nancy school on most things.

It is not suggested that these men worked out their theoretical positions deliberately to accord with their own vanity and self-interest. Processes of psychological motivation and the alignment of theoretical standpoint are much more subtle than that. Today we have similar forces at work. Those who do not wish to acknowledge that hypnosis involves a special state of consciousness decry the idea that harmful and criminal acts can be engineered via the hypnotic state. They are at pains to point out that all manner of anti-social acts may be effectively produced *without* hypnosis. No one would ever deny such a thing, of course. Bullying, lying, and every sort of misdirection have been used from time immemorial to produce anti-social behaviour. Appealing to the worst in men through bribery, and to the best in them through calls to their patriotic and political idealism has always produced the worst crimes from ordinary sorts of people.

It is therefore quite pointless to demonstrate what we know already, as in the cruel and humiliating experiments of Milgram,[19] in which ordinary people were tricked and bullied into behaving in a beastly manner under the misapprehension that they were helping in a genuinely useful scientific experiment. Such demonstrations have no special relevance to what sort of behaviour can be produced under hypnosis.

A fair-minded man must admit that while it would be possible to use hypnosis for anti-social ends, and that this probably does occur in minor instances in everyday life, the difficulties involved are great enough to offer no special invitation to evil-minded persons. They can and do accomplish their nefarious purposes far more effectively through the wide choice of traditional means which are open to them.

Levett and his colleagues at Indiana University have recently argued that the type of experiments carried out in the past by such people as Rowland, Young, Orne and Evans suffered from the disadvantage that the subjects must have regarded the experimenters as basically trustworthy and responsible people and therefore, however dangerous or anti-social the situation appeared to be, the subjects felt *protected* because of the experimenters' presumed benevolence. In order to get over this drawback in a very recent series of experiments planned to test the coercive powers of hypnosis, they have turned to situations in which the subjects are *not* protected.

The acts in question are neither criminal nor dangerous, but are intrinsically unpleasant in themselves for reasons of good taste and because they transgress normal standards of personal propriety. Suggested acts which they have already asked unhypnotized potential subjects whether they would perform in an experiment include masturbating before a large audience, having their temperature taken rectally in public, burning a Bible and cutting up the American flag. They have already experimented with the two last-named acts, and found, to no one's surprise, that there was little difference between hypnotized subjects and subjects instructed to simulate hypnosis. Possibly the subjects' relative degrees of religiosity and patriotism had rather more to do with their willingness or reluctance to perform the acts than their hypnotized or non-hypnotized states.[20] Here we are back in the situation of the young woman in the Salpêtrière Hospital who refused to strip before an audience to please one of Charcot's assistants. We do not seem to have progressed very far in this matter.

Before concluding this topic, a slightly different aspect of the dangers of hypnosis should be discussed, the question of whether hypnosis can have unintentionally unpleasant results. Some people are afraid that if they agree to participate in hypnosis they will fail to wake properly from the trance, or that their will will be weakened or that they will be prone to fall into somnambulistic trances spontaneously. While none of these dangers are quite real, it is best not to dismiss them as old wives' tales, but instead to examine the evidence.

There is no difficulty about waking from a hypnotic trance. If a hypnotized person is left to himself, he will generally fall into a natural sleep of short or long duration, and awaken in the ordinary way. Very occasionally, subjects do not 'awaken' from the hypnotic state immediately the hypnotist asks them to do so, and the most obvious explanation for this is that they are enjoying being in a hypnotic state and wish to prolong it. Occasionally too, it may be apparent after hypnosis that the subject, although discussing things normally, is still in some degree of trance, and this may persist for a while, especially if the subject has been given some post-hypnotic act to perform and he is waiting for the cue without realizing it. After he has performed the post-hypnotic act, his whole demeanour and voice may alter subtly, indicating that he is now fully alert. An experienced hypnotist looks for these signs, because he does not let the subject depart until he is fully in his normal state.

A proper technique of hypnosis always concludes with final strong suggestions that there will be no unwanted after-effects, such as drowsiness or lack of alertness. If these final suggestions are omitted then there may be some unwanted after-effects. Some amateurs and stage hypnotists get up to irresponsible tricks with hypnosis, and then trouble may ensue. Marcuse[21] cites several cases of hypnosis carried out by amateurs which had unwanted after-effects. One typical case was that of a man who appealed to him for help because he had an unpleasant delusion that he was being followed. It transpired that this man had been unwise enough to act as a subject for a stage hypnotist who had entertained the audience with the spectacle of him running around pursued by a hallucinated dog. As there had been no attempt to remove the suggestion, the man was still haunted by this unpleasant feeling of being pursued.

Even where there has been no attempt to induce a temporary, unpleasant hallucination or delusion, there may still be unwanted after-effects following experimental hypnosis. Hilgard *et al.*[22] reported that as many as 2 to 3 per cent of a sample of 220 experimental subjects complained after hypnosis of an intense disturbance of several hours' duration, or of a headache. This is indeed surprising and not easy to explain, for at the Hilgards' laboratory at Stanford University they are very experienced in hypnosis. Perhaps a number of the student subjects reporting with some trouble after hypnosis were individuals with some personal problems and were using the occasion to feel upset and disturbed, and to go to their mentors with an excuse for some psychotherapeutic talk. The author has very occasionally come across student subjects who have complained of some minor symptom after hypnosis, like difficulty in keeping the eyes open or a tendency of an arm to feel stiff, and has removed this symptom by re-hypnosis and strong counter-suggestion. There has generally been an impression that the subject had been so intrigued by the experience of hypnosis that he wished to repeat it.

Such incidents, although uncommon, make it clear that there are dangers in playing around with hypnosis for fun. Some individuals are quite extraordinarily susceptible and can be put into a deep trance by an amateur who knows very little about proper technique. It must be emphasized, therefore, that if people choose to submit to hypnosis with operators who are not properly qualified, they do so at their peril. They are unlikely to be made to jump out of the window, or to do a striptease act to amuse the party, but irritating symptoms may persist for some time afterwards if the hypnotist has not observed the rules of proper procedure.

The risk of unpleasant consequences does not concern only the subject, but also the hypnotist. Some peculiar individuals generate their own fantasies under hypnosis, and afterwards have a distorted memory of what has taken place. Hypnotists must always be prepared to be accused of rape, indecent assault, trying to steal their patients' brains to send them insane, and other unprofessional behaviour. When working at the Maudsley Hospital research unit, the author was covered by a substantial insurance policy to cover just such eventualities. It adds insult to injury to be told by a most unattractive female (or male) that you have been trying to make ardent love for the past half hour!

A recent case was reported by Hartland[23] of a young married woman who brought a charge of criminal sexual assault against a general practitioner who made an obstetric examination of her under hypnosis. The circumstances were such that the jury found the doctor not guilty, although it was quite clear that the woman believed in the reality of the sexual experience which she reported. Her fantasy had apparently created a vivid though improbable hallucination under hypnosis.

Perhaps we should conclude the chapter on a note of warning given in 1892 by the Committee appointed by the British Medical Association to report on the propriety of the medical profession using hypnosis :[24] '. . . under no circumstances should female patients be hypnotized except in the presence of a relative or a person of their own sex.' Whether it was the lustfulness of doctors or the unbridled fantasy of Victorian women that the Committee had in mind, we are not told. That hypnosis offers a threat, or a promise, of unusual behaviour, has always contributed to its fascination.

REFERENCES

1 F. Bjornstrom, *Hypnotism, its History and Present Development*, New York: Humbolt Publishing Co., 1887.

2 J. Braid, *Neurypnology*, op. cit.

3 G. Guillain, *J. M. Charcot, His Life – His Work*, New York: Harper & Row, 1955.

4 J. G. Watkins, 'Antisocial compulsions induced under hypnotic trance', *Journal of Abnormal and Social Psychology*, 42, 1947, pp. 256–259.

5 J. Esdaile, *Natural and Mesmeric Clairvoyance*, op. cit.

6 J. G. Watkins, 'Antisocial compulsions induced under hypnotic trance', op. cit.

7 L. M. Le Cron (ed.), *Experimental Hypnosis*, op. cit.

8 P. B. Field and S. F. Dworkin, 'Strategies for hypnotic interrogation', *Journal of Psychology*, 67, 1967, pp. 47–58.

9 A. R. Luria, *The Nature of Human Conflicts*, New York: Liveright, 1932.

10 M. T. Orne, 'The potential uses of hypnosis in interrogation', in A. D. Biderman and H. Zimmer (eds.), *The Manipulation of Human Behaviour*, New York: Wiley, 1961.

11 E. H. Schein, 'The Chinese indoctrination programme for prisoners of war', *Psychiatry*, 19, 1956, pp. 149–172.

12 P. London, *Behaviour Control*, New York: Harper & Row, 1969.

13 L. W. Rowland, 'Will hypnotized persons try to harm themselves and others?', *Journal of Abnormal and Social Psychology*, 34, 1939, pp. 114–117.

14 P. C. Young, 'Antisocial uses of hypnosis', in L. M. Le Cron (ed.), *Experimental Hypnosis*, op. cit.

15 M. T. Orne and F. J. Evans, 'Social control in the psychological experiment: antisocial behaviour and hypnosis', *Journal of Personality and Social Psychology*, 1, 1965, pp. 189–200.

16 D. S. Calverley and T. X. Barber, 'Hypnosis and antisocial behaviour: an experimental evaluation', cited by T. X. Barber in *Hypnosis: A Scientific Approach*, op. cit.

17 M. T. Orne, 'The nature of hypnosis: artifact or essence', *Journal of Abnormal and Social Psychology*, 58, 1959, pp. 277–299.

18 P. C. Young, 'Antisocial uses of hypnosis', op. cit.

19 S. Milgram, *Obedience to Authority*, op. cit.

20 E. E. Levett, T. M. Overley and D. Rubinstein, 'The objectional act as a mechanism for testing the coercive power of the hypnotic state', *American Journal of Clinical Hypnosis*, 17, 1975, pp. 263–266.

21 F. L. Marcuse, *Hypnosis: Fact and Fiction*, op. cit.

22 J. R. Hilgard, E. R. Hilgard and M. F. Newman, 'Sequelae to hypnotic induction with special reference to earlier chemical anaesthesia', *Journal of Nervous and Mental Disease*, 133, 1961, pp. 461–478.

23 J. Hartland, 'An alleged case of criminal assault upon a married woman under hypnosis', *American Journal of Clinical Hypnosis*, 16, 1974, pp. 188–198.

24 British Medical Association, 'Report of the 1892 Committee appointed by the BMA to investigate the nature of the phenomenon of hypnotism', in 'Medical Use of Hypnotism', *British Medical Journal*, 1, April 23, 1955.

8   *Is Acupuncture Hypnosis?*

> Words are wise men's counters, they do but
> reckon with them, but they are the money of
> fools.
>
> THOMAS HOBBES, *Leviathan*, 1651.

Acupuncture is the practice of inserting needles into the skin and
superficial tissues for therapeutic purposes; it is part of Chinese
traditional medicine. Although known in the West since the seventeenth century, when returning Jesuit missionaries reported on it
and a Dutch doctor, Ten Rhyne, published an account in London,
no extensive knowledge of acupuncture spread until the nineteenth
century, when it began to be practised in France. The French
appear to have been particularly interested in acupuncture; the two
critical accounts by Soulié de Morant, appearing in 1929 and 1930,
were followed by other French publications. There are now various
excellent publications in English, notably those of Stephan Pálos,[1]
Manaka and Urquhart,[2] Matsumoto,[3] and Mann.[4] Accounts of
acupuncture now appear in various learned and more popular
journals in English, covering different aspects of the practice, and
in recent years there has been started an *American Journal of
Chinese Medicine.*

No attempt will be made in this chapter to give a proper review
of acupuncture or of Chinese medicine. All that will be discussed
will be the presumed relationship between acupuncture and hypnosis.
Many important Western and Oriental scientists who have written
on the matter have declared that acupuncture is not a form of
hypnosis. Others have taken a contrary view. Some like Wall[5] have
begun by saying that acupuncture operates through hypnosis, and
later changed their minds to say that it does not.[6] Others, like
Kroger,[7] are perfectly sure that acupuncture is a form of hypnosis.

Now if one says that a whale is not a fish, one must be perfectly
clear about what one means by a fish in order to make the negative
statement. What appears to be at the root of this disagreement over
acupuncture is that the scientists concerned are not all equally clear
about what they mean by hypnosis. Perhaps the reader can come to
a clearer appreciation of the mechanisms of hypnosis by considering
it in relation to acupuncture.

Although an adequate review of acupuncture and Chinese

medicine cannot be given here, it is necessary to give a brief introduction for the benefit of those to whom the subject is quite new.
Acupuncture is alleged to have originated in the stone age in China,
when in a primitive culture men stimulated themselves to relieve
pain and treat disease by thrusting splinters of wood and stone into
the skin. That such a practice should arise is not very surprising, for
children sometimes find out for themselves the pain-reducing properties of sticking a pin into some part of the body other than that
which aches.

The author first encountered a form of do-it-yourself acupuncture
when a clinical psychologist at the Maudsley Hospital. The patient
was a girl who was to be discharged, and came for vocational guidance. The psychometric test which was to be administered neces-
sitated the patient sticking a large needle repeatedly into a printed
pad to record choice among a number of alternatives. This patient
was a beautiful young girl of seventeen, and when handed this
enormous needle she blushed deeply. Having read her case-notes
already, it was obvious why she blushed. She always carried in her
hand a lace handkerchief which concealed an open safety-pin – this
she used to prick her buttocks surreptitiously whenever she felt rising
psychological tension. According to her case notes, her bottom was
covered in scars from her repeated self-stimulation. She was ashamed
of this practice and felt very embarrassed when people referred to it.

This girl's pain had been of a psychological nature, and the self-
perpetuating habit of which she had not been cured was making use
of the distraction technique of acupuncture, which is not so very
uncommon. If one has a terrible sharp pain through barking one's
shin, an automatic reaction may be to bite a finger to relieve the
intensity of the pain in the leg. To bear the pain of a dentist's drill
(in the bad old days when dentistry hurt) some people would dig
their finger-nails into their flesh.

From these early pain-relieving practices the Chinese went on to
develop a whole system of treating not only pain, but every sort of
illness by sticking needles into designated parts of the body.
Matsumoto has made the interesting suggestion that because acupuncture arose among the nomads in the northern part of China
which is cold, they first had resort to those parts of the body which
are uncovered – the hands, face and ears. This may partly explain
why there are so many acupuncture points, said to relate to internal
organs, appearing on the extremities of the body and the ears.

The system of medicine which arose out of these early practices,
which has proved so puzzling to Western scientists, depended upon
elaborate charts of 'meridians' which run all over the body. These
meridians are lines joining acupuncture points, the so-called 'peep-

ing-holes' into the body, and 'passing holes' for energy. The meridians were supposed to be canals along which energy flowed, but in terms of what is known about anatomy, they have no physical existence. The trouble about Chinese medicine is that it grew up under an absolute ban, attributed in part to Confucian philosophy, against dissecting the human body. Although the Taoist magicians did in fact practise dissection in secret, it had no impact upon medical theory. In contrast, the medicine which grew up in Europe out of roots in Greek and Arab science, was empirically based, and though there have been periodic bans on dissection due to Church interference, European doctors have always tried to base their theories, however primitive, on the known structure of the body.

The meridians were the supposed channels of the life energy which operated between the opposing poles of Yin and Yang, which had other opposing implications such as female-male, dark-light and cold-warm. Good health was supposed to depend upon a proper balance between Yin and Yang, and some modern Western writers have sought to compare the system with the known balancing systems such as the sympathetic-parasympathetic system of the autonomic nervous control.

All such details were incorporated into an elaborate theoretical structure based on the number five. In Chinese philosophy the universe is characterized by five elements (wood, fire, earth, metal and water), five seasons, five atmospheric influences, five stages of development and five colours, and into this system medicine has had to fit. There are therefore five outer sense organs, five inner passive organs, five structural elements of the body and five emotions. Our European basis, by contrast, is based on the number four, and the ancient Greek basis of the four temperaments has been adhered to by many historic figures of scientific repute, including the contemporary psychologist Hans Eysenck.[8] We need not, therefore, consider the numerical basis a purely Oriental feature.

It should be mentioned that what the Chinese doctors mean by an 'organ' is not quite the same sort of thing as is meant in Western medicine. As Chinese medicine was not based on any empirical knowledge of anatomy, their 'organs' were more *functional* concepts. Hence we have their delightful-sounding organs such as the 'triple warmer', which has no anatomical reality, and a seemingly absurd classification which puts the heart as a *passive* storage organ and the bladder as an active organ.

While all science has arisen out of magic and is never wholly separate from it, it can fairly be said that Chinese medicine is more of a magical system than a scientific one. This statement is not intended in a derogatory sense, and needs some justification. Magic is all theory, elaborate theory and ingenious theory. A huge, all-embracing and essentially tidy system of the universe is built up, and facts have to be fitted in with this system, or it is just too bad for the facts. Magic is a systematization of knowledge based upon arm-chair theorizing, incorporating bits of knowledge from the past – but only such bits as justify the system. By contrast, science is never tidy, never wholly satisfactory, always doubting and always provisional. Eysenck, who has just been quoted as though he were clinging to the bastion of early Greek science, has written elsewhere of his latest version of a theory of personality : '. . . it is believed that this model is more satisfactory than either of the earlier ones, although still much in need of improvement, and in due course destined for the scrap-heap when it has served its purpose of stimulating sufficient research to make clearer its imperfections.'⁹ In this he shows himself to be a scientist rather than a magician. Some other contemporary theorists of personality, in contrast, write as though they had discovered 'The Truth'.

Chinese learning, somewhat merged with Indian philosophy, spread and dominated the whole of East Asia. Contact with the West, which began to make a significant impression from the sixteenth century onwards, demonstrated that the Western barbarians, for all their crudity, had a system of alien science which paid off in its vigorous technical applications. The result was largely to inspire a well-founded fear that Western science would upset the social order, hence the official policy in both the Chinese and Japanese empires of excluding Western influence, with varying thoroughness in different epochs, for four centuries.

The story of Japan's capitulation to Western influence is well known. After the Meiji Restoration in 1867 ended nearly three hundred years of Shogunate rule which had kept the country locked against Western influence, the new government determined to introduce European medicine. Two German doctors were invited to modernize the School of Medicine at Tokyo University, and by 1884 faculties of Western medicine had been established in the various Japanese universities, and Chinese medicine was proscribed. Within half a century the Japanese had made significant contributions to medical science on a world scale. These Japanese contributions included such early breakthroughs as establishing serotherapy for tetanus, discovery of the dysentery bacillus, extraction of vitamins from rice-bran and, with German collaboration, the development of salversan as a treatment for syphilis. These contributions certainly did not come via Japan's past domination by Chinese medicine.

It appears that even under the Shogunate, there had been

Japanese medical scientists who worked outside the Chinese system. It is generally believed that the first use of chemical anaesthesia was that of nitrous oxide (laughing gas) by the American surgeon William Morton in 1844; yet forty years earlier Seishu Hanaoka in Japan had developed his own general anaesthetic from herbal extracts and used it for surgery. In contrast to the Chinese lack of interest in the details of inner anatomy and physiology, the Japanese, like the Europeans, were carrying out practical investigations at an early date. Discovery of the detailed function of the kidney is usually ascribed to the British anatomist William Bowman, yet it is claimed that in Japan, Soteki Fuseya antedated Bowman's discoveries by nearly half a century.

It is our purpose to relate acupuncture to hypnosis in a scientific manner, which is not easy considering the extra-rational aura that surrounds both topics. A consideration of the Japanese approach may help. The foregoing details of early Japanese medical science have been given to emphasize that although acupuncture was used, and is still used in Japan, the Japanese approach is somewhat different from the Chinese and is not bound by certain philosophical and political considerations which make a rational examination of Chinese medicine rather difficult. The author's personal attempts to investigate acupuncture in Japan were indeed rather farcical, as will be related later, yet it seems reasonable to suppose that from the point of view of empirical science, the riddle of acupuncture will be more readily solved through Japanese rather than Chinese sources.

The twentieth-century history of Chinese medicine is very relevant to the present controversy over acupuncture. According to Wall:[10] 'Tests of the efficacy of acupuncture have not been carried out. If one suggests that these tests are needed, one meets an extremely hostile reaction, as though one were calling an enthusiastic practitioner a liar.' A little later, concerning the use of acupuncture as a method of anaesthesia in surgery, Wall goes on to say: 'My own belief is that, in this context, acupuncture is the effective use of hypnosis.' That Wall partly recanted this statement in a later article, will be discussed later.

Because of their recent history, the Chinese are highly defensive about their native medicine. In 1911 Sonbun formed the Republic of China and repressed native Chinese medicine, hoping that an effective medical service on the Western model could be encouraged to develop, just as it had done so successfully in Japan. But the conditions in China were utterly different. No real technological revolution followed the political revolution, and over the greater part of China the people continued to depend upon traditional methods because they could neither get help from doctors trained in European methods, nor access to relevant drugs and equipment. In the 1930s, the armies of Mao Tse-tung, living off the country in the more remote northern areas, were forced to depend largely on traditional methods for medical service, and, making a virtue of necessity, they claimed that they were thereby affirming China's independence of Western influence.

After the formation of the People's Republic in 1949, the Communist government officially proclaimed the virtues of the traditional methods. To provide so vast a country with anything like a system of medical service on the Western model was in any case utterly impossible. Activities of advanced research in Western medicine were discontinued on the not unreasonable grounds that it was better to advance the general level of the nation's health, even by the spread of 'barefoot doctors', than to make advances in the more sophisticated medical developments. In fact, for many years now, the spread of Western methods in China has been steady, and a compromise between Chinese and European medicine is being arrived at. For purposes of political propaganda and to boost the national morale, the merits of the indigenous methods are being enthusiastically proclaimed, but are being steadily abandoned in favour of the Western methods where they are available. The following figures are given by Wall:[11] 'First, what are the facts? Operations are certainly completed under acupuncture but its use is surprisingly rare and the number of cases is decreasing. In 1973 the most active hospital using acupuncture which we visited had carried out 5,200 major surgical procedures but only 324 (six per cent) were under acupuncture, the rest being done with conventional chemical anaesthesia. The numbers for 1970, 1971 and 1972 were 845, 395 and 350.'

It is not proposed here to discuss the general medical use of acupuncture. As mentioned earlier, it is in theory meant to restore the proper balance between the two poles of the life force, Yin and Yang, and in this the theory is like the European theory of the mesmerists, who declared that all illness was due to a disharmony in animal magnetism, and that the function of mesmerism was to restore the proper harmony. Hence both acupuncture and mesmerism are alleged to be as appropriate for gout as for appendicitis or deafness, the form of the illness being largely immaterial. Properly controlled clinical trials of acupuncture as a general therapeutic method have not been carried out, and therefore we cannot comment on its efficacy in this respect. What can be commented on, however, is its function in the removal of pain, for the evidence in this respect is such that few would contend that it has no such power.

It is with regard to this that we must consider whether it can be regarded, with mesmerism, as a form of hypnosis. If it can be regarded as hypnosis, then our understanding of the mechanisms of hypnosis is enlarged.

Experience of pain is common to us all, but the interesting thing about it is that we do not really know how it takes place. It used to be thought that pain is a special sense like hearing, seeing or smelling and this view still has some proponents. A more modern theory is that of Melzak and Wall[12] who suggest that there is no special pain sense, but that our experience of pain is due to a special sort of patterning of the other stimuli which we receive. One can perhaps compare this theory with our perception of music. Our ears are attuned to receiving certain harmonies, and it feels 'right' to listen to the usual sorts of music that an orchestra will play. But if each musician suddenly went berserk and made noises unrelated to those of his fellow musicians, the result would be a disharmonious jumble of sound which might be quite distressing. Perhaps pain is analogous to that – it is a signal that something is wrong.

The older view that there is a special pain sense implies that we have special pain-receptors in the skin and elsewhere, that is, specialized nerve-endings whose job it is to react to damage such as is incurred by cutting, violent pressure, burning, electric shock and chemical destruction of our flesh. This is a quite reasonable view, but it is difficult to account for some of the odd features of pain and its inhibition by hypnosis, acupuncture and other special means.

There are some very strange sorts of pain which seem to defy any simple explanation. Sometimes if one of our superficial sensory nerves is damaged, we get a severe burning pain that persists for a very long time and does not seem to relate to the place where the damage has taken place. Then there is the strange phenomenon of phantom limb pain. A person who has had an arm or a leg amputated may complain for a long period, for months or years after he has lost the limb, that he has acute pain. Where – in the stump of the limb? No – two feet out in space where the limb used to be. Again, there are terrible neuralgic pains which can occur after recovery from an infection, or even when there is no anatomical evidence that there is anything wrong. Such sufferers are sometimes seen eventually by psychiatric hospitals when all other doctors have given up hope of finding any organic disorder and have suggested to their psychiatrist colleagues that here is a patient who suffers from an insane *delusion* of pain.

It is related that a well-known philosopher once complained of terrible headaches, and after numerous medical tests had been done on him, the consultant physician eventually told him that they could find nothing wrong with him, and that they could not treat him because his pain was *imaginary*. The philosopher retorted that he was not interested in what *names* medical people chose to give his condition, but that he was still in frightful pain and either his doctors could treat him or they must admit that they were incompetent at their job.

Efforts to treat these mysterious burning pains, phantom limb pains and neuralgias have included cutting through nerves either near to the site of where the pain is experienced, cutting nerves where they enter the spinal column, operating on the spinal cord itself at different levels and indeed cutting parts of the brain to intercept the horrible messages of pain, just as we might cut through telephone wires to stop incoming abusive telephone messages. The whole thing is even more puzzling because even when the correct nerve which should have contained the supposed pain fibres has been cut through, stimulation of the far-distant part of the body can still produce a severe pain.

Bad pains can sometimes be produced in a most curious manner just by very gentle stimulation of a part of the body which is sometimes sensitive in an unpredictable manner. Again, the area stimulated and the place where the pain is felt do not always coincide. There is also the strange feature of time-lag. Stroking the skin or applying warmth to it may produce no immediate result, but about half a minute later a sudden pain appears, as though there had been a gradual build-up, as when a condensor slowly charges with electricity and suddenly discharges. All these curious abnormal effects make it difficult to accept a simple 'telephone-wire' theory of pain, and make us suspect that much more complex processes are at work.

Melzack and Wall have named their theory the 'gate control' theory because it envisages the opening and closing of 'gates' which permit the incoming of pain. The theory is rather complex and requires a fairly detailed knowledge of neurology to understand fully. In essence they propose that there are two major factors of significance in the experience of pain. First, the activity which precedes the pain; second, the direct activity which the stimulus provokes in the body. The brain and spinal cord are being continually bombarded by impulses which come in from the outer nerves even when nothing much is happening, and it is this continuous stimulation which, so to speak, holds open the 'gate' by which information about harmful stimuli may enter. The system is held in readiness to respond appropriately to the environment. However, the system is adaptive; when there is a lot going on it may be entirely inappropriate to hold the gate wide open. It has been noted that in battle conditions soldiers can sustain considerable wounding and yet feel no pain.[13] Strangely enough, when treated at the dressing station, such wounded soldiers will be perfectly sensitive to shocks unrelated to the battlefield and complain at clumsy handling by a dresser. This relates to the experiments of Sears described in Chapter 5, where he used hypnotic suggestion to produce analgesia in one leg but not the other.

Possibly relevant to all this is Pavlov's[14] work in conditioning dogs, when in some experiments he used a stimulus which is normally painful, such as electric shock, always given to the same part of the body, to presage the coming of a food reward. Once the dog had been conditioned and salivated reliably on receiving the shock, it apparently lost its pain-producing quality and excited the dog pleasurably, even when the voltage was considerably increased. A shock to any part of the dog's body other than the accustomed one was still painful, however. What hypnosis, acupuncture and conditioning appear to do is to alter the mechanism of pain perception with some specificity to a designated area. Sears' experiments showed that the designation may be entirely a matter of the subjects' psychological expectation, and this may go for acupuncture too. However, Dimond[15] reports that Chinese surgeons say that as well as the designated area being anaesthetized by acupuncture, the patient's general threshold for pain perception is raised.

It seems possible that what the needles do is to create barrages of nervous impulses which close the gates of pain – but from another part of the body. The inserted needles are twirled by the therapists, or activated by an electric current, and the part of the body in which they are inserted is naturally somewhat painful. Feelings of tingling, heat and heaviness are reported in the needled part.

A sheerly physical explanation of acupuncture is generally invoked to explain the action of acupuncture in inhibiting pain, and as this fits in well with the gate control theory of Melzak and Wall it is not surprising that Wall later changed his mind about the mechanism being simply hypnosis – a process he appears to equate with psychological suggestion.

The view of some Japanese acupuncturists, while rejecting hypnosis as an explanatory mechanism, does not quite concur with the localization theory of acupuncture. Matsumoto[16] writes : 'We as well as the Chinese researchers believe that acupuncture is not a form of hypnosis, and that it does alter the patient's perception of both the intensity and quality of pain. Although the Chinese explanations for this phenomenon is that specific blocking actions occur at areas in the central nervous system, we hypothesize that in addition, this aspect of therapy may also partially be the result

F

of a slowing of the electroencephalographic pattern from beta to alpha rhythm.' In other words, they suggest that a *general* change in brain function may be responsible for the lessening of the perception of pain, in addition to the closing of a specific 'gate'. Those who regard acupuncture as a form of hypnosis would agree.

However, this is not the whole story. Sometimes acupuncture just *does not work*. A considerable process of screening and preparation is used in the hospitals before patients are selected for acupuncture anaesthesia rather than conventional Western chemical anaesthesia. As Wall described it after his visit to China :[17] 'Test needlings are carried out. A rapport is developed between patient and staff, especially the acupuncturist. They spoke of the "spiritual aspects" of acupuncture, a surprising subject to discuss in between Marxist-Leninist dialectical materialism. The spiritual value referred to was that patient and therapist must feel like brothers in the Chinese sense. There must be a mutual sense of trust, duty and obligation. If there were any signs of faltering or anxiety on the part of the patient or failure to react to the needles, then he is advised to have conventional anaesthesia.'

Thus acupuncture cannot be deemed to be a wholly physical method. It is a method which depends on a large component of psychological expectancy, trust and indeed what one might call a state of ecstasy. The author has seen operations with acupuncture on film in which the whole proceedings were most dramatic, and indeed inspiring. The patient was clearly the hero of the hour and carried the little red book, *The Thoughts of Chairman Mao*, in his hand as though it were a talisman. All the staff in the operating theatre applauded him by clapping. Dimond[18] describes such an operation he witnessed, and notes that at the end, 'A large adenoma, approximately 2 cm by 3 cm in size, was removed and the wound closed. The patient sat up, had a glass of milk, held up his little red book and said in a firm voice : "Long live Chairman Mao and welcome American doctors." He then put on his pyjama top, slipped to the floor, and walked out of the operating room.'

In modern China then, operations can sometimes be performed painlessly with the use of prior personality screening, careful building up of close trust and empathy between patient and medical staff and the interesting use of political fervour to imply that having an operation without a conventional Western general anaesthetic is to the greater glory of Chairman Mao and all that he stands for. One is reminded of the fervour of the early mesmerist movement in Europe, and how, as Elliotson sadly admitted in his later years, mesmerism lost its power to remove pain when the fervour had died down. The figures for the steady abandonment of acupuncture as an anaesthetic agent, which have been quoted earlier, imply that the fervour is already dying down in China. But just as political fervour permits successful analgesia via acupuncture, so such successful use of Chinese medicine boosts Chinese morale and pride in their present régime. That peasants in the more remote areas simply cannot get the advantages of modern Western medicine because there are not enough trained personnel, equipment and supplies to go round, is a fact. But it is no cause for discontent or feelings of inferiority if it is accepted that traditional methods are as good, and indeed, somehow morally superior.

The political and social usefulness of acupuncture in modern China may partially explain the attempt to magnify its powers, and to resist a cool appraisal of it in terms of an hypnotic phenomenon. In fact, its use as an analgesic agent is generally heavily reinforced by the use of conventional chemical analgesics. Kroger,[19] in his discussion of acupuncture as a form of hypnosis, mentions the extent to which it is backed up by analgesic drugs such as morphine, scopolamine, meperidine hydrochloride and thiopental sodium, administered both pre-operatively and during surgery. In some operations the effect of the acupuncture analgesia is so slight that injection of novocaine into the peritoneal tissues is required. If the old mesmerists had had such an armoury of pain-killing drugs to supplement their efforts to achieve painless surgery, then their critics would have been even more scornful of their claims.

Is acupuncture then nothing more than a form of hypnosis? The question invites a second question – what do we mean by hypnosis? If our concept of hypnosis is limited to the sort of verbal suggestion which is commonly used in modern psychological laboratories and in consulting rooms, then obviously acupuncture is a rather different process. But if we regard hypnosis as an altered state of awareness which may be brought about by such different practices as verbal suggestion, mesmerism, *jar-phoonk* and the manipulations and stimuli which precipitate the physiological changes known as animal hypnosis, then acupuncture is unquestionably a form of hypnosis. That acupuncture may have a beneficial function in addition to its analgesic powers is very likely, for so have other forms of hypnosis. The extent of its curative powers has probably been exaggerated, as were the claims of the mesmerists. Regarding analgesia, it is not to be denied that it may well operate, *to some extent*, by creating barrages of neural impulses which close the gates of pain just in the way that Melzak and Wall suggest, but this does not make it any the less hypnosis, if we regard hypnosis as an altered state of consciousness. Of the many acupuncturists who declare that acupuncture is not a form of hypnosis, the author has not encountered one who feels it necessary to explain himself with regard to what he means by hypnosis.

It has been suggested that the Japanese rather than the Chinese are likely to throw more light on acupuncture eventually. There are two reasons for this. First, the Japanese, although evolving under the influence of Chinese philosophy and medicine, and having centuries of experience in acupuncture, have their own indigenous traditions in empirical science which enabled them to take an entirely realistic view of their own medical practice in order to overhaul it completely once the political power of the Shogunate was defeated. Second, the Japanese have now no social or political need to boost acupuncture, as have the Chinese. They have a long history of its use and are probably best fitted to bring it into perspective in international science.

Having written this, the author must admit his own rather farcical failure to advance his understanding of acupuncture while in Japan. He was told that it was hardly practised on Kyushu, the island where he had an appointment at the University, but that as he was making a short visit to another Japanese city there he would find the Mecca of acupuncture. Perhaps, in view of the rather comic events which ensued, it is best to give this city the fictional name of Kōfuku. It was said that the Kōfuku Institute for Pain Control would be sure to satisfy curiosity about acupuncture.

At Kōfuku, the psychology professor at the University, a very eminent theorist of hypnosis, said that he personally did not know much about acupuncture but that he would effect an introduction to a dentist who practised it. A telephone call brought this dentist immediately to the University to oblige a foreign visitor, an act of typically Japanese kindness which was much appreciated. He brought with him a little instrument which was basically a twelve-volt battery and an electric probe. He explained that the application of the electric probe to the acupuncture point at the root of the thumb on the dorsal side of the hand, would abolish toothache in a specified location. But the author had not got toothache, and pressed for some practical demonstration. When pressed to experiment, to stick this willing guinea-pig full of needles if only he could give some practical demonstration of analgesia, the charming dentist demurred, said that he lacked skill, and his English began to desert him. However, he said that the Kōfuku Institute for Pain Control would be holding a conference at the Grand Hotel in two days time, and the visitor would be sure to be welcome there.

The Grand Hotel was quite the most expensive hotel in the city, which bespoke of the prestige, or at least of the wealth, of those connected with the Institute for Pain Control. The author went there with a European colleague who acted as interpreter. There was certainly a welcome – there was a 1,500 yen entrance fee. First, there were a number of Chinese films of acupuncture, one of which had already been shown on British television. Next, a lecture was given, copiously illustrated with slides, concerning a method of treatment of those who were in a state of debilitated health. The method was of stark simplicity. The debilitated person was joined up in an electrical circuit with someone who was in full health, and thus the life force flowed from the healthy to the sick! This simple point was made by numerous photographs of energy donors paired with energy receivers, and the usual before-and-after pictures of those restored to health. The author looked around for signs of hilarity in the audience, but they, a soberly suited and apparently educated gathering, were receiving the whole thing with perfect seriousness.

Next there was a live show. The speaker, in contrast with most Japanese speakers, was loud and strident in his declamation. He had the authentic voice of a fairground barker. We will refer to him as Dr K. He began by drawing attention to the fact that he had one leg encased in plaster, but remarked that as he applied his own healing methods to himself, a broken leg incommoded him very little, and he did a spirited little dance to demonstrate the fact. Then two or three past patients were introduced, and they testified to the audience how much good Dr K. had done them.

A patient in need of treatment was then produced, a young man said to be suffering from gastric ulcers. Dr K. said that he would cure him without the use of acupuncture needles. The patient was stretched on a table, and Dr K. began to make passes down his body. They were what is known in mesmeric literature as 'long passes' and were made in contact with the patient's body, and for a time it was interesting to watch the ritual which was described by Deleuze[20] in 1825 being practised in modern Japan. Deleuze wrote: 'Many magnetizers shake their fingers slightly after each pass. This method, which is never injurious, is in certain cases advantageous, and for this reason it is good to get into the habit of doing it.' This Dr K. certainly flicked his fingers after each pass, and wiped them on his own buttocks as though he were removing some sticky, evil fluid from the patient. He even made as though to grasp, with cupped hands, the man's breath as it emerged from his nostrils, and to wipe it off on his buttocks.

It would have been interesting if the patient had gone into any sort of mesmeric trance as a result of these proceedings, but he just lay there looking bored. After a time, Dr K. stopped his activities and told the patient to sit up. He asked him how he felt now, and the man replied that he was much better. All this demonstration had proceeded without a flicker of amusement from the audience, who had presumably paid their 1,500 yen to come in. But then the Japanese are a very polite people.

Deciding that any later proceedings would be as unlikely to satisfy scientific curiosity in acupuncture as the first two hours, even though acupuncture needles might be used, the author and his friends left. There were many more interesting things to see in the lovely city of Kōfuku than this prolonged charade.

When back at Kyushu University, the author wrote to the Kōfuku Institute for Pain Control to enquire whether there were any practitioners of acupuncture operating on the island of Kyushu, but received no reply. Thus one foreigner's rather half-hearted attempt to study acupuncture in Japan came to nothing.

In conclusion it may be asked why there is a general reluctance to admit that acupuncture is a form of hypnosis. It is easy to understand why the Chinese resist the idea, for they have a strongly invested emotional interest in claiming that acupuncture is something special and cannot be classed with a world-wide practice which is said to depend largely on psychological phenomena. Japanese acupuncturists like Matsumoto and Manaka may wish to dissociate themselves from the hypnotic antics of practitioners like Dr K., which have been described. In Japan, even though hypnosis is better understood and has more scientific status than in Britain, there are plenty of poorly qualified quacks practising it there. The scientists in Europe and America, who are now looking to far-away China for enlightenment in understanding the mechanisms of pain and their control, might do better to study more closely the phenomena which have gone on so little noticed in their home countries.

It is reported that when the famous authority on animal hypnosis, the Hungarian doctor Völgyesi, eventually paid a visit to Britain, he was astonished to find that we had not erected a statue to James Braid. It is interesting to speculate how Braid and other pioneers of his generation would have viewed acupuncture if it had been widely discussed at that time. Probably, those at the Salpêtrière would have unhesitatingly viewed it as a form of hypnosis, whereas those at Nancy would have been more cautious. Perhaps the truth will always lie somewhere between the rival claims of the Salpêtrière and the Nancy schools.

REFERENCES

1 S. Pálos, *The Chinese Art of Healing*, New York: Bantam Books, 1971.
2 Y. Manaka and I. A. Urquhart, *The Layman's Guide to Acupuncture*, London: Phaidon Books, 1972.
3 T. Matsumoto, *Acupuncture for Physicians*, Springfield, Ill.: C. C. Thomas, 1974.
4 F. B. Mann, *The Treatment of Disease by Acupuncture*, London: Heinemann, 1974.
5 P. Wall, 'An eye on the needle', *New Scientist*, 55, 1972, pp. 29–31.
6 P. Wall, 'Acupuncture revisited', ibid., 64, 1974, pp. 31–34.
7 W. S. Kroger, 'Hypnosis and acupuncture', *Journal of the American Medical Association*, 220, 1972, pp. 1012–1013.
8 H. J. Eysenck, *The Structure of Human Personality*, London: Methuen, 3rd ed. 1970.
9 Idem, *Eysenck on Extraversion*, London: Crosby Lockwood Staples, 1973.
10 P. Wall, 'An eye on the needle', op. cit.
11 Idem, 'Acupuncture revisited', op. cit.
12 R. Melzak and P. D. Wall, 'Pain mechanisms: a new theory', *Science*, 150, 1960, pp. 971–979.
13 See H. K. Beecher, *Measurement of Subjective Responses*, London: Oxford University Press, 1928.
14 I. P. Pavlov, *Conditioned Reflexes*, op. cit.
15 E. G. Dimond, 'Acupuncture anaesthesia: Western medicine and Chinese traditional medicine', *Journal of the American Medical Association*, 218, 1971, pp. 1558–1563.
16 T. Matsumoto, *Acupuncture for Physicians*, op. cit.
17 P. Wall, 'Acupuncture revisited', op. cit.
18 E. G. Dimond, 'Acupuncture anaesthesia . . .', op. cit.
19 W. S. Kroger, 'Hypnosis and acupuncture', op. cit.
20 J. P. F. Deleuze, *Practical Instructions in Animal Magnetism*, Part I, trans. T. S. Hartshorn, Providence, R.I.: B. Cranston & Co., 1837.

A theory of hypnosis stands or falls by its
answer to one crucial question: why do some
subjects quickly and easily experience many of
the phenomena of hypnosis while other subjects
show very little if any hypnotic behaviour after
many attempts by numerous hypnotists?

T. X. BARBER, 'The necessary and sufficient conditions for hypnosis', *American Journal of
Clinical Hypnosis*, 1960.

Throughout this book, in many different contexts and settings, we
have seen that all people are not equally susceptible to hypnosis.
This is a puzzling feature of the phenomenon, and it must be frankly
admitted that no one has yet come up with a very satisfactory
answer to the question of why this should be so. Such individual
differences in susceptibility were found among the patients of the
mesmerists, and occur equally among the patients of modern
acupuncturists, and indeed among individual animals of the same
species which have been the subject of experiments in animal
hypnosis.

Degree of susceptibility is a very enduring trait of personality.
The various studies which have attempted to discover what sort of
personality is related to susceptibility to hypnosis have really been
doing two things: first, investigating the sort of thing hypnotizability is; and second, finding meaningful ways of describing personality. Take the question of suggestibility: it has long been
assumed that hypnosis is largely a question of suggestibility, the
subject accepting the suggestions of the hypnotist. It would logically
seem to follow that more suggestible people could be hypnotized
more easily, but in terms of everyday observation, this has *not* been
found to be true.

Psychologists became interested in devising tests of suggestibility,
for if people varied in their suggestibility, just as they varied in their
height, weight, intelligence and hair colour, then their degree of
suggestibility could be measured and recorded. Various ingenious
tests were devised. Binet,[1] who was not permitted to continue his
researches on hypnosis in French schools, turned to devising suggestibility tests, one of which, the Progressive Weights test, is worth
describing in detail.

The subject is given fifteen little boxes, all of which are of equal size. He is asked to pick up the first, then the second, and to say which is the heavier. He is then asked to compare the weight of No. 2 with that of No. 3, No. 3 with No. 4, and so on. In fact, the boxes get progressively heavier from 1 to 5, but thereafter they are all the same weight. The fact that the boxes get progressively heavier over the first part of the series suggests that this increasing weight may persist for the whole series, and as it is very difficult to decide about the objective reality when trying to discriminate between tiny differences in weight, a suggestible subject is likely to report a continued increase in weight in the series long after he has reached the point at which the weights are actually the same.

Further tests of suggestibility have included other senses – suggestibility for odours, sounds, perception of light and changes in warmth. With such a battery of suggestibility tests at their disposal, experimenters were disappointed to find that although people differed reliably in their degree of suggestibility, those scoring higher were not more susceptible to hypnosis.

Hull[2] advanced the theory that there are two types of suggestibility, which he referred to as the 'prestige' and 'non-prestige' varieties. He thought that certain types of suggestibility depended upon the prestige of the person making the suggestion, and that the induction of hypnosis by verbal suggestions was of this variety. Other tests, such as Binet's Progressive Weights test that has just been described, depend for their success on the suggestion implicit in the material and the method of procedure, and not on the prestige of the person administering them.

Hull's theory of prestige suggestibility is not borne out very well in practice, for a prestigious professor who is well known for his experience in hypnosis will have no more success in inducing hypnosis than a young research assistant who has just been trained as a hypnotist – a fact which some eminent hypnotists do not like to admit.

That it was a mistake to view suggestibility as a single, unitary trait had been proposed by psychologists for some time (for instance, by Prideaux[3]), but it was still a matter for argument for many years. A considerable advance was made when psychologists began to apply the statistical methods of factor analysis to increasingly diverse tests of human ability and performance. Eysenck[4] gave a battery of suggestibility tests to sixty neurotic patients, in an investigation of the supposed higher suggestibility of those diagnosed as hysteric. Factor analysis of the results revealed that there were two clearly distinct groups of suggestibility tests. The first group included the Body Sway test (described in Chapter 4), suggestions that an outstretched arm would float up or sink down, and the Chevreul Pendulum test in which a pendulum held by the subject is made to swing by the verbal suggestions of the administrator. All the tests in this group are rather hypnosis-like in their administration, and Eysenck referred to them as tests of 'primary' suggestibility.

The second group that Eysenck identified as being factorially independent of the first included Binet's Progressive Weights test and a similar test which involved the judgement of the length of progressive lines. This group of tests appeared to measure a trait of naïveté or gullibility, and this Eysenck referred to as 'secondary' suggestibility. In a later and larger experiment in which he worked with Furneaux,[5] ten tests of suggestibility were used, and an attempt was made to hypnotize the subjects. As before, analysis of the results showed separate factors of primary and secondary suggestibility, and only the former predicted susceptibility to hypnosis.

These results have been confirmed by later experimenters. Stukát[6] found the same distinction between the tests of primary and of secondary suggestibility, and elucidated the whole matter still further. It should be noted that all the tests of primary suggestibility were tests in which a muscular movement, apparently unwilled, is produced in the subject by the verbal suggestions of the experimenter. This is known as 'ideomotor' movement, and when people make it they may be quite unaware that they have made any movement, as when the pendulum that hangs from their hand begins to swing from side to side in response to the tiny unconscious lateral tremors produced by suggestion. It should be noted that most techniques for inducing hypnosis depend initially on ideomotor suggestions – suggestions of complete muscular relaxation, of heaviness and irresistible closure of the eyes, immobility of the limbs, and perhaps later of automatic, unwilled levitation of an arm.

In Eysenck's discussion of his study that has been referred to, he pointed out that the actual response to a test of primary suggestibility depended on two aspects of the subject, his attitude and his aptitude. Obviously, if he had a negative *attitude* he could resist giving any response, just as he could resist being hypnotized, but if he was lacking in *aptitude*, however positively he might feel about the test, nothing much would happen. So it takes a combination of both positive attitude and adequate aptitude to manifest much primary suggestibility or to experience hypnosis. Ernest Hilgard[7] has likened insusceptibility to hypnosis, in spite of a positive attitude, to sexual impotence in the male; the man tries hard but performance and experience escape him.

The present author came upon the problem of the degree to which different people are susceptible to hypnosis, when working on the Nuffield Hypnosis Research Unit at the Maudsley in the 1950s. In a study by Faw and Wilcox[8] it had been found that students who were well-adjusted were more susceptible to hypnosis than those less well-adjusted. In addition, there were some rather complex relationships between scores on a personality test and hypnotizability. We wanted to see if these relationships held in London, using the Maudsley Personality Inventory (usually called the MPI) which Eysenck had developed. This is a paper and pencil test which gives measures of extraversion and neuroticism, and it was beginning to be used a great deal in research.

The research laboratory used by the Nuffield Unit was a trailer caravan, suitably equipped with apparatus and a hypnosis couch, and it served very well for the purpose as it could be towed anywhere, and parked where a source of subjects was to be had. Part of the research was carried out with the caravan parked in a quiet cul-de-sac in Bloomsbury, the majority of subjects coming from University College, London. Another and smaller group of subjects was recruited from the readers of two anarchist papers, and this was part of an investigation of the sort of personality that anarchists of the more intellectual variety tend to have. A third group was composed of mediums, spiritualists, faith-healers and students of the occult, and was recruited by attendance at spiritualist churches and through a body called the College of Psychic Science.

This third group, though vastly interesting, proved to be generally too weird in personality to be included in the main study. All the mediums were phenomenally susceptible to hypnosis, and in their trance would chatter away in the person of their 'spirit guides', Red Indians, Chinese and Russians being the favoured nationalities of the spirits. Sometimes they would talk in a sort of broken English, and sometimes in gibberish, which may or may not have resembled the tongues of the nationalities they represented.

Among the various findings of this research, it was evident that two contrasting types of personality were relatively more susceptible to hypnosis. If people were high on the neuroticism scale of the MPI, then the introverted types were the more susceptible. For those low on neuroticism, the more extraverted were more susceptible.

A further complication was introduced by the implications of the Lie scale of the MPI.[9] This is a series of questions which are sensitive to whether people tend to lean over backwards in trying to create a picture of themselves in terms of improbable moral perfection. It was found that 'liars' tended to be especially *insusceptible* to hypnosis. The possible reason for this is that people who are highly guarded and suspicious will tend to be less willing or indeed able to enter into close enough rapport with another person (let alone a psychologist!) for hypnosis to be induced, even if they desire the experience.

The publication of these interesting findings[10] came to the attention of Ernest Hilgard at Stanford, and in association with a research assistant, he tried to repeat them. The results were indeed surprising, for although the MPI still predicted susceptibility to hypnosis to a significant degree, the relationships with personality scores were entirely different. In particular, not only were the American subjects higher on the Lie scale, but the 'liars' were more susceptible than average – and this to a highly significant degree![11] Hilgard suggested that Americans might respond differently to the MPI, but did not develop the point, and no adequate explanation of the difference between the Maudsley findings and those at Stanford has ever been advanced. Most of Hilgard's subjects were 'compulsory volunteers' and others were hypnotized in groups, a less reliable procedure than the individual method which was used at Maudsley.

Later work by the present author, working with different colleagues,[12] has basically confirmed the earlier Maudsley findings, but added some complications. The Lie scale has still indicated those who are insusceptible, but in males only. Getting a high Lie score is partly a matter of the particular situation, and a certain sort of masculine pride might result in both striving to resist hypnosis and trying to create an improbable image of perfection on the questionnaire. Perhaps it is unwise to speculate further when we still need more research in this matter.

It must not be thought that by using a personality questionnaire one will be able to predict with much confidence the extent to which an individual will be susceptible to hypnosis. Such research work merely establishes tendencies. To take a useful analogy, it is a very reliable fact, for instance, that males tend to be taller than females, but one cannot reliably predict the sex of any individual if one is simply told that person's height. The object of such research is not to screen people for hypnotic susceptibility, but to try to find out more about the reasons why people differ so much in their degree of susceptibility. For instance, as it was found that the relationship between level of extraversion and hypnotic susceptibility depended in a paradoxical way on the level of neuroticism, it was decided to try the experiment of giving a tranquillizing drug to lower the operative level of neuroticism. Subjects whose degree of hypnotic susceptibility had already been determined were given the drug valium on a second occasion, and their reactions to hypnosis then compared with their undrugged reactions.

A lot has been written about the effect of drugs on hypnotic susceptibility, some writers, like Horsley,[13] claiming with complete confidence that susceptibility is increased by the use of certain drugs. In fact, the literature on the subject is extremely confused and contradictory. As Vingoe[14] has pointed out in an excellent review of the subject, the custom of referring to certain drugs as 'hypnotics' (because they send people to sleep) has created the erroneous impression that they increase susceptibility to hypnosis.

A study which the author and his colleagues[15] carried out with subjects given valium, matched against a control group given a placebo, established quite clearly that the tranquillizing drug did affect susceptibility more than the placebo did. The drug made subjects either significantly *more* or significantly *less* susceptible. There was also a complex interaction with the personality type of the individual, with males and females reacting rather differently, and it did appear that the tranquillizing drug was reducing the operative level of neuroticism. It is a little too early to say much about the implications of this study, for it must be repeated, preferably by other experimenters in other laboratories, before one can feel too sure about the reliability of these results. However, the study does highlight the fact that it is not a meaningful question to ask whether a certain drug increases or decreases susceptibility to hypnosis, for the answer must be – it depends on the individual personality make-up.

People accustomed to working with the effects of drugs on behaviour will not be surprised at the results of the study just quoted, for drugs in moderate dosages often affect people differently according to their personality. Many of us may have noted how the familiar drug alcohol affects our friends very differently. Some get more friendly, and some morose. The most surprising people get amorous, yet some inexperienced virgins can drink their would-be seducers under the table without turning a hair. Professor Drew and his colleagues[16] investigated the effects of alcohol on driving skill, and found that the way alcohol affected skill very much depended on the individual level of extraversion. It is useless, however, to plead in court that a stated level of alcohol in the blood has increased rather than decreased one's road safety, because of one's introverted personality! The law takes no notice of such individual differences, however relevant.

Some writers have been extremely critical of the whole attempt to establish the essential personality correlates of hypnotic susceptibility.[17] The emphasis of such writers is generally on the details of the immediate situation and the transient motivation of the subject. This, of course, is what was discussed earlier in terms of Eysenck's component of *attitude*. It has been consistently maintained in this book that this is only half the story, and the really interesting thing for researchers to investigate is the other component of *aptitude*. Aptitude refers to deep-rooted personality constitution, and is perhaps largely determined by the biological basis of our make-up. It must be admitted that we are a long way from having any very accurate techniques of measuring personality, and those like Guilford, Raymond Cattell and Eysenck who have devoted a great part of their careers to developing measures of personality are quite ready to admit how far psychologists have yet to go. They have not only to develop better techniques, but also to evolve more adequate explanatory schemes for describing meaningful differences in personality. Our understanding of the personality differences which underlie differential susceptibility to hypnosis can be no further advanced than the psychology of our time.

One interesting personality difference relating to hypnotic susceptibility concerns the extent to which individuals can become imaginatively involved in everyday life. This refers particularly to involvement in reading, watching dramatic performances, listening to music or simply day-dreaming. Some people habitually become 'lost' in such activities, and unaware of other things in their environment. Such a capacity is essentially child-like, and can be likened to the total involvement of a child in a game of make-believe so that he is so utterly unaware of anything else that he is deaf to adults calling him, or oblivious to the passage of time. There is some evidence to show that people who have this capacity for trance-like involvement make good hypnotic subjects.

Shor[18] gave a questionnaire concerning 'hypnotic-like' experiences occurring in everyday life to 145 university students in an attempt to find the frequency with which such experiences occur. His questionnaire contained 44 items such as, 'Have you ever had the experience of seeming to watch yourself from a distance as in a dream?' and 'Have you ever lost intervals of time when you cannot remember what you have done?' Shor writes as though he were discovering the actual frequency of these occurrences, and such an assumption is somewhat naïve. What he was really doing was establishing the extent to which his subjects *alleged* they had these experiences, which is by no means the same thing. People's reports on their own behaviour and experiences often differ very significantly from what they actually do and experience. Deliberate falsehood is not the only factor which distorts the reliability of self-report; all sorts of other factors are involved – a sense of the dramatic, a taste for exaggeration, an inventive memory and a tendency to guess wildly when memory fails. If one were to ask a large group of seven-year-old children a number of questions about their experiences and capacities and included the question, 'Do you ever jump six feet in the air when you are very pleased?', a certain percentage would probably reply in the affirmative.

Although the results of Shor's study cannot be taken at their face value, the study was important in directing people's interests to this sort of personality difference in their search for the indicators of hypnotic susceptibility. Josephine Hilgard[19] interviewed students about a wide range of experiences, both currently and in their childhood, and related their reports of such experiences to the ease with which they could be hypnotized. In general, it was found that those who could become 'lost' in the manner described above, were the more susceptible. This type of personality was related, to some degree, to the sort of upbringing they had had as children, and how they had related to their parents. Other researchers, like Coe,[20] have confirmed at least some of Josephine Hilgard's findings, although some other findings were actually contradicted.

It should be noted that what Josephine Hilgard was dealing with was students' *reports* about their current experiences and memories of childhood, rather than observations of what actually occurred. This point was made earlier when her study was referred to in Chapter 6, with reference to the developmental aspects of animal hypnosis. But it does not matter if such reports were totally erroneous and dependent on fertile imaginations rather than factual occurrences. If the giving of certain types of report is reliably predictive of high hypnotic susceptibility, then we are getting some useful indices. An interesting example of this question of reports being a useful indicator is in the surprising finding that those students who reported that they had been severely punished in childhood were more easily hypnotized. This finding was so inexplicable that Josephine Hilgard repeated her study on a further sample of students, and she found that the relationship still held.[21]

One student reported that she had been regularly spanked about twice a week around the age of eight, and it is interesting to speculate how this might relate to her later high susceptibility to hypnosis. Perhaps a vivid imagination might provide the clue.

The suggestion which arises out of much of Josephine Hilgard's work is that in childhood most people have a capacity for becoming totally absorbed in the preoccupation of the moment, and lost to the other demands of the environment. Maturing in the sort of social environment that our technologically based civilization has created, necessitates growing out of this habit of trance-like indulgence in reverie and absorption in creative if impractical fantasy. More and more the child is forced into the way of reality-testing as he grows older, and hence he loses the capacity for going into a trance and experiencing the make-believe world that can be conjured up by the suggestions of a hypnotist. This is an interesting way of looking at hypnotic susceptibility – regarding it as a capacity which we all have had in childhood, but have lost to a greater or lesser degree through the experiences of growing up.

The evidence that children are more susceptible to hypnosis when young, and lose that susceptibility with maturation, is fairly clear. Liébault found it over a century ago[22] and modern experimenters have confirmed it. One must be cautious about studies that deal with children, and report large numbers with age norms, for sometimes they do not deal with *susceptibility to hypnosis* but merely with *suggestibility*, which is not the same thing at all. Barber and Calverley[23] published norms for 484 elementary school children and 119 high school children, which showed an impressive drop in suggestibility scores between the ages of nine and fifteen, on a test known as the Barber Suggestibility Scale. However, as discussed earlier, there are two types of suggestibility, which Eysenck and Furneaux distinguished as *primary* and *secondary*, only the former correlating with hypnotizability. Children are certainly more naïve, gullible, eager to please and subject to intimidation than adolescents and adults, and it is much more difficult to separate the primary from the secondary components of suggestibility with younger children. Stukát, who has taken great care in keeping the two types of suggestibility separate, reported on testing 319 children for both primary and secondary suggestibility, and while he observed an impressive drop in secondary suggestibility between the ages of eight and fourteen, with primary suggestibility he found nothing like the striking drop reported by Barber and Calverley. It seems likely, therefore, that the Barber Suggestibility Scale is more concerned with secondary suggestibility in children, and does not tell us much about their hypnotizability.

In order to find out about the hypnotizability of children one must do the obvious thing – to try to hypnotize them. It is not always easy to get permission to do this in practice, because parents, schoolteachers and other guardians of the young frequently have a strong reluctance to give consent. At worst these guardians fear sexual seduction of the children, but less extremely they express a fear that hypnosis 'won't be particularly good for him'. The author, in the course of an investigation of some hundreds of children, did not dare to apply to the local education authority for permission to use hypnosis, but did use the Body Sway test. He was surprised to learn from a social worker that one mother reported that 'Melvyn is reading much better since Dr Gibson hypnotized him.' This mother at least had a shrewd appreciation of the nature of a test of primary suggestibility, even though she guessed wrongly at its purpose.

London and Cooper[24] reported on the results obtained by hypnotizing some hundreds of children in more than one study. As found by Liébault, the children were certainly more hypnotizable than adults, the greatest susceptibility being between the ages of nine and fourteen. Before the age of nine, they are rather less susceptible, probably because their verbal understanding is still rather underdeveloped and so they are less aware of the ideas that the hypnotist tries to convey to them. The same goes for people of abnormally dull intelligence and, for a different reason, those who are suffering from a severe mental illness.

An interesting aspect of comparing the hypnotic reactions of children with those of adults is that although they are generally more susceptible, children are much less easily influenced by the initial suggestions in the induction procedure that they will find their eyes closing irresistibly. They are more susceptible to hallucinatory experiences in hypnosis, and more subject to post-hypnotic amnesia than adults. This is a very important field of research, and might reveal a great deal about the tantalizing question of individual differences in susceptibility, so it is a pity that children are generally not given the opportunity of choosing whether they would like to try the experience of hypnosis.

The question of whether males or females are more susceptible to hypnosis is rather difficult to answer because of traditional prejudices associated both with hypnosis and with sex differences. Because of Charcot's erroneous teaching that hypnosis was an hysterical phenomenon, and because hysteria has traditionally been supposed to be a female complaint, so the stereotype of the easily-hypnotizable hysterical woman has arisen. In reaction to this, many modern writers firmly allege that there is no difference between the sexes in hypnotizability. This somewhat distorts the facts, which are very interesting.

As recorded by Bramwell,[25] the inevitable source of wisdom, Ambroise Liébault, reported that females were *slightly* more susceptible than males, and the same finding has been reported by many later investigators. Hull[26] was intrigued by this regular, slight difference and, by an ingenious piece of mathematics which was typical of his concern for precision, worked out that females exceeded males in susceptibility, on average, by one fifteenth of the degree to which males are, on average, taller than women.

Weitzenhoffer[27] reviewed a number of studies on the sex difference in hypnotizability, later than Hull, and noted the regular slight superiority of females. We may wonder, therefore, why some authors state that there is *no difference* between the sexes. Here we come upon the point that may vex the lay reader and convince him of the old saying that there are lies, bloody lies and statistics. Some writers have the habit of saying that there is 'no difference' when they have shown a difference which is 'not significant'.

This magic word *significant* refers to probability statistics. If one does an experiment and finds that red cows eat more than black cows on average, then one is faced with the problem of how likely it was that this was a mere chance finding, or is breed of cow really related to hay consumption? Obviously the degree of reliance placed on the results depends on the number of cows in the experiment. If there are only five cows of each breed, and four of the reds are the biggest eaters, then the results are not very convincing, for they could easily have arisen by chance. If however, one has fifty cows of each breed, and forty of the reds turn out to be the biggest eaters, then it would be very unlikely that this was a mere chance occurrence. Statisticians have worked out methods by which the precise chance expectancies can be determined in experiments, and it is usual to be on the safe side and dismiss results that have a probability of more than one in twenty of having occurred by chance. They are 'not significant'.

Occasionally researchers mislead themselves and others in the following manner. Having found that there is 'no significant difference' between two sets of figures on the basis of their calculations, they then go on to assert that there is 'no difference'. Thus Barber,[28] on page 40 of his book states : 'Effects of Sex. Analysis of variance and Duncan Range tests . . . showed that males and females did not differ *significantly* on Objective scores either overall (total sample) or at any one of the specific age levels.' But he goes on to say : 'The sexes are *equally* responsive to standardized test-suggestions [italics added].' One is left wondering if some were more equal than others, and one would want to see the actual figures before being convinced that his study really differed from most.

The fact is that if a certain tendency, however small, occurs again and again in the same direction in different studies, one can be pretty sure that it is a real tendency and in need of some explanation. The greater susceptibility of females may be cultural in its origins, or biological, or both. In the Gibson and Corcoran study referred to earlier, it was suggested that among males there is a minority who view hypnotic susceptibility as being inconsistent with their masculine image of themselves. Such an expression of *machismo* would lower the attitudinal component of susceptibility.

Very little good work on sex differences in hypnotizability has been carried out, and because a somewhat mistaken feminist pressure in seats of learning has implied that it is somehow 'wrong' to investigate sex differences, researchers do not always analyse their results with respect to sex as fully as they might. It is not that males and females differ so much in their degree of susceptibility, as that relationships of personality differences with susceptibility may be quite different for the two sexes. Thus Bowers[29] matched 36 men with 36 women for degree of hypnotizability, taking subjects at all levels of susceptibility, and tested them on measures of 'creativity'. It was found that for men creativity was slightly *negatively* related to hypnotic susceptibility, but for women there was quite a strong *positive* association. Further experiment with most of the same subjects showed quite striking differences between the sexes. Among all subjects whose susceptibility was relatively high, the relationship between creativity and hypnotizability was specially high for women and specially low for men.

A few other modern studies have highlighted intriguing differences between the sexes in respect of the different sorts of relationships one finds between personality and hypnotizability. Those researchers who have tended to gloss over sex differences, and to claim that much of the work on the personality correlates of susceptibility has been wasted effort, have simply overlooked a vast source of potential information. It is possible that the social and biological factors involved in sex differences will be one of the important areas of the future for research in hypnosis.

An important, though quite invalid reason for neglecting sex differences in research, is that by such neglect the researcher can get away with doing just half the amount of routine work! Since the sexes are educated, work and play together nowadays, randomly recruited samples of experimental subjects will be of mixed sex, and as probability statistics largely depend on the absolute number of subjects in the sample studied, in order to take note of sex differences the researcher must double his numbers and his work to get adequate results. It is therefore tempting to demonstrate that there is 'no significant difference' between the sexes, and then proceed as though there were really *no* difference. This is perhaps an over-cynical way of looking at it, but research workers are human like the rest of us and want to get publishable results without doubling their effort.

The work of Bowers, referred to above, has treated sex as a 'moderator variable', that is, a factor which governs the relationships between degree of hypnotizability and other personality factors. The studies which have stemmed from the original one of Furneaux and Gibson,[30] have treated the personality trait of neuroticism as a moderator variable determining the relations between hypnotizability and extraversion, and, as has already been discussed,

the latest attempt has been to see the effect of lowering the operative
level of neuroticism with a tranquillizing drug.

Obviously a great deal of earlier work attempting to relate
hypnotizability to differences in personality produced ambiguous
results because the techniques used by the experimenters were not
sophisticated enough to investigate the results in terms of moderator
variables. Rosenhahn[31] has urged very strongly that all investigators
should take note of the possibilities of elucidating the problems of
individual differences in hypnotic susceptibility by scrutinizing the
results of their research for the action of moderator variables.

There is a growing body of experimental work indicating that
hypnosis, like sleep and other states of altered awareness, has
measurable physiological correlates, and that from measurement of
very fundamental facts about a person's make-up one can predict
his degree of susceptibility. It used to be thought that there were
no reliable physiological indices of the state of hypnosis, and indeed,
the earlier evidence was very ambiguous owing to the relatively
crude techniques of measurement which were used, but such a view
is hardly tenable today.

Studies in the physiology of hypnosis have been criticized,[32] but
the volume of such work is growing to the extent that it cannot be
neglected. A recent study by Morgan and her colleagues[33] establishes
fairly clearly that more hypnotizable subjects *before they are
hypnotized* show more alpha brain activity when their eyes are
closed, as measured on the electroencephalograph (EEG), than do
less hypnotizable subjects. Similarly, Galbraith[34] and his colleagues
found that subjects high in hypnotic susceptibility had more slow
EEG activity, which in the circumstances of the experiment was
supposed to relate to the capacity to ignore selectively stimuli
irrelevant to that which was the focus of attention. This may well
be an important underlying feature of *capacity*.

One explanation of why people vary so much in their hypnotic
susceptibility is that they were born that way. This simple explanation will not commend itself to those who like to think of us all
being born as alike as peas out of one pod, and then becoming as
different as we are due to our varied experiences in life. One fact
that is well known, however, is that basic right-handedness or left-
handedness is inborn, and relates to the structure of the two hemi-
spheres of the brain. The question of 'handedness' is rather complex
and people differ in their degree of ambidextrousness, but, even so,
it is one of the clear indicators of the asymmetry of the organization
and function of the brain, which is determined prenatally. Some
remarkable experiments by Bakan[35] have indicated that brain
asymmetry is related to hypnotic susceptibility.

One of Bakan's early experiments consisted of sitting opposite subjects and asking them to do a number of mental problems, and also to try to get a mental image (a person crying) with their eyes open. When people try to do problems they generally avert their eyes to the left or to the right away from the direct gaze of the interrogator. The left or right preference relates to the way in which their individual brain is asymmetric. Having noted for each subject whether he was a left-gazer or a right-gazer, Bakan then checked on their hypnosis scores, which had been obtained by another experimenter. He found that the left-gazers were significantly more hypnotizable than the right-gazers. Moreover, the left-gazers tended to be higher on all those rather vague things that Josephine Hilgard has catalogued about people more susceptible to hypnosis – being more highly imaginative, preferring humanities to hard science, and being subjectively rather than objectively oriented. Now Josephine Hilgard has implied that all these things are in some way *caused* by childhood experiences, but might it not be that the causal origin is even earlier – in the basic organization of the brain? Perhaps the type of child one is, imaginative and dreamy or hard-headed and practical, relates to the type of brain one is born with.

Bakan's results have since been independently confirmed by other research workers, and he has gone on further to investigate the question of asymmetry of brain function in relation to sex.[35] Such an investigation is entirely necessary in view of the findings that the sexes differ in hypnotic susceptibility in relation to a range of personality differences.

It will be seen that the future of research in hypnosis, and specifically the question of the meaning of differential susceptibility, is now developing in the borderland of psychology and physiology. It is an area in which researchers with different sorts of training must collaborate, and we are progressing far beyond the era in which a 'hypnotist' on his own could expect to make much contribution to the sum of knowledge. The study of brain function in relation to hypnosis and personality opens up exciting possibilities, and by interdisciplinary research we may solve problems which have caused pessimistic hypnotists to wonder whether we know as much about hypnosis as we are ever likely to. In reality, we are merely on the threshold of knowledge.

REFERENCES

1 A. Binet, *La Suggestibilité*, Paris: Schleider, 1900.

2 C. L. Hull, *Hypnosis and Suggestibility*, op. cit.

3 B. Prideaux, 'Suggestion and suggestibility', *British Journal of Psychology*, 10, 1919, p. 228.

4 H. J. Eysenck, 'Suggestibility and hysteria', *Journal of Neurology, Neurosurgery and Psychiatry*, 6, 1943, pp. 22–31.

5 H. J. Eysenck and W. D. Furneaux, 'Primary and secondary suggestiblity', *Journal of Experimental Psychology*, 25, 1945, pp. 485–503.

6 K. G. Stukát, *Suggestibility; A Factorial and Experimental Analysis*, Stockholm: Almquist & Wiksell, 1958.

7 E. R. Hilgard, *Hypnotic Susceptibility*, New York: Harcourt, Brace & World, 1965.

8 V. Faw and W. W. Wilcox, 'Personality characteristics of susceptible and unsusceptible subjects', *Journal of Clinical and Experimental Hypnosis*, 6, 1958, pp. 83–94.

9 H. B. Gibson, 'The lie scale of the Maudsley Personality Inventory', *Acta Psychologica*, 20, 1962, pp. 18–23.

10 W. D. Fureaux and H. B. Gibson, 'The Maudsley Personality Inventory as a predictor of susceptibility to hypnosis', *Journal of Clinical and Experimental Hypnosis*, 9, 1961, pp. 167–177.

11 E. R. Hilgard and P. M. Bentler, 'Predicting hypnotizability from the Maudsley Personality Inventory', *British Journal of Psychology*, 54, 1963, pp. 63–69.

12 H. B. Gibson and J. D. Curran, 'Hypnotic susceptibility and personality: a replication study', ibid., 65, 1974, pp. 283–291; H. B. Gibson and M. E. Corcoran, 'Personality and differential susceptibility to hypnosis: further replication and sex differences', ibid., 66, 1975, pp. 513–520.

13 J. S. Horsley, 'Narcotic hypnosis', in L. M. Le Cron (ed.), *Experimental Hypnosis*, op. cit.

14 F. J. Vingoe, 'More on drugs, hypnotic susceptibility and experimentally controlled conditions', *Bulletin of the British Psychological Society*, 26, 1973, pp. 95–103.

15 H. B. Gibson, M. E. Corcoran and J. D. Curran, 'Hypnotic susceptibility and personality: the consequences of diazepam and the sex of the subjects', *British Journal of Psychology*, in press.

16 G. C. Drew, W. P. Colquhoun and H. A. Long, 'Effect of small doses of alcohol on a skill resembling driving', *British Medical Journal*, 5103, 1958, pp. 993–999.

17 See, for example, N. P. Spanos and T. X. Barber, 'Towards a convergence in hypnotic research', *American Psychologist*, 29, 1974, pp. 500–511.

18 R. E. Shor, 'The frequency of naturally occurring "hypnotic like" experiences in the normal college population', *International Journal of Clinical and Experimental Hypnosis*, 8, 1960, pp. 151–163.

19 J. Hilgard, *Personality and Hypnosis*, op. cit.

20 W. C. Coe, *Personality Correlates of Hypnotic Susceptibility*, paper presented at the meeting of the Society for Clinical and Experimental Hypnosis, Montreal, October 13, 1974.

21 J. Hilgard, 'Imaginative involvement: some characteristics of the highly hypnotizable and the non-hypnotizable', *International Journal of Clinical and Experimental Hypnosis*, 22, 1974, pp. 138–156.

22 See H. M. Bernheim, *Suggestive Therapeutics: A Treatise on the Nature and Uses of Hypnotism*, op. cit.

23 T. X. Barber and D. S. Calverley, ' "Hypnotic like" suggestibility in children and adults', *Journal of Abnormal and Social Psychology*, 66, 1963, pp. 589–597.

24 P. London and L. M. Cooper, 'Norms of hypnotic susceptibility in children', *Developmental Psychology*, 1, 1969, pp. 113–124.

25 J. M. Bramwell, *Hypnotism: Its History, Practice and Theory*, op. cit.

26 C. L. Hull, *Hypnosis and Suggestibility*, op. cit.

27 A. M. Weitzenhoffer, *Hypnotism: An Objective Study in Suggestibility*, New York: Wiley, 1953.

28 T. X. Barber, *Hypnosis . . .*, op. cit.

29 K. S. Bowers, 'Sex and susceptibility as moderator variables in the relationship of creativity and hypnotic susceptibility', *Journal of Abnormal Psychology*, 78, 1971, pp. 93–100.

30 W. D. Furneaux and H. B. Gibson, 'The Maudsley Personality Inventory as predictor of susceptibility to hypnosis', op. cit.

31 D. L. Rosenhahn, 'Hypnosis and personality: a moderator variable analysis', in L. Chertok (ed.), *Psychophysiological Mechanisms of Hypnosis*, New York: Springer-Verlag, 1969.

32 See, for example, F. J. Evans, 'Hypnosis and sleep: techniques for exploring cognitive activity during sleep', in E. Fromm and R. E. Shor (eds.), *Hypnosis: Research Developments and Perspectives*, op. cit.

33 A. H. Morgan, H. MacDonald and E. R. Hilgard, 'EEG alpha: lateral asymmetry related to task and hypnotizability', *Psychophysiology*, 11, 1974, pp. 275–282.

34 G. C. Galbraith, P. London, M. P. Leibovitz, L. M. Cooper and J. T. Hart, 'EEG and hypnotic susceptibility', *Journal of Comparative and Physiological Psychology*, 72, 1970, pp. 125–131.

35 P. Bakan, 'Hypnotizability, laterality of eye movements, and functional brain asymmetry', *Perceptual and Motor Skills*, 28, 1969, pp. 927–932.

36 P. Bakan and W. Putnam, 'Right-left discrimination and brain lateralization: sex differences', *Archives of Neurology*, 30, 1974, pp. 334–335.

INDEX OF NAMES

GENERAL INDEX